Songs of Dzogchen Trekchö

A Detailed Commentary on Shabkar's *Flight of the Garuda*

Dzogchen Pema Kalsang Rinpoche

Translated by Christian A Stewart

Mahasandhi Publishing

Mahasandhi Publishing
37 Maresfield Road
East Cowes
Isle of Wight
U.K.

www.dzogchen-monastery.org

© 2020 Mahasandhi Publishing

Cover photograph of Pema Kalsang Rinpoche by Mura Rinpoche
Design and typeset by Mahasandhi Publishing

All rights reserved. No portion of this book may be reproduced by any means without prior permission from the publisher.

SONGS OF DZOGCHEN TREKCHÖ
A DETAILED COMMENTARY ON SHABKAR'S *FLIGHT OF THE GARUDA*

By Dzogchen Pema Kalsang Rinpoche
Translated by Christian A Stewart

First edition

ISBN: 978-0-9568596-4-8

The companion volume to this teaching is the restricted text

SONGS OF DZOGCHEN TÖGAL
A DETAILED COMMENTARY ON SHABKAR'S VERSES ON DIRECT CROSSING

Authorised practitioners can request copies by emailing:
info@dzogchen-monastery.org

Contents

Translator's Foreword 1
Brief Introduction to Dzogchen Pema Kalsang Rinpoche 3

Teaching Day One 11
    Opening Words 11
    The Freedoms and Endowments 14
    Goodness of the Beginning—the Introduction 23
    Goodness of the Middle—the Meaning of the Text 33
Song One: the Essence of Enlightenment 33
Song Two: the Nature of Rigpa 41
Song Three: the Arising, Abiding, and Disappearance of Mind 47
    Closing Words 51

Teaching Day Two 55
    Opening Words: Precious Human Rebirth & Impermanence 55
    Main Teaching 61
Song Four: the Nature of the View 62
Song Five: the Introduction that Determines Delusion 65
Song Six: Fundamental Nature 73
Song Seven: How the Five Kayas, the Five Wisdoms, and so on, are Complete in Rigpa 83
Song Eight: Fourfold Imperturbable Presence 91
    Summary of the Teaching 99

Teaching Day Three 113
    Opening Words: Samsaric Suffering and Renunciation 113
    Main Teaching 119
Song Nine: the Ordinary Introduction 119
Song Ten: Introduction to Appearances as Mind & Mind as Empty 123

Song Eleven: Self-liberation of Non-dual Appearances & Emptiness .. 133
Song Twelve: the Three Kayas of Ground, Path, and Result 141
Song Thirteen: Self-liberation of the Five Poisons 147
    Summary of the Teaching 157
    Closing Words 164

Teaching Day Four 169
    Opening Words: Karma 169
    Main Teaching 175
Song Fourteen: Self-liberation of the Sixfold Group 176
Song Fifteen: Non-duality of Proliferation and Abiding 181
Song Sixteen: the Single Emptiness of the View 185
Song Seventeen: the Key Points of Meditation 191
Song Eighteen: Elucidation of Naked Rigpa 205
    Closing Words 215

Teaching Day Five 221
    Opening Words: Liberation 221
    Main Teaching 227
Song Nineteen: Conduct that Liberates from Defiles 228
Song Twenty: the Signs of Mastery 237
Song Twenty-One: Yogic Practice 241
Song Twenty-Two: the Result 255
Song Twenty-Three: the Fundamental State of Liberation 257
    Goodness of the End—the Conclusion 265
    Final Words 267

Translator's Foreword

This teaching on Shabkar's *Flight of the Garuda* was given by Dzogchen Pema Kalsang Rinpoche in Gerong Monastery, Amdo, Tibet, in the summer of 2015. The Tibetan transcript was prepared by Jenrong Tenzin and Ratie Tulku Thubrot, and published in 2018 as volume twenty-six of the *Collected Works of Dzogchen Pema Kalsang Rinpoche*, with the title *'od gsal rdzogs pa chen po khregs chod lta ba glu dbyangs sa lam ma lus myur du bgrog pa rtsal ldan mkha' lding gshog rlabs kyi zhal khrid rig stong rdo rje'i rang sgra zhes bya ba bzhugs so* by Gansu Nationalities Publishing House.

This English translation was prepared based on both Pema Kalsang Rinpoche's oral teachings and the transcribed text. My numerous questions were patiently answered by Pema Kalsang Rinpoche's nephews Mura Rinpoche Tenzin Khachab Dorje and Dzogchen Rinpoche Tenzin Longdok Nyima. The translation was made possible by the kind generosity of Mr Ang Keng Lam.

It should go without saying that these direct and profound instructions must only be read by those who have already been authorised and empowered into the main Dzogchen practices by a genuine master. As Pema Kalsang Rinpoche mentions in this teaching:

> Having read this book, if someone were to realise the complete profound meaning and see the essence of ultimate wisdom, this would be due to their own innate faith, the self-present blessings of the teachings, and a previous karmic connection that has become awakened. If someone does not have this realisation and these letters and words become a mere reflection, then perhaps we can say this has been decided by the method of self-secrecy. Those unaware of the presumptuousness of accessing restricted Dharma teachings without permission and who do not engage in any contemplation or analysis of their meaning should perhaps avoid the teachings of Secret Mantra.

Royalties from the sale of this book go directly to Dzogchen Monastery and its numerous beneficial projects. May this virtue enlighten all beings!

Christian A Stewart
May 2020

Lotus Ground Retreat Centre
Dzogchen Monastery, Tibet
www.dzogchen-monastery.org

Brief Introduction to Dzogchen Pema Kalsang Rinpoche

Dzogchen Pema Kalsang Rinpoche is one of only a few surviving masters who grew up in Tibet before the 1950s. He had the fortune to receive a traditional spiritual education with some of the most eminent masters of the 20th century, and became twelfth throne holder of Dzogchen Monastery while still a teenager. Throughout the bleak period of the 1960s and '70s, he managed to maintain and practise the Dharma in secret, and as soon as circumstances permitted, he completely rebuilt Dzogchen Monastery, Shirasing Buddhist College, and established the Lotus Ground Great Perfection Retreat Centre. He now devotes his time to teaching Dzogpa Chenpo to tens of thousands of students from all over the world, and to date, thirty-two volumes of his teachings have been published in Tibetan, with a growing number also becoming available in translation.

Pema Kalsang Rinpoche was born in the summer of 1943 in Dzachuka, Eastern Tibet, the homeland of many exceptional masters, including the great bodhisattva Patrul Rinpoche and the incomparable scholar Mipham Rinpoche. Lama Rinpoche's mother was the sister of the accomplished Dzogchen master Adro Socho, and she bore many signs of a dakini. Rinpoche's maternal uncle, the fourth Mura Rinpoche Pema Norbu, named the child Pema Kalsang.

When Pema Kalsang reached the age of five, Dzogchen Kontul Rinpoche, who had been very close to the second Pema Banza, travelled to Dzachuka and arrived at the family camp. As soon as the young Pema Kalsang saw the master, he went to him very joyfully, as if he was a good friend. He also recognised the knife strapped to Kontul Rinpoche's belt, saying 'That's mine!' The knife had belonged to the second Pema Banza. The names of Rinpoche's parents, his place of birth, and other details were found to correspond with the prophecies of Jamyang Khyentse Choki Lodro, the sixth Dzogchen Rinpoche, and other genuine masters, and Pema Kalsang was recognised as the third incarnation of Great Khenpo Pema Banza.

The first Dzogchen Pema Banza, also known as Padma Vajra or Pema Dorje, was considered the most learned master of his time. He presided as Head Khenpo in Shirasing Buddhist College for many years, and in the latter part of his life, lived and taught in the Dzogchen Lotus Ground. He was amazingly realised, and in particular, in visions of the wisdom body of All-knowing Jigme Lingpa, attained indications of realising the ultimate lineage, thereby receiving direct transmission of the Heart Essence teachings. Great Khenpo Pema Banza had many eminent students, including Mipham Rinpoche, Jamyang Khyentse Wangpo, the fourth Shechen Gyaltsab, Do Khyentse, the third Dodrupchen, Adzom Drukpa, the fifth Shechen Rabjam, and the treasure revealer Lerab Lingpa.

Pema Banza is in turn considered to be the emanation of Zurchen Choying Rangdrol, who was the Tantra master, root guru, and Dzogchen master to none other than the Great Fifth Dalai Lama. Thus he is a very important and influential figure in Tibetan Buddhism, numbering many eminent masters of the seventeenth century among his students.

While Pema Kalsang Rinpoche was growing up, he lived and studied with his root guru Khenpo Yonten Gonpo, and the sixth Dzogchen Rinpoche, in the Lama Palace of Dzogchen Monastery. Together they also travelled to the monastery of Dzongsar Khyentse Jamyang Choki Lodru to receive empowerments of the old and new traditions, Sutras, Tantras, and treasure texts. In 1955, Lama Rinpoche, together with Khenpo Yonten Gonpo and the sixth Dzogchen Rinpoche, travelled to Central Tibet and Tsang on extensive pilgrimage and met many great lamas, including a young 14th Dalai Lama. Following their return, from the age of fourteen to sixteen, Lama Rinpoche lived in the Long Life Retreat Centre above the Dzogchen valley with great Khenpo Pema Tsewang, who taught him personally. This was to be the last opportunity Lama Rinpoche had to study with his masters.

In the autumn of 1958, when Lama Rinpoche was seventeen, Dzogchen Rinpoche took him to Gyalgi Drakkar, famous for one of Guru Rinpoche's retreat caves and the site of Great Khenpo Tupten Nyendrak's retreat centre. With tears in his eyes, Dzogchen Rinpoche requested the khenpo to give Lama Rinpoche seventeen long life empowerments, corresponding in number to the years of his age. Dzogchen Rinpoche said to the khenpo, 'Very soon the Buddhist tradition will face great obstacles, and destruction. At that time don't worry about me, focus your attention on this young one', and he pointed to Lama Rinpoche. It was only a few days later the political situation deteriorated into violence.

During the winter of the following year, Lama Rinpoche, Dzogchen Rinpoche, and Khenpo Gonre were imprisoned in Dege for political re-education. At one stage, because he was still only a boy, Lama Rinpoche was allowed to return to Dzogchen. This was the last time he saw either Dzogchen Rinpoche or his root lama Khenpo Yonten Gonpo. Lama Rinpoche himself recalls a brief exchange he had with Dzogchen Rinpoche several years earlier:

Introduction to Dzogchen Pema Kalsang Rinpoche

One day, as we were sitting together, Dzogchen Rinpoche turned and said to me quite emphatically, 'I have no other heir but you. Do you understand?' I didn't know it at the time, but later I realised what Rinpoche said to me that day was prophetic.

The next twenty years brought terrible suffering, even before the turmoil of the Cultural Revolution. Dzogchen Monastery and Shirasing Buddhist College were completely razed to the ground and Lama Rinpoche was sent to live in Dzogchen village. From 1959 to the late 1970s, under extreme duress and with no personal freedom, Lama Rinpoche was allotted the heaviest manual labour, forced to move earth and stones, make roads, and build houses for the communist Chinese.

During the worst years, not only was he allocated heavy work during daylight hours, but the nights were filled with terrible political education sessions. Every so often, Lama Rinpoche was arrested and threatened with imprisonment, or even death, if he did not conform. He was often singled out as an object of intimidation, repression, and struggle. During the years of the Cultural Revolution, Lama Rinpoche was accused of various anti-revolutionary crimes, and forced to live in conditions worse than anyone else. It was only many years later that he was given the less demanding work of tailoring. In the words of Lama Rinpoche himself:

> More devastating than all of this was the complete waste of the crucial time when my youthful mental faculties were at their sharpest. My progress in studying general areas of knowledge and science, and in particular the traditions of Tibetan Buddhism, came to an abrupt end under the Cultural Revolution. The little knowledge I have of Dharma does not extend beyond that which I had when I was sixteen years old. If I had completed my education, I believe I would certainly have been able to write a few more Dharma-related books and leave a positive legacy which would benefit many future generations. However, the lives of my parents and family were taken when I was young, and my holy tutors, spiritual companions, and master khenpos were separated from me by force, leaving me alive but orphaned from their wisdom and love.

During this time, Dzogchen Pema Kalsang Rinpoche prayed day and night for the revival of the precious Buddhist teachings. He risked everything to store secretly even the smallest piece of scripture or representation of the Buddha which came into his possession. He did not waste any time resting from the exhausting daily labour, but tirelessly practised the approach and accomplishment of the yidam, and the practices of generation, perfection, and Great Perfection. In this way he embraced the bad conditions into the path of Dharma to enhance his realisation. In Rinpoche's own words:

> Despite all the physical and mental hardship and suffering that I endured, I also realised many beneficial aspects of those experiences, true teachers which cannot be found in the words of books. These included true renunciation of samsara, realisation of the impermanence and unreliability of worldly pursuits, the way to find inner happiness from undefiled samadhi, and non-separation from the lama who resides in the centre of the heart.

During the years 1978 and 1979, limited freedom to travel was allowed, and Lama Rinpoche took the opportunity to make pilgrimage to almost all the important holy sites of the Central and Tsang regions of Tibet. Travelling widely on foot, he managed to recover many important texts and statues which had escaped destruction. These he saved, and often carrying them on his back, brought them back to Dzogchen. In this way, he managed to preserve many sacred items which otherwise would have been lost or stolen.

Returning to Dzogchen, Lama Rinpoche gathered resources to build a small mantra wheel house on the site of the now ruined Dzogchen Monastery, where only a few collapsed walls remained. This was barely permissible at the time, but he managed to complete its construction. Eventually, Lama Rinpoche was able to move back to the monastery grounds where he lived in a tent. Small pujas began to be held in makeshift buildings, and finally monks were permitted to wear robes once again.

In 1981, Lama Rinpoche began reconstruction of the ground floor of the Dzogchen Lama Palace. He based the design on the original building and began construction on the original site, finishing the ground floor the same year. This was the crucial first step in the revival of Dzogchen Monastery.

In the same year, Dzogchen Pema Kalsang Rinpoche and Zankar Rinpoche managed to get permission to establish the first Tibetan language college of Sichuan Province, on the original site of Shirasing Buddhist College. Lama Rinpoche went to great lengths to invite senior non-sectarian masters, the surviving holders of the Dzogchen teaching lineage, to give instruction on Tibetan language and other key subjects. Because Dzogchen is historically such an important monastic seat, these eminent lamas and khenpos were willing to act as school teachers in the new Tibetan Language School.

INTRODUCTION TO DZOGCHEN PEMA KALSANG RINPOCHE

At first the school was merely a few tents pitched on the site of the original college. Only later was it possible for basic classrooms and accommodation to be built. The school served as a lone outpost of learning and culture to educate a generation of Tibetans who otherwise would have had no opportunity to receive an education, or even study their own language. At that time, becoming a monk or nun was prohibited, so the school also served as a refuge for young men and women, where they were able to dedicate themselves to concentrated study. Later, the Tibetan Language School was moved to Dartsedo, where it continues to provide comprehensive learning opportunities for young Tibetans; opportunities which are still very difficult to find elsewhere in the region.

In 1982, at the age of thirty-nine, Lama Rinpoche set out to travel on pilgrimage to India, but on the way was involved in a terrible car accident. He was seriously injured and almost died. In Lama Rinpoche's own words:

> I had managed to survive all the obstacles that threatened my life. I was the only one left of all the lamas and monks who had lived in the Lama Palace of Dzogchen. That I was able to continue to work for the Dharma at a time of extreme decline was certainly due to the power of Dzogchen Rinpoche's prayers, and the blessings of Khenpo Tupten Nyendrak's seventeen long life empowerments.

Lama Rinpoche was forced to spend a year in hospital where he underwent multiple operations to pin together broken bones, some of which had to be repositioned over and over again. Not disheartened, Lama Rinpoche recovered his strength, and relying on two walking sticks, travelled to India and Nepal, working for the teachings and making pilgrimage to all the major holy sites. During this time he was also reunited with His Holiness the 14th Dalai Lama. From India he visited Europe and the United States, where he also gave teachings to many fortunate Westerners.

Having returned to Dzogchen, Lama Rinpoche took responsibility for the completion of the upper floors of the Lama Palace, as well as the reconstruction of the Grand Temple of Dzogchen Monastery. Despite the physical hardships, he once again joined in the manual labour on the construction site. Lama Rinpoche was also able to build a golden reliquary stupa to enshrine the relics of the sixth Dzogchen Rinpoche, which he had risked his life keeping hidden for twenty-five years. The stupa is now enshrined in the newly rebuilt Dzogchen Palace.

From a prophecy of the Great Treasure Revealer Pema Namdrol Lingpa:

> On the supreme fearless lion throne
> Of Shri Singha Dharma Centre,
> Padma's mind emanation, named Pema,
> Will illuminate like the sun
> The excellent and enlightened qualities
> Of all the Buddha's teachings,
> And the thousand-petal lotuses
> Of many young Pemas will bloom.

This prophecy was fulfilled when reconstruction of the great Buddhist College of Shirasing began in the fortunate dragon year of 1988. Lama Rinpoche used the small amount of money he received in compensation from his road accident to start the building work. In the past, the college was a highly specialised establishment accommodating only fifty or so of the most exceptional and promising tulkus and monks, together with the most eminent khenpos and lamas. Lama Rinpoche saw the opportunity for expansion, and constructed buildings to accommodate five hundred monks, and a large temple which could hold a thousand people. Again, Lama Rinpoche laboured personally on the construction to the extent that the soles of his feet cracked open.

When the building was complete, he invited many of the surviving senior and most learned masters from all schools of Tibetan Buddhism to revive the teaching lineages, and so Shirasing Buddhist College attracted students from all traditions. This was a very fragile time for the Dharma in Tibet, but Lama Rinpoche managed to bring up a new generation of monks, tulkus, and khenpos in the true Dharma, educating them to the highest possible standard. He spent the next ten years living in the college, focused on educating the younger generation, so there would be qualified teachers to spread the Dharma in the future.

Lama Rinpoche also revived the tradition of ordination in Tibet, and was the first master to give the vows of ordination in Samye Monastery after the Cultural Revolution, in the same temple where the first ever Tibetans became monks. Travelling extensively, he was invited to give teachings and empowerments in the great monastic seats of Dorje Drak, Mindroling, Palri, Jigme Lingpa's seat at Tsering Jong, Samye, and Drigang, as well as over a hundred of Dzogchen's branch monasteries. Lama Rinpoche also established extensive community aid and education programmes through his charitable organisation, the Kalsang Foundation.

Introduction to Dzogchen Pema Kalsang Rinpoche

In 2003, Lama Rinpoche completed the Lotus Ground Great Perfection Retreat Centre in Dzogchen Pema Tung, the site of his previous incarnation Pema Banza's retreat centre. It is from here that he now shares the blessings of one of the closest and most pure Longchen Nyingtik lineages in the world. Only five lineage holders connect All-knowing Jigme Lingpa with Lama Rinpoche, all of whom were truly eminent masters.

Despite being still very active in teaching, writing, and travelling, Lama Rinpoche now spends most of his time in silent retreat, rising early every day to engage in sessions of prostration, writing, and meditation. Working with all the tremendous hardships and challenges he has faced throughout his life, Lama Rinpoche fully embodies the activities of Buddha body, speech, and mind. With his body he rebuilt Dzogchen Monastery from the foundations up, with his speech he teaches the enlightened view of the Great Perfection, and with his mind he never ceases to benefit all sentient beings by transmitting realisation of Dzogchen Great Perfection.

Teaching Day One

Opening Words

Through the strength of our combined accumulation of positive karma and aspirations, this Sangha of many excellent yogis has been brought here today, together in one Dharma. With great happiness which comes spontaneously from the teachings, I would like to give respectful greetings to everyone here, all brothers and sisters in the Dharma. Allow us now to begin discussing our aims for this teaching.

There are well over three thousand people in attendance here today, from many different regions of Tibet. Many of you are from Amdo, I know some of you have come from Central Tibet and Kham, and there must be a few people who have travelled from even further afield. Such diverse regions vary not only in environment and landscape, but also the people from these places exhibit different dialects and customs. Although this is the case, if we look at all the ways in which we are similar, we all come from places that are home to Tibetan Buddhism, and we most probably come from a family that has devotion to and faith in the sacred Dharma. Moreover, what is truly the same for every single one of us is that we desire happiness and do not wish to suffer. Not only that, but we spend all our days and nights, months and years, in pursuit of this happiness. Thus, to the extent that we are all sentient beings, living and breathing, we are all identical.

Among all of us here, some of you are advanced in age and others are still in their prime. Regardless of whether we are young or old, when we look back at the time of our youth, now past, and summarise our lives up until now, the appearances of this worldly life, neither happy nor miserable, appear before our eyes: after every summer came a winter and, as one year ended, a new one began, many of which have now already passed. However many years of life we have already lived, that many are already gone. Remembering in this way, at the time when we were small heedless children, our parents brought us up. We had no concept of prioritising things for the future. However, when the time came for us to walk and run, and as some of us went to school to learn how to read and write, each of us grasped our own potential for action.

Most of us here are no longer young, but not yet extremely old. We have passed middle age and are now approaching our fifties and sixties. Compared to the average length of human life, so much of our lives have already passed. With the exception of the few holy masters in attendance, during that time, what truly meaningful things have we accomplished for ourselves and others, for the present and the future? Having been given a Buddhist name, not only are you now present in the seated lines of the assembled Sangha, but you may have already ascended to the head of the row. However, when we get to the real point of inner practice, when tomorrow's sun is not going to rise and tonight is our time to die, have we arranged things suitably well so that we will not fall down to the lower realms of samsara in our next life, and are able to go to a happy and joyful place? The same applies to our family and friends that we rely on, as well as the monks, nuns, and students who rely on us. In short, what beneficial things have we done for those with whom we are connected? What legacy will we leave them?

Additionally, if we use our powers of analysis to think carefully about what is good and bad, positive and negative, in the case of the average person, each day and night passes in complete distraction. Burdened by suffering and misery, such people tend to stray further from virtue, not knowing how to make good use of their independence. It is as if they are about to leap from the top of a towering rocky precipice. But, having arrived at such a perilous moment ourselves, we need to actually identify the danger.

Whether it was good or bad, the past has gone. We may recall it, but it is not coming back. Whatever happiness or misery, goodness or bad, may have occurred on the path of our human life, it all fades into memories in the reflections of the mind. However, by using these experiences in the future, now when we travel down the path that lies before us leading towards a new destination, we need to seize upon such positive and negative examples, and put our practical experiences to good use.

As we practise the sacred Dharma, obviously we hope that we can accomplish something. However, when we look back, if what we have done has been nothing more than a mere semblance of practice, and in fact we have not made any progress in the actual accomplishment of Dharma, then it difficult to distinguish whether it belongs in the category of virtuous or unvirtuous activities. Not only that, but we cannot be certain it will not prove to become nothing more than a mere addition to our samsara-producing karma. Our teaching today is the holy Dharma of Dzogpa Chenpo, the victorious summit of the nine vehicles. Ati Yoga is called the 'resultant vehicle', and in terms of its meaning, it truly is so. However, for an ordinary person, if they have not accumulated the conditions to accomplish these teachings accordingly, then even an excellent teaching may not end up being very beneficial.

Regarding the peak of all Dharma vehicles, the top of a mountain is its lofty summit, however the mental capacity of an ordinary person is low. Moreover, if those in the valley below are struggling, unable to get free from the mud of attachment, aversion, and ignorance, then as the saying goes: *you may tie your head up high, but your neck will snap below.* Therefore, in this case the fault lies with the individual. So, before receiving teachings, it is very important to cleanse and purify the Dharma vessel, which is our mindstream. As it is taught:

> Secret Mantra is like lion's milk.
> If poured into another inferior container,
> Not a precious vessel of gold,
> The container will break and the essence will be lost.

This not only applies to the resultant vehicle of Secret Mantra, but even if we wish to enter into the path of the common causal vehicle, the lesser vehicle of the path of arhats and pratyekabuddhas, there is no way not to accumulate the accordant conditions necessary for the vessel of our mindstream. Without motivation that renounces samsara, even the lesser vehicle vows of individual liberation cannot be received. Samadhi does not develop in a mindstream that is not disciplined by vows. Without samadhi there is no wisdom, so it is difficult to grasp even the start of the common path to liberation. Generally, in this Dharma lineage of ours, and specifically, even if I was only going to teach four lines of verse, that which is first taught at the beginning, and the key point which we need to grasp, is the teaching of the mind trainings.

In the *Utterly Pure Chariot* the All-knowing Lord of Dharma gave the following instruction:

> Without clairvoyance you have no capacity to benefit others,
> So strive for your own sake while considering the benefit of others.
> Do not let your mind be seduced by the distracting excitements
> Of this demonic deception; it is essential to strive in practice.

For an ordinary person like me, who has not got things well-arranged even personally, the time has not come for me to be teaching the Dharma to others. I do not measure up to such a noble activity. However, because of the upheavals of the period after I was born, at this time when the Dharma is undergoing such change, waxing and waning, developing and declining, the responsibility and fortune to possess, protect, and promulgate our Dharma lineage has fallen upon me. But, when taking up the burden of teaching the Dharma, someone who does not have clairvoyance has no means of knowing the mind of others, and so it is difficult to teach the appropriate Dharma in the right way. However, because our mindstreams are not secret to ourselves, we must take knowing our own mindstreams as the foundation of our practice. I am speaking about taking oneself as an example, which is the only method on which to rely when there is no better alternative.

The Freedoms and Endowments

Initially, when we begin to speak about the mind trainings, it is the custom to teach the difficulty of finding the freedoms and endowments as the first of the four mind changers. With this in mind, before knowing how to enumerate the complete freedoms and endowments of a precious human rebirth, I personally think it is important first to understand the value of our human life, or in other words, to understand how we should cherish ourselves. There is no creature living that does not cherish their own life. Our life is more important than all the riches in the world. Without life, what is the use of money? The basis upon which our life depends is this body. For these few days, before this body and mind are driven apart, we are called a 'living person'. But whatever we do, ultimately this body is not something reliable, on which we can depend forever. Having become connected, mind and body remain together, but we do not know when our life, more cherished than all the riches in the world, will become separated from this precious body. Ultimately, however long the body may last, it is still not wholly reliable.

Thus, during the minutes and seconds of this short human life, which are more precious than gold and which we will never see again, how is it we are still preoccupied with trifling, petty activities, and we neglect what is really important? When our time comes to die and we have not gained anything from the precious opportunity of our human life, it goes completely to waste. In the guidance instructions this is what is known as 'gaining nothing from the freedoms and endowments'. In fact, this is because we do not understand the difference in good karma between us humans and the wild animals of the mountains, or the cattle and yaks in the fields. Up until the day they die, even herd animals know how to survive, eating grass and drinking water. After death, if we have not accomplished any benefit for ourselves or anyone else, then regardless of whether we ate delicious food instead of grass, except for the difference in our individual perceived awareness of deluded appearances, in fact we humans are just the same as animals, in that we did not consider any long-term implications. As it is taught:

> At best this body is a boat to liberation.
> At worst this body is an anchor to samsara.

In that case, based on this understanding of the way we need to cherish ourselves, we need to search for the value of human life based on the foundation of the Dharma scriptures. Therefore, we need to begin our practice of the Dharma by first analysing whether or not we have the eight freedoms and the ten endowments. The eight freedoms are established by what we are free from, and the ten endowments are established by what we have. It does not follow that if we have the complete eight freedoms, we also have the ten endowments, but it does follow that if the ten endowments are complete, the eight freedoms are also complete. This time we have not been born in the three lower realms, and we have not been born as a long-life god. However, if our mindstream is conceited with barbaric views or corrupted by wrong views, one of the main foundations of our practice will be the need to rectify these points. Although we may not have actually lost faith in the Three Jewels, if we have not found conviction in the workings of cause and effect with the deep certainty that thinks 'This is true', then it is difficult not to fall among the ranks of those who have wrong views.

Similarly, from the aspect of the circumstantial endowments, for the majority of us they are complete. But in terms of the personal endowments, it is difficult for us to pass the test to say they are complete, to be sure we do not have a corrupt way of life, and to be certain that we have faith in the teachings. Why is that? It is said:

That actions are untrue is known through conduct.

By getting lost in the distractions of worldly activities, what gets neglected is practice of the holy sacred Dharma, so that all of our most productive time is spent engaging in mundane tasks. When it happens that only the leftovers of our resources are used to pay the tax of gathering the accumulations, the freedoms and endowments are not complete. Blue stone posing as turquoise needs to be outed.

To get to the main point, when we wish to be true practitioners of Buddhism, based on training the mind in the preliminaries of the four mind changers, we need to establish the foundation of taking refuge in the Three Jewels which eliminates wrong paths. Then arouse the supreme mind of bodhicitta which avoids lesser paths, and maintain it in our mindstream without it diminishing. Based on this, we follow an authentic lama, mature our mindstream with the four empowerments, and liberate it with the liberating instructions. Doing so, we follow the profound method of the swift path and actualise in this life the wisdom of the unity of the four kayas. In this way, if we practise the holy Dharma without separating from a diligent attitude, then it can be accomplished.

For this reason, from the start, in terms of the right motivation and manner in which to listen to the profound guidance of the holy Dharma of profound Secret Mantra, the motivation is the vast attitude of bodhicitta to establish all mother-like sentient beings in great enlightenment. The vast skill in means of Secret Mantra is to keep in mind the ongoing all-encompassing purity of appearance and experience. Thus we need to maintain this experience while we listen.

The Subsidiary Topics of Exposition

Now the time has come to begin the teachings of Shabkar Tsokdruk Rangdrol. From his two collections of songs on the two stages of Dzogpa Chenpo, trekchö primordial purity and tögal spontaneous presence, we will teach *Songs of the Trekchö View*, which is famously known by the beautiful title '*Flight of the Garuda*'. However, in order to teach this correctly, in addition to the actual topic of exposition, we should first consider the subsidiary topics of exposition. These include the method of exposition of the teaching master, how students should listen, and how both master and student may do these correctly.

The Teaching Master's Method of Exposition

Those referred to as 'spiritual masters' are not all the same; there are different categories of master. The masters of the past were the Buddha, the arhats, and the panditas, and their successors today need to follow after them. Therefore, at the time the Buddha taught the Dharma, he possessed the ten powers, together with the ten strengths, and his insight, clairvoyance, and miracles were totally unimpeded. So, by the threefold means of the miraculous manifestation of his body, the miracle of his mind to communicate with all, and the miracle of his speech to teach the listener, he gathered a large retinue of beings to be tamed who had faith. Fully-knowing the minds and capacities, including the latent potentials of those to be tamed, the Buddha taught whatever Dharma was appropriate to guide them with the sixty aspects of melodious speech.

If the spiritual master is an arhat, then they teach by means of the three purities. An arhat has clairvoyance that knows the minds of others. The first purity makes pure the recipient who listens to the teachings. The second purity, when referring to an 'arhat', is that they are free from the obscurations of the afflictive emotions including attachment. Therefore, not mixed with attachment and the other afflictive emotions, their words of expression are unsullied and they teach with pure signs and melodious tones. The third purity is that, with perfect recall, they are able to repeat whatever their teacher, the fully enlightened Buddha teaches, without missing or adding any words, and without any mistake or confusion in meaning.

Teaching Day One

How do master panditas teach the Dharma? In ancient India, the land of the noble ones and source of this holy Dharma, when the Buddha Dharma dawned like the rising sun, there were two renowned monasteries: the glorious monastery of Nalanda where panditas had one way of teaching, and Vikramalashila Monastery where panditas taught in another way. As I am just an ordinary person of these end times, at this period of decline in the general and specific teachings, someone who sincerely holds the teachings and wishes to continue to revive their Dharma lineage must maintain them foremostly with sincere faith and devotion. What is more, when teaching the Dharma, although the one doing the teaching may be an ordinary average person, what they speak is still the Buddha Dharma, therefore there is no way not to adhere to these previous traditions of teaching. Therefore, here we primarily follow the way the panditas of glorious Nalanda Monastery taught, and adhere to the following five headings: the person who composed the teaching, the sources from which it was compiled, which areas it incorporates, what the overall meaning is from start to finish, and for what purpose and whose benefit it was composed.

The Five Headings to be Included:
The Person who Composed the Teaching

As is necessary to teach with regard to these five headings, for the first which concerns the person who composed this text, we begin with an outline of Shabkar's life. This will be a new teaching for those who have not heard it and a reminder for those who are already familiar with it, which also links into the purpose of its composition. Generally, it is customary to teach the biographies of holy masters using three divisions: outer, inner, and secret, with respect to ordinary and extraordinary students. The outer biography is the established common perception of ordinary students which is known to all, but the inner biography transcends the average worldly attitude. It is an account of engaging in practice with study, diligence, and accomplishment, as well as how the actualised result of accomplishment was achieved for the benefit of both self and others.

In addition to demonstrating this author's great qualities, with pristine faith and devoted intent we need to grasp the key points which allow us to engage in listening to the meaning of this text. As well as having confident faith in the author, when devotion and a naturally-arising longing grows for the Dharma that they bestowed, the words of the scriptural transmission arise and the actual transmission enters our heart. Experience and realisation that has not yet arisen newly arises, and there is hope that having arisen, they will increase even more.

This being the case, the place where Shabkar Tsokdruk Rangdrol was born was in this snowy land of Tibet, in the Lower Amdo region known for its horses, in Rebkong County, Sermug District, in the area of Shorong Lakha, Nyengya Town, which is close to where we are now. This area is south of Tsongkha Kyeri, where the lord of the Dharma of the three realms, Victorious Tsongkhapa, was born. It is also connected to the eight sacred places of accomplishment in Rebkong, and the places where Easterly Lord Kalden Gyatso attained accomplishment. Shabkar's father was the mantra holder Dorje Namgyal, and his mother, the matriarch of the Damtsang clan, was called Tashi Tsek.

Shabkar was a holy master, who was prophesied in the teachings of Sutra and Tantra. Among the many prophecies that predict him by name and significance, the main one from the treasure tradition is found in the general prophecies revealed by Treasure Revealer Dudul Dorje, which gives an indication of his enlightened activities:

> The glorious vajra will fly to the east.
> Named Rangdrol, he will be wise in the genuine truth.

In terms of our own Dharma tradition, he is mentioned more than once in the prophecies of the Lord of Siddhas Dzogchenpa Kunzang Shenpen and others.

The full details of Shabkar's life are recounted in the first volume of his own collected works, around section fifteen, in both poetry and prose. Foremost among his many activities is the way in which he followed his lama, how he engaged in practice, and subsequently how he trained his students. It also describes how Shabkar engaged in practice, not just in his homeland, but on Tsonying Mahadeva, the island in the heart of Lake Kokonor, around the sacred mountain of Amnye Machen, and in Drakkar Dreldzong, the White Rock Monkey Fortress.

Not only that, but he engaged in practice and worked for the benefit of beings in Central Tibet, Tsang, Nagri, and Ladakh. He retreated in Upper Tibet in the famous and snowy Mt. Kailash of White Lion-face, the sacred place of enlightened body. In Central Tibet, he retreated in the authentic source, Mt. Lapchi of Striped Tiger-face, the sacred place of enlightened speech. In Lower Tibet, he retreated in unparalleled Tsari of Black Sow-face, the sacred place of enlightened mind, as well as in Nepal, Central Tibet, and Tsang. In these places he engaged methodically in accomplishment for his own benefit, and also devoted himself actively to the benefit of others. The extensive tales of how he nurtured the teachings and sentient beings with beneficial enlightened activity is recorded in great detail in his collected songs.

Teaching Day One

It is recorded that Shabkar was born in the eighteenth century, in the year of the Female Iron Ox (1781), less than three hundred years ago. For the benefit of later generations of students, he left over ten volumes of collected teachings. Chiefly among these are the eight emanated scriptures: *the Marvellous Emanated Scriptures, the Emanated Scriptures of the Bodhisattva, the Wondrous Emanated Scriptures*, and so on. As well as these, he composed foremost instructions which focus on the view, meditation, conduct, and result of the peak of the nine vehicles, Dzogchen Ati Yoga, which is the section of Dharma that we are currently studying. These are extraordinarily special teachings.

While we discuss the life story of the author of these teachings, we should mention that when Shabkar was young and living at home he was named Ngawang Tashi. When he became ordained and renounced his home for the state of homelessness, he received the name Shamba Tashi, and he was given the name Tsokdruk Rangdrol when he received Secret Mantra empowerment.

Sources from which this Teaching was Compiled

The songs of the enlightened view that this author composed, including both *Flight of the Garuda* and those pertaining to tögal, are compiled from the teachings of the great charioteer of the teachings of Dzogchen in the land of snow mountains. This of course refers to Victorious Longchenpa, who was like the second buddha of the doctrine, and his spiritual son Jigme Lingpa, who are sometimes referred to as the father and the son. These songs also originate from all the traditions of Padmasambhava and Vimalamitra, the essence of the enlightened mind of Samantabhadra. In particular, *Flight of the Garuda* is based upon Guru Rinpoche's *Self-liberation through Naked Perception*, taught as an additional ornament of the foremost instructions of Victorious Longchenpa, father and son, which unify the enlightened intent of the three sections of Dzogpa Chenpo.

Areas this Teaching Incorporates

Within which section of Dharma are these teachings included? They are included within unexcelled Mantra of Mahayana Secret Mantra, which is divided into four common tantra sections. In the classification of the six unique tantra sections, these teachings are included within the inner tantra of Ati Yoga.

The Overall Meaning

Overall, what is the essential meaning of this text? In addition to the main purpose of setting forth the view of the Dzogchen Mind, Space, and Foremost Instruction Sections, this text also serves as a meaningful and detailed presentation of ground, path, view, meditation, conduct, and result.

Those to be Benefited by the Composition

For whose sake was this text composed? In general, this text is for those fortunate enough to be tamed by this spiritual approach as a whole. In particular, for such practitioners who have as yet not engaged in extensive study, contemplation, or training, the special characteristic of this teaching is that the terminology is simple to understand and the meaning is easy for the mind to assimilate. So it is a text for all people, whether of superior or lesser experience. In this way, we should say that it is a Dharma teaching that brings liberation to all ordinary and extraordinary beings to be tamed by Dzogchen, both those whose mind state is one of self-manifest rigpa and those whose mind state is one of objective appearances. This is also how the master who teaches this text should explain it.

How Students Should Listen

How do students who receive a teaching need to listen to it? The general motivation and conduct for listening to the Dharma was already mentioned at the beginning of this session. In particular, do not be without the Mahayana arousal of supreme bodhicitta. Especially, the distinctive method of Secret Mantra motivation is that the universe and its contents are the all-encompassing purity of pure realms and immeasurable celestial mansions. Forms are enlightened body, sounds are enlightened speech, and thoughts are enlightened mind. Without suppression or cultivation of whatever manifests, undistracted and free of grasping, trained yogis need to listen while maintaining the state of the unmistaken actual fundamental nature without separation.

In terms of conduct to be accepted or rejected, having entered into a gathering of the holy Dharma and when listening to the teachings, with a mind of faith and devotion, apply the four metaphors: that you are sick, that Dharma is medicine, and so forth. Moreover, we must listen having abandoned the three defects of the pot, the six defilements, the five wrong way of remembering, and so on. In summary, the one who teaches the Dharma and all those listening need to do so by means of all six transcendent perfections, as well you know.

Teaching Day One

How Both Master and Student May do These Properly

With this kind of good motivation and conduct, the manner in which both master and student engage in teaching and listening needs to be explained as outlined by the fivefold or threefold framework, which is of course the general way. There is a way to explain the fivefold framework in connection with the meaning of the title, which also relates to the general meaning of the text.

To connect the meaning and the main subject of the text, and discuss it according to the intent stated in the scriptural authority of *Well Explained Reasoning*, the first point of the fivefold framework is the purpose, which is as follows: generally speaking, all sentient beings possess the essence of enlightenment. If they have the potential to be free of defilements and manifest enlightened qualities, then the purpose is for all beings wandering in delusion to realise the undeluded actual fundamental nature and actualise enlightenment. In particular, the purpose for beings with sharp faculties to be tamed by Dzogchen is to actualise attainment of liberation in this life.

Second is the summarised meaning. This text summarises all the key points of ground, path, and result, and view, meditation, and conduct. Third is the meaning of the words. Through the arrangement of the expressed names and words, the object of expression, the foremost instructions of the three sections of Dzogchen, is taught and easy to understand. Fourth is the connection. The earlier and later objects of expression and the expressed are taught without confusing the order. Fifth is the objections and refutations. Like the lion's roar, the deafening sound of the utmost peak of the Dzogchen view spontaneously intimidates all lesser and inferior views, like herds of forest animals, with its splendour.

Alternatively, we can speak in terms of the great threefold framework, which is to cover the length of the subject, to stress the words of phrasing, and to summarise the sections. These three are taught with three examples: the leap of a tigress, the plod of a tortoise, and the poise of a lion. To describe this in more detail, unlike the scuttles of a pika which do not cover the ground of the meaning which is taught, to cover the full length of the subject is like the leap of a tigress. Also, unlike speaking roughly using generalities and losing the key points of meaning, to stress the words of the textual meaning is like the plodding of a tortoise. Also, unlike not differentiating the meaning of earlier and later sections like an uneven and poorly woven ball of yarn, to summarise the intermediary sections is like the poise of a lion. In this way, this text also possesses such unrivalled great elegance.

The Actual Topic of Exposition

As for discussing the actual subject to be explained here, this particular teaching discloses the hidden meaning of the ultimate essential truth of the Tathagata's instructions. If we ask 'What are the features of the Tathagata's instructions?' They inherently resolve all defects and gather all positive qualities. They comprise the goodness of the beginning, the goodness of the middle, the goodness of the end, true excellence in meaning, true excellence in words, and so forth. Likewise, this text that we are studying needs to be described in terms of the outline of the great threefold framework, which is the goodness of the beginning, the goodness of the middle, and the goodness of the end.

Teaching Day One

Goodness of the Beginning—The Introduction

First is the goodness of the beginning, which comprises three sections: explanation of the title, the expression of homage, and the author's pledge of composition.

Explanation of the Title

The title is taught to be:

Flight of the Garuda, Songs of the Trekchö View of Luminous Dzogpa Chenpo, Capable of Swiftly Traversing the Paths and Levels without Exception.

This clearly named title combines both name and meaning. Those wise with sharp faculties, upon merely seeing or hearing this title, can determine the entire meaning of the scripture. Those with middling faculties whose discerning knowledge is not fully matured can approximately understand to which of the greater or lesser vehicles, Sutra or Tantra, this text belongs, and how swift or slow the path may be. As for those lesser individuals with very dull faculties, based on the connection between name and meaning, even they can easily find this section of teaching and the scriptural volume, so there are these purposes.

For us at this time, we are discussing a combination of essential instruction and practical guidance for Dzogchen, in the manner of a maturing guidance. So at this stage, it would not be suitable for me to read the text straight through like an oral transmission. For this devotional guidance it would also not be suitable to receive the teaching just in name, without any of the positive qualities, and say 'We got through it and made it to the end', or to say 'It was read through and we heard it'. If these methods of transmission are unsuitable, how then should we cover this text? We need to study it all completely, in connection with the four great rivers of Nyingma transmission. As this is necessary, we need to mature our mindstreams by conferring the river of maturing empowerment and introduction. So, at this stage of guidance on the main practises of both trekchö and tögal, we need to give a Dzogchen empowerment of the early Heart Essence.

Some people may be wondering, 'Wasn't an empowerment already given the other day? And before that, there was another empowerment on the day just after we arrived. Why are there so many empowerments?' We should know that empowerments are not all the same; there are many different kinds. The first empowerment that was given was a public longevity empowerment connected with the common class of Sutra and Tantra. Following that, the empowerment given to the monastic community was of Yumka Queen of Great Bliss, connected to the unexcelled common completion stage yoga of the channels, essences, and energies. In particular, that practice is connected with the path of method, mainly with the practice of blazing and trickling down melting bliss to bring to maturation the generation of the wisdom of bliss and emptiness, connected with mother tantra Anuyoga generation sadhana practice.

This time, the intended meaning of the six million four hundred thousand tantras of Dzogpa Chenpo, the inner essence of the seventeen great secret tantras, essentialised in the four profound volumes, is being given as a revealing instruction of trekchö primordial purity and tögal spontaneous presence. This is based on the teachings of Shabkar, in the manner of an extensive instruction on the Dzogchen Heart Essence of the Great Expanse. At this stage in our tradition, empowerments are referred to as 'elaborate, unelaborate, extremely unelaborate, and utterly unelaborate', and the fourth empowerment is called the 'precious word empowerment'.

Without receiving this higher, profound, maturing empowerment which incorporates all the lower empowerments, a student is not suitable to be taught the stage of instructions that bring liberation. For example, for someone who wants to brew beer, without adding yeast to the barley, the beer cannot be brewed. Empowerments are the same. Also, it is not acceptable to say 'I think I've received this empowerment sometime in the past', or to put it off saying 'I'll get it later'. First the empowerment is given. Then based on the unbroken samaya commitments of the empowerment, when the teaching is given, not only do these two become interlinked, but together they become something very meaningful.

As for the empowerments of the *Four Volumes of Heart Essence*, the two mother and two child, on some occasions I give the full set, at other times I give the empowerments individually in rotation. In this case, this year I am considering giving the ultimate essence of all, the *Profound Ultimate Essence* empowerment. Having matured the mindstream by means of granting the maturing river of the four empowerments together with the introduction, both the full-length explanation of the river of scripture, together with commentaries and essential expositions, and the instructional river of practice, together with the revealing instructions and crucial notes, are combined together. Then, with the method to liberate that which has been matured, the three: tantras, transmissions, and foremost instructions comprise the foundation. Following that, the true nature beyond mind, the actual mode of presence, primordially pervasive Dzogchen, truth without depth or width, needs to be introduced by recognising your own nature.

Together with this, the river of practice and accomplishment, including the additional activities, is taught, and the integration of the Tantra section and the sadhana section into one is accomplished automatically. If we are unable to join together these methods of Tantra and sadhana, we lack the nail of unchanging intention, so the view, realisation, and samadhi of the other three nails become mere words, like a baseless result or a wall without a foundation.

Getting back to the text, let us explain the meaning of the word 'luminosity' in the title. This term is the same as that which appears in unexcelled Mantra; at the stage of the six qualities of the common completion stage the essence of the path is called 'luminosity'. However there are differences in ground, path, and resultant luminosity, example and true luminosity, and so forth. 'Luminosity' is not the aspect empty of true existence, the non-affirming negation. It is not fixation on attached experiences of bliss, clarity, and no-thought. It is the nature of mind, naturally occurring wisdom, and so this title refers to 'luminous Dzogpa Chenpo'. As basic space is inherently luminous, from this aspect it is luminosity. From the aspect that it is not mere emptiness or nothingness, it is taught to be naturally occurring wisdom, the ground from which all wisdom arises. Thus it is clarity without grasping, emptiness' natural state of clarity, and emptiness' unimpeded natural radiance, and should be understood as luminosity of metaphor and actuality connected.

Because of this, the terms 'empty luminosity of trekchö primordial purity' and 'manifest luminosity of tögal spontaneous presence' come about, and these are the key points that need to be discussed when we recount the way things are, and when we differentiate that from the way things appear. However, in fact, the way things exist is beyond all limits of elaboration of similarity and difference, appearance and emptiness, and any positivity or negativity of grasping and fixation, and so on. In a single state of great primordial perfection of evenness, all phenomena of samsara and nirvana are subsumed perfectly and completely, thus it is taught to be Dzogpa Chenpo or Great Perfection. This is the ultimate fundamental nature of all phenomena.

Although this essence does not have divisible categories, from the perspective of supported phenomena, when we divide these through terminology we get the threefold presentation of Dzogchen ground, path, and result. However, at the time of the ultimate result, this is not a mere nirvanic exhaustion of samsara. However it was at the time of the ground, so it is at the time of the result, and its timelessly present qualities become apparent. For example, a genuine sword possesses the quality of sharpness which enables it to cut. However, if it is not drawn from its scabbard, this is not apparent. A clear mirror has the potential and qualities to give rise to reflections, but without taking it out of its box, these are not apparent. Similarly, a jewel has attractive shiny qualities, but if covered in mud, these qualities cannot become evident, yet when free of everything that conceals it, the jewel is apparent just as it is.

Likewise, to speak in terms of the ground of separation and the result of separation, what is known as 'the subject matter of actual Dzogchen' does not contradict with the accomplishment of possessing the twofold purity. Even among beings to be tamed with sharp faculties, it is never the case that they exhibit no variation in sharpness or dullness. Therefore, from among the expressed words of Dzogchen—the six million four hundred thousand tantras, and the corresponding number of scriptures and foremost instructions compiled and taught from them—if we gather together the essential meaning stated in the three Mind, Space, and Foremost Instruction Sections, the stages of the path of practice of trekchö primordial purity and tögal spontaneous presence are subsumed within this inseparable primordial purity and spontaneous presence. As this needs also to be explained through conventional designation, terms, and phrases, the manner in which the single nature is represented through attributes is done with a progression of phrasing, which is explained in stages.

Following this, next from the title we explain *Songs of the Trekchö View*. All elaborations of grasping and fixation are thoroughly or directly cut through, like a rope of plaited grass burnt by fire, so this is taught to be 'trekchö' or 'thorough cut'. Such rigpa of self-arising wisdom is itself the ultimate wisdom of all buddhas. From the perspective of a yogi whose mind state is one of self-manifest rigpa, whether things appear as pure or impure, whatever appears to them, its nature is primordially pure without concepts of samsara or nirvana. These ordinary appearances, without shedding their coats or changing their colours, reside in enlightenment. So, for a yogi with lofty realisation of the view that whatever manifests arises as pure, these songs of the view correspond to their realised experience.

As mentioned in the *Tantra of Heaped Jewels* and elsewhere, as expressed by the twelve great vajra laughters, there is the tradition of singing songs of realisation, vajra verses of spiritual realisation composed of words that mix verse and prose. For example, all of glorious Saraha's meditative experiences of realised mind are taught in vajra verses or doha. This composition also corresponds with the confidence and demeanour of the view to be sung with a melodious tone, and can be called both song and doha. In Shabkar's own words:

Teaching Day One

> For me, the yogi Tsokdruk Rangdrol,
> Whatever happens, happiness or sorrow,
> It is in my nature to sing.

Thus, this text is also referred to as *'Songs of the Trekchö View'*.

Regarding the phrase *'Capable of Swiftly Traversing the Paths and Levels without Exception'*, for the threefold ground, path, and result of Dzogchen, the ground is primordial purity and spontaneous presence, the path is trekchö and tögal, and the result is the kayas and wisdoms. Regarding the words 'without exception', as explained earlier in the meaning of the name Dzogpa Chenpo, however many approaches there are to the profound and vast Dharma of the Victorious One, from the lower vehicle of the shravakas to the upper vehicle of Secret Mantra, there is nothing that is not subsumed or incomplete within the innermost essence of this doctrine, the Dzogpa Chenpo state of inseparable basic space and rigpa. As this wisdom fully pervades samsara and nirvana, it is called *'chenpo'* or 'great'. In this way, this is a path that subsumes the key points of all paths without exception and is swift to traverse.

Although the aim of the ultimate level to be attained and the goal that is the destination are identical, there are different examples of how to travel there: travelling like cattle, travelling like elephants, and travelling as fast as the coursing of the sun and moon. Similarly, it is possible that in the short period of one lifetime, or mere years and months, that which has not been found for many aeons since begininglesss time, the ultimate result of the blissful path of enlightenment, can be reached. Just as it is said:

> A single lamp can dispel the darkness of a thousand years.

The statement *'Swiftly Traversing the Paths and Levels without Exception'* mainly demonstrates the function of this teaching. This is connected to the example of the capacity of the teaching, which is compared to the soaring garuda, hence its name *'Flight of the Garuda'*. The garuda is said to be the powerful king of birds, also known as the great garuda. When this powerful king of birds soars high in the sky, at that time it exhibits four special features. The first is that it is capable of pursuing a lofty flight-path. The second is that the ground, and all the mountains and rivers, are subsumed beneath its presence. The third is that although there are things on the ground below which can be seen, they remain unconnected to it, and the fourth is that there is no doubt or fear of falling down into the ravines or steep cliffs below.

As in this example, the view of the peak resultant vehicle of Dzogpa Chenpo is lofty. Within this, when view, meaning, and meditation are gathered together, the exalted teachings of the eight lower vehicles are implicitly complete. At the same time, although the view is lofty, conduct is refined. As karmic causality is extremely subtle, based on pure refined conduct, when Dzogchen rigpa, naturally occurring wisdom, appears laid bare free of contrivance and corruption, hope and doubt, and without the cage of fabrication, the defiles of fear of straying, fear of error, and fear of loss do not exist. Just as it is said:

> At the level of all-good there is nothing not good,
> Thus the one Samantabhadra is without distinctions of good and bad.

Thus, this text entitled *'Flight of the Garuda'* combines the enlightened meaning of the tantras, a fundamental summary of the scriptures, and the essence of the foremost instructions. The subject of the actual body of the presentation is clearly taught by this title. It is a foremost instruction with an illustrative symbolic title that cannot be mistaken for any other. This completes explanation of the meaning of the title.

The Expression of Worship

Now, in the expression of worship, there first appears the homage to the lama, which is in accordance with the general sutras and tantras:

NAMO GURUBHY

Just as it is taught:

> In a time before there were any lamas
> The name 'buddha' also did not exist.
> The buddhas of a thousand aeons
> Appeared in reliance on the lama.

Thus the root of blessings is the lama. The object signified by this expression of worship is the ultimate lama who is inseparable from the dharmakaya nature of mind itself, and to whom homage is paid with the faith of the view that knows one's own nature. This homage is made in the Sanskrit language with the purpose of receiving blessings of the authentic source of the Dharma, which is in accordance with and corresponds to a general translator's homage of Sutra and Tantra, Kangyur and Tengyur. Following this, there are additional expressions of homage, in which Shabkar pays homage to his three lamas in three stanzas that mention their names. The first of these is:

> **From the seven steed-drawn sun disc of your all-illuminating wisdom and love,**
> **Immeasurable rays of compassionate light radiate forth**
> **Which instantly dispel all the darkness of beings in the three realms.**
> **I pay homage to Chokyi Gyalpo.**

The object of this expression of worship is Shabkar's extraordinary root lama whom he praises here. This is Bontsang Dalai Deching Wang Ngawang Darge Palzangpo Chogyal Ngakgi Wangpo, who at that time was said to be a king in Mongolia. Here homage is offered in the form of beautiful objects: in the expanse of his enlightened mind, the all-illuminating basic space of the sky, the sun of wisdom and love arises. Rays of light of immeasurable compassion without limit radiate forth tremendously and unobstructedly. The three realms refer to the apparent, the unapparent, and the semi-apparent realms. For the limitless gathering of beings, who are not abandoned by the tremendous wisdom activities of the Victorious One, the great demon of ignorance at the root of existence is eliminated either directly, indirectly, or through its own strength, by the singular great manifestation of the compassionate wisdom of awareness. Just as it is said:

> Enlightened qualities equal those of all buddhas,
> Yet the protector's kindness surpasses them all.

First the lama guides us in the generation stage deities in connection with the vase empowerment. Then they guide us in the channels and energies of yogic inner heat tummo, in connection with the secret empowerment. Following that, the lama guides us in bliss emptiness Mahamudra in connection with the wisdom knowledge empowerment. Finally, they guide us in trekchö and tögal in connection with the precious word empowerment. Not only does the lama grant the complete empowerments, including those of permission and the guardians of the teachings, but continuously every day they bestow instruction and the key points of practice in connection with the four empowerments, as if filling a vase to the brim. This is the lama who possesses the three kindnesses, the manner of which is just as recorded in their respective biographies. It is for this reason that Shabkar offers respectful homage, bowing down first to this master.

The second expression of worship pays homage to Ngakchang Dorje Namgyal. This is Shabkar's father, the great khenpo of Tsodu. The manifestations of enlightened body, speech, and mind which are established in the common perceptions of those who act through the three doors, depend on a father for the factors to give rise to their holy body, speech, and mind. It is from these that their outstanding, especially exalted enlightened qualities are accomplished. Therefore, the father of Shabkar's enlightened mind is Chogyal Ngakgi Wangpo, and the father of his enlightened form is Ngakchang Dorje Namgyal, so the second expression of worship is dedicated to him:

> **In the vast sky of your empty luminous dharmakaya,**
> **Clouds of compassion and love amass.**
> **Upon the earth of fortunate ones to be tamed,**
> **You expertly pour a rain of Dharma. I pay homage to Ngakchang Dorje.**

Here the expression of worship can be understood to mean 'in the sky of dharmakaya, vast clouds of sambhogakaya wisdom and compassion amass. Upon whichever fortunate beings are to be tamed, Ngakchang Dorje is the master who satisfies them with whatever they desire with rains of Dharma.'

The third expression of worship is to Jamyang Gyatso. He was the root guru of the region where Shabkar was born, and revered by all as their crown jewel. For Shabkar, by practising the nectar of this master's teachings and oral instructions, he was brought up as the main disciple of his speech. Due to his kindness, he is the subject of this third expression of worship:

> **On the ship of the view, the central great sail of supreme intention is hoisted.**
> **Driven by the wind of diligence across the ocean of existence,**
> **You establish all drowning beings on the jewel island of the three kayas.**
> **I pay homage to the captain, Jamyang Gyatso.**

From the endless vast ocean of samsara, the view is lofty realisation of the view of Secret Mantra. Conduct is the actions of the bodhisattva children of the Victorious Ones, the six perfections. Without separating from the realisation and conduct of the supreme intent of bodhicitta, the ship of method and wisdom which are the two accumulations, manifest and non-manifest, is propelled by the wind of diligence. Wandering beings sinking and drowning in the samsaric sea of suffering are guided to and set upon the shores of omniscient liberation of the jewel island of the three kayas. Such is this meaningful expression of worship.

These three stanzas of homage are presented using the forms of the sun, pleasant rain, and a great ship, which are connected to threefold wisdom, compassion, and capacity, and the three kayas. This completes the expression of worship.

The Author's Pledge of Composition

From the wisdom and love of the seven steed-drawn sun disc of these three,
Warm rays of potent blessings radiate.
Striking this fortunate white lotus renunciant,
Rigpa was revealed and a thousand petals of experience and realisation bloomed.

These songs of the view, nectar essence that liberates on taste
Welling up wonderfully in the flower of my mind,
I offer to the swarm of bees, my fortunate students.
Enjoy it with devotion to your hearts' content.

In the above expression of worship, from the sun disc-like wisdom of knowledge and love of these three lamas, rays of light still warm with the power of blessings, radiate forth. They strike Shabkar, the karmically fortunate renunciant who is like a white lotus, and like sunlight bringing a lotus flower to bloom, his rigpa awareness was revealed. Thus the thousand petals of his enlightened qualities of experience and realisation bloomed and blossomed. Here 'rigpa' needs to be understood as the dynamic energy of the wisdom of naturally occurring rigpa which was revealed, or becoming free from obscurations, became manifest.

By the power of practice for accomplishment for personal benefit, the qualities of experience and realisation developed from within. Through engaging in enlightened activities for the benefit of others, the comprehensive conclusion is to fulfil the hopes and desires of beings to be tamed. Thus, from the centre of the pollen bed of his lotus mind the heart essence welled forth wonderfully, and from the brimming treasury of his enlightened mind he recited these songs of Dzogchen trekchö.

Meditation, together with conduct and result, is like honey, the essence of reviving nectar which overcomes the chronic disease of samsara. This he offers to his fortunate students who are likened to bees, all those with karma to be his students, and also those who are yet to become his students, with each one receiving an appropriate share. He instructs them to 'enjoy' it with an attitude of faith and devotion, allowing the insatiable to become satisfied.

This teaches the author's pledge of composition and his expression which encourages those with fortune towards the Dharma. It also implicitly teaches the origin of the Dharma of the three lineages. The general and specific transmission of the doctrine can be understood to be indicated here implicitly. This completes the goodness of the beginning, the introduction.

Goodness of the Middle—The Meaning of the Text

Second is the goodness of the middle, the meaning of the text, which in twenty-three sections covers view, meditation, and conduct, and also gives a presentation of the ground, path, and result. In addition, in a continuous and integrated manner, the enlightened intent of the Mind, Expanse, and Foremost Instruction Sections of Dzogpa Chenpo are taught in accordance with beings to be tamed of sharp, middling, and dull faculties. This is primarily suitable for the minds of those who have as yet not engaged in extensive study, contemplation, or training, and is taught through refined means.

Song One
The Essence of Enlightenment

The first song teaches how the fundamental continuum of the essence of enlightenment is primordially present within us:

> **EMAHO!**
> **I, the spacious, carefree, and serene renunciant**
> **Sing a song of the view *Flight of the Garuda*,**
> **Which facilitates swift progress of the levels and paths**
>   **without exception.**
> **Fortunate heart children, listen carefully.**

Rejecting busy samsaric worldly activities, Shabkar is spacious and carefree. Having mastered non-fixated unfettered rigpa, he is serene. Having the confidence of the renounced conduct of a yogi, he teaches the view of Dzogpa Chenpo. This begins first with 'EMAHO', an exclamation of amazement. What is amazing is taught by the seven kinds of amazement:

> **Like the thundering roar of the dragon, the renown of**
>   **'Buddha'**
> **Resounds throughout both samsara and nirvana.**

This teaches the foundation of amazement, the Buddha. Regarding the Buddha it is taught:

> Because he has awakened from the sleep of ignorance,

And because his mind has expanded to include that which can be known,
His understanding blossoms like the petals of a lotus.

When the enlightened qualities of abandonment and realisation are perfected, this is called 'buddha', therefore:

**Continuously present in the mindstreams of the six types of beings,
How amazing we are never separate from its company even for a moment!**

So, what is the first way this is amazing? In the Second Buddha Master Padmasambhava's foremost instruction *A Garland of Views*, when he discusses the view that all phenomena are enlightened in the representational mandala, he teaches by making distinction between the buddha of nature, the buddha of realisation, and the buddha of accomplishment. Of these, the buddha of nature is further divided into three: the buddha of the cause of birth, the buddha of the support of birth, and the buddha of the full manifestation of birth.

Regarding the buddha of the cause of birth, it is the cause which brings about body and mind. Regarding the buddha of the support of birth, these are the elements of the parents' bodies and minds. What is taught to be the buddha of the full manifestation of birth is established at the time of fully establishing our bodies. Moreover, the buddha of realisation refers to those who reside on the vidyadhara levels, and the buddha of accomplishment is established upon actually perceiving suchness. These are taught in this way, distinguished as natural and circumstantial.

Connecting this to what Shabkar teaches above, not even an iota of unenlightened phenomena can be identified, however of course there are still divisions and differences. Because there is a difference between being unrealised and realised, being unfamiliar and familiar, we need to train our minds to actualise the level of buddhahood. If that is the case, how are sentient beings called buddhas? How does enlightenment reside continuously in the mindstreams of the six types of sentient being? Moreover, how is it never separate for even a moment? When we discuss Dzogpa Chenpo, we need to know the mode of presence of the ground from the very beginning.

The ground, the manner of delusion, the manner of pervasion,
The place, the paths, the doors, the object,
Practice, its measure, the bardos,

Teaching Day One

The state of liberation itself: the eleven.

This indicates the entire threefold ground, path, and result, as well as the view, meditation, and conduct of Dzogpa Chenpo in a summarised form. In this case, in the very beginning, the ultimate primordial fundamental nature of the luminosity of the ground is also the ultimate true nature of all phenomena. It is from within this state that all appearances of samsara and nirvana arise. However, in the very course of their arising, they do not waver from this state, and there are no other phenomena that exist beyond this. This is also the ultimate level of liberation, and so is described as the fundamental nature of ultimate dharmakaya.

Then, as the two obscurations together with adventitious habituations are purified, at the final stage of possessing the two purities, the truth of cessation of the supreme vehicle, this is called 'svabhavikakaya'. For such ground, because there is no different duality of what is known as 'liberation' or 'delusion', it is natural vast evenness. On this ground, not even a mere speck of elaborated characteristics is to be found, so it is primordially pure. Not mere emptiness or nothingness like space, it is impartial self-luminosity, without limit or bias, and is therefore spontaneously present. As it is the source of all apparent phenomena in samsara and nirvana, it is taught to be 'all-pervasive compassion'.

The ground is characterised by being endowed with the three wisdoms: empty essence, luminous nature, and all-pervasive compassion. From the vast luminosity of this ground as basic space, without wavering in any respect, any expressive manifestation of apparent phenomena in samsara and nirvana can arise. When wandering unrealised in samsara, all variety of appearances of grasping and fixation appear. Dualistic appearances of self and other, happiness and sadness, good and bad, and so on, all arise. At the time of realisation of nirvana or total enlightenment, realising the natural mode of presence of the nature of phenomena as it is, whatever myriad appearances manifest, they arise as primordially and totally liberated, non-dual vast evenness, nothing other than the nature of enlightenment.

For this reason, from the perspective of realisation of the very nature of phenomena, the totally pure fundamental nature, all totally pure appearances are the nature of enlightenment and undeluded, ascertained and established by infallible rigpa of true nature. Although when examined by a dualistic deluded mind things are not like this, such examination by dualistic deluded mind does not harm non-dual pure mind.

Do not rely on consciousness, rely on wisdom.

This is the statement of someone who has reached authentic understanding. Thus, enlightened nature which resides continuously in the mindstream of sentient beings, which has never been separate for even an instant, is not just particularly noteworthy, it is the most amazing and wondrous state. Therefore at the beginning of expressing all this, Shabkar utters the words of amazement 'EMAHO!'

The second expression of amazement is:

> **Not knowing that buddha exists within,**
> **How amazing they search for enlightenment elsewhere!**

This is the second great expression of amazement. The term 'sentient being' refers to beings that possess a conscious mind. Therefore, living beings with consciousness are called 'sentient beings'. The true nature of consciousness from the very beginning is the nature of enlightenment, but sentient beings who do not know that buddha exists within themselves are likened to a prince who goes wandering off. Whether a prince lives in the kingdom or not, he is still a prince. There is no changing that. However, when he does not stay in the palace and goes wandering the lands, he takes on the appearance of a wandering vagabond. If he returns to the palace, he can still rule the kingdom. His nature does not change, either when he is ruling the kingdom or roaming the plains. Whatever his status was before, he holds the same status later on, but the way his appearance manifests can differ. So, while we wander as vagabonds not knowing that we are actually princes or princesses, we cannot transcend having the appearance of a vagabond.

To call searching for enlightenment outside while all the time having it within 'amazing' is an ironic and scornful reproach. If we are sentient beings, then sentient beings have minds which are comprised of the eightfold group of consciousness. Consciousness and wisdom are not the same, so does that establish a third aggregate comprised of both good and bad? No. By the strength of training on the path of practice, when a yogi realises and masters the true nature of mind, present primordially without meeting or parting, in its presence there not even an iota of what is known as an 'independently existing' eightfold group of consciousness. Consciousness itself arises as wisdom, and likewise, all phenomena arise as purity. As it is taught:

> Free of purity and attainment, mind is Buddha.
> Unchanging and immaculate, it is the Dharma,
> And its spontaneously present qualities are the Sangha.
> Therefore your own mind is supreme.

In name it is Dzogchen. In actuality the path is based on mind. Given this, except for generally maintaining the classification that mind is the eightfold group of consciousness, this is only so because its true nature is unapparent. Unable to find even a trace of what is called the 'unconditioned luminous nature of mind', wherever it may be, is what Shabkar is referring to here.

> **Directly manifest, like the radiant orb of the sun,**
> **Yet how amazing so few see it!**

This is the third great expression of amazement. The nature of mind, essence of dharmakaya, is present within us from the very beginning. When this true nature of luminous wisdom is seen by someone who knows how to look, it is clear and limpid without obstruction. To give an example, no darkness exists in the orb of the sun, and similarly no distortion of obscuration has ever mixed with it. Possessing the radiance of one hundred thousand brilliant suns, it is manifestly pure and independently luminous. However, except for those who are fortunate, endowed with eyes of wisdom, and who have already accumulated merit, it cannot be seen. This is said to be 'amazing'.

When a practitioner sits motionless in the seven-point Mt. Meru-like posture, with sense faculties unstirring like a lake reflecting the stars and planets, and with mind unwavering and free of all elaborated extremes, then as All-knowing Victorious Longchenpa taught:

> Dharmakaya, without references of grasping or fixation,
> The immaculate luminous orb of the sun,
> Arises without limit or centre: bliss, clarity, and no-thought.

When all concepts and thoughts are placed in the state of the true nature of phenomena without straying, conceptualisation dissolves into the basic space of phenomena, grasping and fixation become naturally eliminated, and together with the bliss, clarity, and no-thought of luminous Dzogpa Chenpo, self-arising innate wisdom dawns. Thus pristine lucid unwavering no-thought realisation of dharmakaya arises from within.

> **Our parent-less mind is buddha itself.**
> **How amazing it is unborn and deathless!**

From the *Mahayana Treatise Uttaratantra*:

> This luminous nature of mind

Is space-like, changeless.

Just as space is unborn and deathless, the very nature or actual nature of mind has no parents. It is self-arising and timelessly abiding. This abiding is like space, empty luminosity without limit or centre, beyond birth and death, ageing and decline, and therefore it is taught to be amazing. The *Mayaguhyagarbha* also teaches this meaning:

> EMAHO!
> Amazing marvellous Dharma,
> Secret of all perfect buddhas.
> Everything is born from the unborn;
> Birth itself is unborn.

In this case, if the fundamental nature of self-arising wisdom, the meaning of Dzogpa Chenpo, is not realised just as it is, mind will not be enlightened. Well then, why do we need to train our mind on the path, progressing through the stages of study, contemplation, and meditation to ultimately attain enlightenment? Isn't it pointless to teach all these paths and vehicles? No, it is not pointless. The minds and inclinations, the constitutions, faculties, and attitudes of beings to be tamed are multitudinous, therefore there is no way not to teach the various stages of the path of provisional meaning.

However, all these supporting vehicles, which are supported by the methods and paths, are for the sake of supporting this one truth, therefore except for basing the path on the ultimate wisdom of definitive truth, the meaning of Dzogpa Chenpo, the self-arising wisdom of rigpa, any enlightenment is impossible. Because of this, our own limitless mind is buddha.

But what is the reason that mind has never been born and knows no death? This wisdom is the nature of mind, not something that arises from it. The fundamental nature of all things is emptiness. This is the way things exist, not something that arises from them. What we refer to as 'realising' or 'not realising' emptiness, 'seeing' or 'not seeing' true nature, is not about adding the true nature of the ground onto ourselves. The ground is the ground of realisation which abides in suchness. At the time manifestations of the ground arise from the ground, if they are realised as such, liberation occurs, if they are not realised then delusion occurs. Depending on this, the terms 'sentient being' and 'buddha' arise. This is just the way things are and the way things appear.

As for this realisation or non-realisation, when the true nature of mind that resides in the ground is realised by the consciousness of mind which realises, the true nature of mind which is realised is not required to be conceptual mind. When the unborn nature of mind is realised, there are no separate aspects of conceptual mind or consciousness that are left behind. Unobstructed self-luminosity of luminous rigpa, essence of the unity of appearances and emptiness, is called the 'true nature of mind'.

> **Whatever myriad joys and sorrows are experienced,**
> **How amazing that it is not improved or impaired in the slightest!**

This is the fifth great expression of amazement. 'Mind', 'consciousness', 'conceptual mind', whatever term we use for it, experiences all variety of joyful and sorrowful perceptions. In particular, the way that everything manifests in samsara is not free from the three sufferings. Because the mind that meditates also needs to develop from the threefold collection of sense objects, sense faculties, and consciousness, then it is subject to arising and cessation, and therefore experiences manifold compounded happiness and suffering of the path. However, from the perspective of fundamental true nature, it is far beyond terms of existent or non-existent, compounded or uncompounded. That which is seen by individual self-knowing is without transition and change throughout the three times, and it does not become improved or impaired whatsoever. Just as Lord Maitreya taught:

> However it was, later it will be so:
> Unchanging true nature.

By means of the five great expressions of amazement, the above mainly discusses wisdom of primordially pure emptiness. Now this is taught in combination with luminosity of spontaneously present appearances:

> **This unborn, primordially pure nature of mind,**
> **How amazing it is unfabricated and spontaneously present from the beginning!**

In general, primordial purity and spontaneous presence are inseparable, the epitome of a unified single essence. As it is primordially pure, so it is spontaneously present, and because it is spontaneously present, it dwells in primordial purity. As for the direct significance of this, the nature of the ground when applied to freedom from transition and change is unborn and unimpeded from the very first, the unchanging nature of mind pure from the very beginning, which is not newly made from nothing into something by anyone, nor fabricated into being something that it is not. Spontaneously present exactly however it was originally, this is said to be 'amazing'.

This kind of nature that is pure from the very beginning and present spontaneously, this self-arising wisdom, is unconstrained so has no need to be freed again, which is the final expression of amazement:

> **This originally liberated self-knowing nature,**
> **How amazing it is liberated by leaving whatever arises to be!**

Here 'original' has the meaning of having no permeation, action, or effort. From time without beginning or end, it does not originate from or reside anywhere. It does not go anywhere or possess any nature. It is self-knowing wisdom beyond the realm of fetter and liberation. This abiding nature, originally transcending eternalism, nihilism, and so forth—all elaborations of the eight extremes—when left self-settled for whatever arises to be, is primordially liberated. This state of liberation is like, for example, gold which from the very beginning is intrinsically golden. Gold does not need to become golden.

The above completes the section of the meaning of the fundamental continuum of the primordially unchanging essence of enlightenment, enlightenment that dwells within us, as taught by the seven great expressions of amazement.

Teaching Day One

Song Two
The Nature of Rigpa

Now, in connection with the way in which the manifestations of the ground arise from the ground as liberation or delusion, we address the preliminaries for the main Dzogchen practice of introducing the nature of rigpa, which include investigation into mind and searching for its hidden flaw.

> **EMAHO!**
> **Fortunate children of the family, listen without distraction.**

Here, through several consecutive examples, thorough investigation of mind is taught as follows:

> **The Victorious Ones of the three times without exception,**
> **Teach the eighty-four thousand divisions of Dharma, and so forth,**
> **Countless teachings, equal to the limits of space.**
> **Yet they are for the purpose of realising your own mind.**
> **The Victorious Ones do not teach anything other than this.**

All enlightened actions and activities of the Victorious Ones of the three times, those that have passed on, those that are currently manifest, and those that are still to appear without exception, are united solely for the benefit of sentient beings. To unite all beings with their undeluded actual fundamental nature comprises the single method to purify delusion primordially, demolish samsara from the foundation, and conquer suffering from the root. Thus, the three collections of Vinaya, Abhidharma, and Sutra, together with the fourth collection of vidyadhara Mantra Tantra, comprise the remedy to overcome the afflictive emotions and the three poisons equally, and encompass the teachings of the buddhas which are equal to the extent of space.

However many profound and vast modes of Dharma there are, if we summarise the meaning of them all based on this momentary mind of ours, when the demarcation between samsara and nirvana, liberation and delusion is revealed, some teachings do so directly, some do so in passing, and some indicate it implicitly. In short, there is not one teaching, whether provisional or definitive, that is not a method to bring about realisation of the essence of the true nature of our own mind and its undeluded and uncompounded nature. Not one of the victorious perfect buddhas has ever taught anything different and will never do so. This point is taught through examples as follows:

> **For example, when the single root of a tree is cut,**
> **A billion branches and leaves wither all at once.**
> **Similarly, when the single root of mind is cut,**
> **The leaves of samsara: grasping, fixation, and so on, wither.**

Just as Gyalwa Longchenpa taught:

> You may strive at acceptance and rejection with the lower vehicles,
> But they are not accomplished in aeons; this is terribly exhausting.

The paths of the lower vehicles of Sutra and Mantra each have their own distinctive features, however for some, such as the causal vehicles, it is necessary to wait for the result which comes about elsewhere. For some other vehicles, although they may be included among the resultant vehicles, they do not contain the complete key points of the path and so do not embrace the actual crucial point. Because those are not systems of decisive instruction, when leaves and branches are cut, this is unable to eliminate the trunk of a tree entirely.

In the above example of cutting the roots of a mature tree, the thousand branches and leaves automatically wither. Any partial remedies for afflictive emotions, such as renunciation, transformation, incorporation into the path, and so on, can do nothing except merely suppress afflictive emotions in part. In contrast, by means of the key point of afflictive emotions becoming purified in wisdom and the nature of mind becoming liberated in dharmakaya, we are taught that grasping and fixation are naturally eliminated, samsara is primordially pure, and mundane existence is merely a name, liberated beyond the extremes of existence and nothingness.

The above example uses numbers to convey the point. Now to speak in terms of time:

> **An empty house may be dark for a thousand years,**
> **Yet it is illuminated in an instant by a lamp.**
> **Likewise, the instant luminosity of mind is realised,**
> **Negativities and obscurations accumulated over countless aeons are purified.**

The discovery of genuine innate wisdom is the mark of gathering the accumulations and purifying obscurations. All the lower paths of Sutra and Tantra are like the rivers of the land which all flow into the sea.

None of them is anything other than a method and a path to discover all-knowing wisdom. Through embracing extraordinary method and wisdom, in the very moment a single lamp is lit, the gloom of ancient darkness in a thousand-year-old empty house is completely dispelled. Likewise, in the very moment the luminosity of our mind is recognised—self-arising wisdom pure from the very beginning—through the strength of this powerful accumulation of undefiled virtue of knowing our own nature, countless aeons of accumulated negativities and obscurations are purified. It is implicit that when darkness is lifted, appearances become clear and do not need to be searched for. Similarly, it is taught that as the two accumulations are completed, the two kayas are attained at the same time.

An example of the reason for this is taught as follows:

> **The nature of the radiant orb of the sun**
> **Cannot be obscured by a thousand aeons of darkness.**
> **Similarly, the luminous nature of your mind**
> **Cannot be obscured by aeons of delusion.**

To think 'the sun has become obscured by clouds' is only what appears to have happened from our distant external perspective. Other than this, in fact there is no way the radiant orb of the sun can be covered by clouds. What is even more unlikely is for the illuminating sun disc, the sole means of dispelling darkness, to become covered by darkness. In the same way that this is impossible, our mind has a true nature of purity, which is the essence of primordial luminosity itself. However long it may have experienced delusion, many aeons upon aeons, the essence of luminosity has never been sullied by delusion. Due to this, it is taught the nature of luminosity has never been deluded.

To teach this by means of a different example:

> **The nature of the sky transcends limits of colour and shape,**
> **It does not become sullied by white or black clouds.**
> **The nature of mind transcends limits of colour and shape,**
> **It does not become sullied by white or black phenomena of**
> **   virtue or non-virtue.**

The spacious aspect of empty space whose extremes cannot be reached is called 'the sky'. If we want to describe its nature, shape, colour, or scale, none of these can be measured. Whatever appears in the sky, not just white or black clouds, but hailstones, thunder and lightning, or rainbows and so forth, it does not become sullied in the slightest. It is unable to be benefited or harmed, much less made happy or sad. Likewise, the nature or true state of mind, the characteristic of unchanging luminosity, does not become sullied by any virtuous or unvirtuous phenomena.

As taught in the tantras, in the Dzogpa Chenpo seven or eight secret or great expressions of amazement, there is not the slightest difference between two people, one of whom takes the lives of a billion sentient beings, and the other who engages continuously in the ten transcendental perfections. This is similar to the key point of self-knowing unchanging freedom from birth and death.

Our nature may be like this, but just being like this is not enough. If we do not practise the key points of the path, we will not be liberated. This is taught as follows:

> **For example, milk is the causal factor of butter,**
> **However, without churning, butter will not form.**
> **Likewise, the essence of enlightenment is the causal factor of all beings,**
> **But without practice, sentient beings do not become enlightened.**
> **If they practise this, all will be liberated,**
> **Regardless of sharp or dull faculties.**
> **Even a cowherd will be liberated if they practise.**

Every single kind of sentient being, from the lowliest micro-organism upwards, is pervaded in their fundamental continuum by the essence of enlightenment, just as a sesame seed is pervaded by oil. All samsaric sentient beings are able to become enlightened. However, as in the example of milk being the cause of butter, without passing through the action of churning it, butter will not materialise. If sentient beings do practise this path, then they will all be liberated and escape from the bonds of samsara. There is no difference between those who in this life have studied Buddhist logic, and so forth, or whether or not they have all kinds of knowledge and learning, or sharp or dull faculties. As an example of stupidity, even if an uneducated cowherd enters this genuine path and practises with steadfast faith and samaya, they will be liberated.

> **When you directly realise the truth of the luminosity of your mind,**
> **There is no need for experts to explain it,**
> **Just as when you are eating muscovado,**
> **You do not need to be told how it tastes.**
>
> **Without realising this, even panditas are deluded.**
> **Even if they are skilled at explaining the entire nine vehicles,**

**It is like telling tales of the distant and unseen.
Enlightenment is more distant than the sky from the earth.**

From Rahula's *Praise for the Mother*:

> Indescribable, inconceivable, and inexpressible transcendent
>   perfection of wisdom,
> The unborn, unimpeded essence of space,
> Is the domain of individual self-knowing wisdom,
> Mother of the Victorious Ones of the three times.

Dzogpa Chenpo and Mother Prajnaparamita are synonyms for the same meaning: individual self-knowing wisdom free of description, conception, and expression. As the truth of the luminosity of our mind transcends description, conception, and expression, without realising this truth even the most eloquent scholars cannot explain it. But if you have actually realised the truth of the luminosity of your mind, there is not any need for eloquent scholars. For example, having put some muscovado into your mouth, while experiencing its taste you do not need to look to others to explain its flavour.

If this point is not realised correctly, even if someone has the title of pandita or even mahapandita, if they have not been able to transcend delusion, then however skilled they are at explaining the nine vehicles with empty verbosity, it is all tales of the distant and unseen. This is not something they have actually seen, only what they have heard. Repeating what you have heard is nothing more than guessing at shapes under snow, or a blind person trying to get their bearings. Thus, it is taught the attainment of buddhahood remains as distant as the sky from the earth.

> **If you do not realise the genuine luminosity of your mind,
> Even if you maintain discipline for an aeon,
> Or meditate on patience for an age,
> You will not rise above the three realms of samsara.
> Therefore strive to sever the root of mind.**

If you do not realise the actual luminous mode of presence of your mind itself, genuine nature in the way that it is, if you have not actually seen the face of the dharmakaya nature of mind, however long you strive at other practices of generosity, discipline, patience, diligence, and so on, even if you do so for an aeon, then like a group of blind people trying to find their way, you do not rise even one step above the three realms of samsara. All such actions accomplish only samsara and nothing more.

If you have the actual essence of realisation of the actual fundamental nature of your mind, vast accumulations of merit and wisdom are reconciled in an instant, and you become liberated from the realm of samsara. Thus, the unmistaken focus for great effort and diligence is to see the nature of mind. Therefore Shabkar teaches us and followers in later generations to strive at this. This completes the section of teaching on cutting the root of mind and searching for its hidden flaw.

Teaching Day One

Song Three
The Arising, Abiding, and Disappearance of Mind

Now the main introduction of the common preliminaries, searching for the arising, abiding, and disappearance of mind, is taught:

> **EMAHO!**
> **Listen again, all my fortunate noble children.**
>
> **Without resolving the root of your mind,**
> **Whatever spiritual practice you do will not reach the key point.**
> **For example, it would be like putting a target in front of you,**
> **But shooting an arrow in a distant direction.**
> **It would be like leaving a thief in your home,**
> **But searching frantically for them outside.**
>
> **It would be like ignoring a demon at the eastern gate,**
> **But offering an effigy at the western gate.**
> **It would be like a pauper, unaware their hearthstones are gold,**
> **Going to beg for alms from others.**
> **In this case, fortunate children of my heart,**
> **Resolve the root of your mind like this.**

This teaches the direction in which we should search for our mind. It does not depend on the need to train for countless aeons on the Sutra path. The wisdom that is attained by applying the key points of extraordinary means of Mantra with characteristics over an extended period of a few lifetimes, is simply introduced on the path of Dzogchen by the lama's foremost instructions, through which one passes onto the level of actualising the fundamental nature. This comes down to knowing or not knowing the secret essential point of mind.

When the secret of this essential point is not known, this is like not being able to identify the core parts of an engine, and being under the impression that the auxiliary components are more important. In such confusion, whatever spiritual practice you do is ineffective. This is likened to placing a target nearby but firing an arrow far away, leaving a thief inside your home but searching for one outside, or ignoring a demon in the east while casting an effigy to the west, all of which are totally ineffectual.

If we resolve dharmakaya essence, the nature of our mind, upon our own mind, then this is taught to be a great discovery. For example, if a pauper does not know that the hearthstones in his house are all made of gold, then he will not be free from the suffering of poverty his whole life. However, the moment he realises what they are, he is no longer poor but has become wealthy. As long as he actually picks up the gold and makes use of it, then his wealth will be abundant. Likewise, when we discover enlightenment in our mind, we do not need to search for another place of refuge. Without mistaking what is important with what is meaningless, by relying on the quintessence of the lama's foremost instruction in this way, we are taught to resolve the root of our mind.

As for the actual method to search for the arising, abiding, and disappearance of mind, it is taught as follows:

> **This so-called 'mind', which moves to and fro knowing this and that,**
> **If pursued is not caught, but vanishes, elusive as mist.**
> **If set down does not stay, but flits about and moves away.**
> **Without definition as 'this', it is insubstantial emptiness.**
>
> **Our mind, experiencer of various joys and sorrows,**
> **From where does it first arise, what is its source?**
> **External phenomena of mountains, cliffs, rivers, trees?**
> **The wind in the sky, or anything else, solid or insubstantial?**
> **Ask 'Where does it come from?' and investigate its root.**
> **Or if you think 'Does it come from my parent's blood and semen?'**
> **Analyse how that would happen.**

What is known as 'mind' exists while not existing, is manifest without basis. It perceives objects and is aware of discursive thoughts, the stirring of all kinds of thoughts. If mind is chased after in pursuit, there is nothing to catch. If it is set down, it does not stay where it is left. Flustered by too many thoughts, there is nothing it will not think. If we want to grasp and show 'it is this', it is insubstantial emptiness, without anything to grasp or hold on to. In truth, does this mind, which has experienced multitudinous joys, sorrows, and everything in between in this samsaric realm from beginningless time until now, exist or not?

If it does not exist, then why is a living person different from inanimate earth, stone, and wood? If it does exist, and we examine where first it comes from, in the middle where it remains, and where it goes in the end, then it is impossible to demonstrate how it could initially arise from external earth, stone, mountains, cliffs, rivers, trees, or the sky. The internal causes and conditions of a mother and father bring a physical body into being, but is there anything that can be found to make you think that mind also arises in such a way? Shabkar teaches us to look carefully, to think and analyse this in detail.

> When analysing in this way, having not found a source,
> In the middle, where does it currently reside?
> In your upper or lower body, sense organs, heart, and so on?
> If in the heart, does it reside in the top or bottom?
> What kind of shape, colour, and so on, does it have?

Having not found a source, we cannot yet determine that mind does not exist. Can we find a place where it resides? We think it should surely be somewhere within our body. In that case, where in the body does it reside? In the head or body, the upper, middle, or lower frame, in the five sense organs, the five vital organs, or the six hollow organs? If we think it resides in our heart, is it in the upper, middle, or lower section? In modern times many people consider the mind to reside in the brain. In that case, dividing the brain into regions, in which section does it exist? If we discover where it resides, we will have found that which is residing, and so we will be able to say what kind of shape and colour it has.

> Having analysed carefully, when a dwelling place is not found,
> In the end, when the mind goes,
> Through which sense organ does it leave?
> And in the instant it takes to arrive upon an external object,
> Investigate does the body go or only the mind?
> Do mind and body go as a group, or...?

If at first we cannot find a source of mind, and in the middle we cannot find where it resides, then it is difficult to say where mind goes to in the end. However, with the understanding that thinks 'mind projects onto objects', Shabkar teaches us to investigate through which sense door mind leaves and the manner in which it leaves. When the mind moves onto an object, does the body go or just the mind, or alternatively do mind and body go together as a group?

> Moreover, when an afflictive emotion or thought arises,
> From where does it first arise, and at present where does it remain?
> Look if it has any colour or shape.
> Finally, when it subsides of its own accord and disappears,

> Investigate where it went when it disappeared, and so forth.
>
> At the time of death, what happens when mind departs?
> Analyse carefully until you have determined with certainty
> That it is intangible, free of birth and death, coming and going,
> Empty, pristine, and inexpressible.

Especially when fierce afflictive emotions and thoughts arise and increase, are they easy to find? At that time, at first, where did they come from? Where are they currently residing? If they are present, what kind of colour and shape do they have? Particularly in the end, when afflictive emotions and thoughts subside of their own accord and disappear, how and to where did they disappear? Most especially, at the time of death, what happens to the mind? Where does it go? Examine carefully and investigate these things.

If, in the end, we are left without being able to say 'I found this', that is still not enough. What is the essence of this thing, about which we cannot determine anything or find anything to say? Shabkar is teaching us to investigate until we reach a definitive conclusion that all birth and death, coming and going, about which we cannot say 'It is this', is empty, pristine, and inexpressible. Investigate until we can say 'The way it is determined is like this...'

> The dry examples and explanations of others
> That say 'It is emptiness' are of no use.
> For example, in a place reported to have tigers,
> Even if others say there are none,
> You will not be convinced.
> Likewise, you will be in two minds and doubt.
>
> To have carefully determined and established
> The root of your mind yourself,
> Is like having gone to the valley where tigers are said to live.
> Having searched everywhere, high and low,
> To determine their presence,
> When you do not find any, then you are certain.
> Likewise, in future, you will have no doubt
> And think 'There are tigers in that place'.

In doing this, when we search for the arising, abiding, and disappearance of mind, there is nothing to show that 'mind arises in this way, and goes away here'. Also, when we cannot find anything to say as to where it has disappeared, Shabkar teaches us it is still not suitable to listen to others who say 'Mind is emptiness'. If someone were to say 'There are tigers in such and such a place, I saw them', how do we know that this is actually true? And if someone else were to say 'There aren't any tigers there, I saw that there aren't any', then how can we know that this is true? Just as we believe the existence or absence of something if we see for ourselves, we are also taught to resolve the arising, abiding, and disappearance of mind for ourselves.

Closing Words

We will finish today's teaching here. During our practice sessions this afternoon and tomorrow, go alone to an isolated spot, such as a hillside or among the cool shade of trees, under a house's awning or in a corner of a park, and so on, wherever you want and wherever is comfortable. Then search for the arising, abiding, and disappearance of mind. If you find mind does not exist, you need to be able to explain 'The reason it does not exist is this...' If you find mind does exist, you need to be able to explain 'The way in which it exists is this...' You need to find your own certainty. Otherwise, to repeat what others say, or to ask your companions what they would say and to give the same answer is not suitable.

As I have mentioned on previous occasions, when the opportunity to receive such an important Dharma teaching comes, do not just leave the temple thinking 'There was this teaching that I attended today. It didn't take very long and so didn't delay this and that important worldly activity that I'm off to do now, which is good. I've added it to my list of Dharma teachings that I've received.' Without any actual mark of receiving something or any sign of experience, adding the title of this text to the list of teachings that you have received is of no use.

To receive a lot of teachings but only meditate on them a little is the real cause of becoming resistant to Dharma. In that case, if you do not intend to teach the Dharma, then do not teach it. If you do not intend to study the Dharma, then do not study it. However, if you do embrace the start of a Dharma teaching and begin to listen, from that point forward you need to see if you can learn and practise it appropriately and authentically until you actually manage to do so.

As for the meaning of 'guidance instruction', this is like taking the hand of a blind person and guiding them along the path until they arrive at their intended destination. This is called 'guidance'. For these guidance instructions which we are receiving now, we also need to engage in guidance practice. When a child is taught how to walk, a grown-up needs to help them stand up by holding their hands. A child also needs to see if they can walk by themselves. Likewise, when guidance teachings are given, no benefit comes from just hearing and understanding them. Anyone can understand the mere meaning of words. To connect the meaning of what is being contemplated to the crucial point of meditation is to actually engage in 'guidance practice'.

When I teach Dzogchen, I do not teach it in the manner of the vehicle of characteristics, through engaging in revision of analytical clarification. Up until now, we have been following objective factors through mental elaboration and intellectual analysis, but this is like a blind bird that will never reach the edge of the sky, and so will eventually be unable to fly. Therefore, we need to learn the unified manner of the unelaborated limit of elaboration, the inexpressible limit of expression, and the non-referential limit of referential concepts. Therefore, first, we begin with the correct manner in which to sit. Then, whether we understand or not, whether we know what to meditate on or not, we need to control our mind and begin to meditate.

First in meditation we need to find the one who is meditating, and today's guidance practice is to search for the meditator. Today, while we are searching for the arising, abiding, and disappearance of mind, we ask what is this mind which has been deluded since beginningless time until now? Who is the one looking at the key point of undeluded true mind? Where are they? What are they doing? Up until this point, we have never turned inward but only looked outwards. We have been watching the external show of appearances, and we have seen hundreds of distant phenomena. But now turn inward and look at your own mind which you have never seen. Looking inward, you need to see the single nature of mind.

In modern times, science has completed some research into the way superficial form exists. However, in terms of determining the way inner consciousness exists, and the true nature of knowing and objects of knowledge, science has not yet even arrived at an entry-level of understanding. Having arrived there, except for categorising it with the term 'the hidden secret of the mind', nothing much beyond that has been achieved. Why has scientific method not arrived at a deeper understanding of the mind? Current research methods are unable to traverse the boundary which is cut through by atemporal secret methods. In this case, that which society's laboratories are unable to research through scientific method, that which cannot be observed by any kind of detection equipment, is our inner mind, the root of the joys and sorrows of samsara and nirvana.

The method to realise the secret key of the mind has been known since ancient times on the plateau of the Land of Snows. In mountain hollows and rocky caves there were those who were liberated in the rainbow body, and only left behind their hair and nails. When the remainders of their corporeal elements transformed into the subtle essence of light, how did the sixfold group of consciousness and their sense faculties transform into something else?

This physical body is a collection of atoms of the four elements. That it is a city of microorganisms is also now able to be demonstrated by biologists. When a practitioner vanishes into light in the rainbow body, and especially when one passes into the body of great transformation, many sentient beings included in their own experience and the experience of others, up to and including the microbes of their body, are liberated from the control of deluded manifestations, karma, and afflictive emotions. What is the secret key to this? Theists say there is a god, atheists say there is no god, but this is irrelevant. All knowable phenomena in their entirety need to be determined upon our single mind, as we sit here.

In this case, if we had a hundred days to engage in guidance practice, then we should allocate a few weeks just to search for the arising, abiding, and disappearance of mind. However, this time, during this short teaching, we only have enough time to devote four practice sessions to search for mind. Having completed this brief guidance practice on the entire preliminaries and main practice, I do not know if you will feel that you have gained some benefit which you previously lacked, but at the very least it will teach you how to engage in practice sessions in future, just like pointing out the direction of a mountain. And although time is short, through the blessings of the assembled Sangha, I believe these sessions of group practice will be different from your regular solitary practice.

With so many people coming here especially to receive these teachings, travelling from Amdo, Central Tibet, and Kham, and enduring hardship for the sake of the Dharma, you have made it a truly marvellous and unique event. As it is said: *the people of Ling do not assemble every day; horses do not race every day.* As for this place where we are currently gathered, it is here in times past that Choying Topden Dorje, Shabkar Tsokdruk Rangdrol, Gerong Natsok Rangdrol, and many other great masters placed footprints and handprints of the teaching and accomplishment of Dzogpa Chenpo. Therefore, it is suitable for us to have faith that we too can discover a new inheritance of experience and realisation here.

To tell you the truth, without even mentioning the complete qualities of a genuine lama who teaches the Dharma of Dzogchen, it is difficult even to possess the complete qualities of a worthy student vessel. However, having been entrusted with this Dharma lineage, having had it conferred to me by enlightened holy masters of the past, the responsibility to continue the flow of Dharma at this time has fallen automatically upon myself. So like a tailor who cannot sew or a smith who cannot work metal, I have needed to adopt a similar manner in terms of teaching the Dharma.

Our main aim, of course, is to arrive at a method to give birth to unprecedented realisation in each of our individual mindstreams. That is the fundamental point. This being so, as it is difficult for any of us to encounter this teaching, having met with it, not to seize the key point of practice would be to let the complete freedoms and endowments go to waste, or to be in line for a share of a vast inheritance but then to lose our fortunate entitlement. We can call this fortune the individual benefit for us ordinary people, or the shared benefit of the teachings in general. We can call it repaying the kindness of our parents or bringing benefit to mother-like sentient beings. As such, this teaching combines a hundred meaningful features, so I humbly offer an encouraging reminder not to forgo this truly remarkable opportunity.

Teaching Day Two

Opening Words
Precious Human Rebirth and Impermanence

In order to practise the sacred Dharma authentically with the wish to reach the essential goal in this lifetime, although it is very important to receive instructional guidance teachings on the main practice, it is even more important to establish a firm foundation in the preliminaries. If we slip into the main practice before the foundation of the preliminaries is firmly established, and in the end we have not developed anything in our mindstream, then when the time comes to die we will end up needing to search for a source of refuge elsewhere.

Someone who wants to fulfil their true potential as a human being should have faith in the authentic view and accept the workings of subtle cause and effect. Except for those who have eyes which can see far into the future, while we are living on this planet we do not know how to accomplish even inner mental happiness or well-being. With our impure perception everything we see, all appearances, are false, but it is not impossible for this to change. These impure perceptions belong to a mind which has not trained in the Dharma of the mind changers, or in other words, any Dharma that we have studied has not been assimilated into our mindstream. Dharma and our mindstream are still separate. Whichever scriptural traditions we study, whichever Dharma is most profound, the essential point of the practice which arises from the instructions needs to be applied to our mindstream. For the majority of people, what they learn is left as theory, and the meaning of what they study is not applied to their mindstream in contemplation. We can, of course, observe such kind of people.

In this case, turn your mind away from this life and the next with the four mind changers. With the mind of bodhicitta for the benefit of others, turn your mind away from, or reverse it against, self-centred mental processes. If you get to the point which is like a nauseous person suffering from jaundice who is offered oily food, then the key points of training in the main practice will also come to be determined.

You may be thinking that whenever I sound the conch of Dharma, I always seem to talk about the preliminary practices. There is good reason for this, and when we do discuss the subjects of the mind changers, do not dismiss them assuming you already know their purpose. You need to place yourself as the focus of the mind changers and engage with them directly. The root of self-cherishing, that which is known as 'life' which we hold so dear, together with its basis: the physical mass of the four elements and the gathering of body and mind, is the basis of designation for what we call 'I'. This is considered the most precious thing among everything we cherish.

However, the true value of this body in all succession of lifetimes, both now and in the future, lies in enabling happiness and well-being to arise in the continuity of our mind. This mind accompanies each one of our successive physical bodies, whichever we may adopt. Every one of our parents, relatives, and friends, all people in our region and land, and if we look still further, all living creatures without a single exception, desire happiness and fear suffering in each and every lifetime. Therefore, considering that whether or not we can help ourselves and accomplish meaningful benefit for others comes down to our current physical basis, we need to understand the value of possessing a body with the complete freedoms and endowments.

However, there is no direct benefit from the conducive factors of a precious human rebirth merely assembling once, at some point. According to the foremost instructions of the All-knowing Lord of Dharma, even if the eight unfree incidental circumstances, the eight unfree states that cut the mind off from Dharma, and so on, are not currently present, it is easy for them to appear suddenly. Even if the freedoms and endowments are currently complete, due to adventitious circumstances, they can quickly become incomplete. Because of this, to look for scarce riches outwardly with mental attachment to worldly wealth, is like a small child who mistakes hailstones for jewels. For these most childish of children, who think the attitude and behaviour of ordinary people is appropriate, they need to understand the truth.

The difficulty of finding the freedoms and endowments is a teaching that concerns the physical body. If they have so far not been complete, make them complete now. If they are currently complete, guard them well, so they do not break down in future. At this time, while we have these precious freedoms and endowments, by gathering the accumulations of merit and wisdom, consider that we need to accomplish the capacity to establish all limitless sentient beings in happiness and well-being. We need to have firm resolve, so that even if we are threatened with a spear to the chest, we will not turn back.

If we think back over the time that has already passed in our life, it is not as if we do not believe in cause and effect, or that we have never turned our mind towards the holy Dharma and never practised it. Yet still we think 'Maybe not today, but I'll surely do some practice tomorrow. Let's wait this year, next year will be more conducive. After I've done this and that important task, then I'll turn my attention to the Dharma'. Whoever we are, we cannot estimate the length of this impermanent life.

Unable to calculate the time when the noose of the Lord of Death will hang before us, we live in its shadow. Most people lack the Dharma and depart empty-handed, void of any means to take with them the wealth they have accumulated in life. Without having already gathered virtue and engaged in purification in preparation for the next life, such people do not have anywhere to place their hopes, and any regret at the time of death is useless. Most people are like this when they arrive at that final place of demarcation. If you happen to encounter such a person, it is apparent that this is what they are going through while in the throes of death.

Why do some people end up like that? It is because a sense of urgency has not developed in their mindstreams. Even if they are not foolish enough to think that they will never die, they believe that death will not happen anytime soon, convinced that nothing could happen to them in the next year or two. Continuously thinking this year after year, eventually this is where they end up. We ourselves do not see this underlying threat, as time passes through the stages of life, from youth to middle age, and then into old age. If you compare a photograph of yourself from years ago to now, you may not even recognise yourself having changed so much, but still you do not plan on dying. Even if you will not see the year out, it is as if you feel sure you will not die for a hundred. Deceived by the mundane phenomena of this life and the eight worldly concerns, whether they are positive, negative, or variegated, we lose the value of the freedoms and endowments. Thus the root of all our failure comes down to clinging to permanence.

When we contemplate the guidance on the impermanence of life, the outer container of the universe is not permanent, it undergoes the three aeonic stages of formation, existence, and destruction. The sentient beings contained within the universe are also impermanent, and have uncertain time and indeterminate circumstances of death. Not only do we understand the theory of this very well, but if it comes to teaching it, we are fluent in the subject. Yet still it does not become assimilated into our mindstreams. We turn our backs on what we learn and leave it in the realm of theory. We are known as those who are 'stubbornly resistant to Dharma'. Until the messengers of the Lord of Death arrive, we do not realise enough to be afraid. To tell the truth, we are really foolish, ready to go along with the yaks to the slaughter. When yaks are led into the slaughterhouse, they do not know they are about to have their throats slit. Even if they did, it is already too late. There is no way for them to escape or hide.

Currently we have the physical basis of a human from the higher realms. This is obviously better than the physical basis of an animal. We can speak and comprehend meaning, and we are intelligent. From the aspect that all beings with a physical body cannot escape death, we are the same as yaks in the slaughterhouse. However, using our human intellect, despite not having any means to avoid death this time, we must consider that we need to find a method to ensure we never need to experience the suffering of death in the future. We need to find a way so that this time when we die, we do not have to experience the suffering of going to the lower realms. Such a method can be searched for, and we need to seek it out. Otherwise, if while we are alive we know nothing except eating, sleeping, and lounging around, like a yak that just wanders around lying down wherever it wants, then at the time of death we also will probably have to die like a yak, writhing in acute pain.

In short, the concluding activity of human life is to be struck down by death. So, at the time when we take our final breath, without prior training in the Dharma, there is not one single possible beneficial outcome of death. Accompanied by the suffering of non-virtues the size of Mt. Meru, unable to climb out from that dark cavernous pit, we have no choice but to go downwards. There is no alternative path stretching out in front of us.

When we contemplate these terrifying things, it is no wonder no one even wants to mention the word 'death'. However, if you do know how to practise, and can follow the holy sacred Dharma to attain the warmth of engaging in the profound instructions, then death becomes the great door to happiness. You can embrace the entrance to the path which leads to the destination of a pure realm. Moreover, individuals of the very highest calibre with sharp faculties, wisdom, and excellent capacity, by following the swift path of the Dharma of Dzogpa Chenpo and these profound guidance instructions, do not even need to die. By training in the practice of trekchö primordial purity in this life, their body vanishes into atoms, which is said to 'leave nothing behind but hair and nails' in the accomplishment of the rainbow body. Not only that, but by gaining confidence in the practice of tögal spontaneous presence, and perfecting the four appearances in this life, without abandoning this body they can arise in the enlightened form of the light body of great transference, and upon this basis work continuously for the benefit of sentient beings until samsara is emptied.

It is not the case that some people are allowed to do this and others are not. Whoever has the diligence and determination, and if someone is capable, there is no lack of Dharma instructions. These drops of the nectar of the profound instructions are the only medicine needed to alleviate the chronic disease of samsara. They are the supreme healing which connects to the lifeline of liberation. When we meet with something as profound as this, it brings meaning to our human life. By embracing the beginning of the path to liberation we accomplish benefit for ourselves and others. By not deviating from the eternal goal, everything we do, we do according to the holy Dharma. In short, do not waste or squander this extraordinary physical basis for the accomplishment of enlightenment. The search for the path to liberation is the greatest kindness we can do for ourselves, so not a moment should be lost to laziness. We need to rouse this kind of intent towards enlightenment not just when we first start to practise the holy Dharma, but we should never part from it, in the beginning, middle, or end.

Together with developing the mind trainings in our mindstreams, at every stage of listening to, contemplating, meditating on, and practising the holy Dharma of Mahayana Sutra and Tantra, we can never be without the three excellent principles. First, embrace roots of virtue using skilful means with the excellent principle of the preparation by arousing bodhicitta. Then, prevent roots of virtue from beings destroyed by circumstances with the excellent principle of the main practice with non-conceptuality. Finally, allow roots of virtue to increase evermore with the excellent principle of the completion with dedication. Furthermore, make the vast attitude of bodhicitta motivation and the vast means of the attitude of the Secret Mantra naturally complete. With the pure conduct to receive Dharma teachings, we need to assemble these qualities according to the teachings of the sutras, tantras, and the Buddha's words and their commentaries, and listen to the Dharma.

For an ordinary person, when they hear of these things that are required at the time of a Dharma teaching, they may think 'Is all this really necessary?' One quality of sentient beings is that their mindset is not yet workable, so at first it is not necessarily easy for them to perceive what is true. However, there is nothing that does not become easier through familiarisation. If at the early stages something is contrived, but at the later stages it becomes familiar, then a mindstream can be corrected. However, if someone has already rejected selflessness, then even after a hundred years of trying to turn their mind in the direction of goodness, it would not be possible.

Teaching Day Two

Main Teaching

On day one of teaching *Flight of the Garuda, Songs of the Trekchö View of Luminous Dzogpa Chenpo, Capable of Swiftly Traversing the Paths and Levels without Exception*, we discussed the auxiliary subjects, as well as the goodness of the beginning, the introduction. Additionally, from the goodness of the middle, the meaning of the text, we completed the instructions on the fundamental continuum of the essence of enlightenment which pervades all samsara and nirvana, as taught by the seven great expressions of amazement. We searched for the hidden flaw of that which at the time of unrealised delusion is labelled 'mind'. We investigated the root of this mind and searched for its arising, abiding, and disappearance. Following that teaching, we engaged in practice sessions for several days to actually search for the arising, abiding, and disappearance of mind, according to the tradition of practical guidance.

Now today, we come to the main introduction to the nature of mind. There are two terms which we use to describe this in the oral tradition: 'introduction to the nature of mind' and 'introduction to the nature of rigpa', which we can explain as having the same meaning. In terms of what is called 'introduction to the nature of mind', this mind, in which delusion manifests evidently, has the nature of undeluded mind, rigpa wisdom. In this case, whether we introduce the nature of mind or the nature of rigpa, we can say it basically means the same. But, to explain the difference, although dharmakaya wisdom is the same regardless, from the perspective of beings to be tamed who receive introduction, although in general, practitioners of Dzogchen all have sharp faculties and have already accumulated merit, among them there are still differences in the sharpness of their faculties. Because of this, for those whose mind state is one of objective appearances, we say 'introduction to the nature of mind', and for those whose mind state is one of self-manifest rigpa, we refer to 'introduction to the nature of rigpa', but as I said, these are congruous in meaning.

Likewise, here we are presented with ways to introduce this nature in stages and also in no particular order. First, following the explanation of the title of this text *Songs of the View, Flight of the Garuda* and its meaning, to alight upon the view of Dzogchen is likened to the garuda landing upon the top of a wish-granting tree. Based on both introduction to determine the nature of the view—timeless freedom, primordial purity—and introduction to determine delusion, the nature of the actual view is introduced for those whose mind state is one of self-manifest rigpa. Of these, first is the introduction which determines the nature of the view.

Song Four
The Nature of the View

EMAHO!
Once again, listen here my fortunate children.

Having examined and analysed in this way,
When you have not found even an iota of substantial existence,
Which you can point to and say 'This is mind',
This finding nothing is the supreme discovery.

This is the summary. Following that:

Our mind has no initial source.
It is timelessly empty, so has no identifiable essence.
In the middle, it has no dwelling place, shape, or colour.
In the end, it goes nowhere, and there is no trace to show where it went.
Its movement is empty movement, its emptiness is empty appearance.

The root of both samsara and nirvana comes down to this mind, so until it is properly resolved, however much seemingly spiritual practice we do, or however grandiose we make a spiritual approach sound, although that may not necessarily be a meaningless or wrong path, it is still not the direct and close path. This is the key point which is taught here. When we search for our mind, we cannot find its source. Whether in the outer environment or inside our body, wherever we search an initial source for mind cannot be found. In the middle, a place where this mind remains, of which we can say 'It is here' also cannot be found outside, inside, or somewhere in between. At first, mind comes from nowhere, and in the interim we are unable to demonstrate where it remains, so of course, a place where mind goes in the end cannot be found either.

Regarding the arising, remaining, and departing of mind, there is also nowhere to point to and say 'It exists'. If we wanted to say that mind does not exist, like the horns of a rabbit or the child of a barren woman, that is also problematic because mind is not the same as some inanimate object, like earth or stone. Therefore, between being existent and non-existent, we are unable to determine what mind is and we do not know what to say. At this point, mind has not been found not because the one doing the searching is feeble, but this is what it is truly like. So seeing its nature, this finding nothing is actually the supreme discovery. For this reason, Shabkar teaches that mind's movement is empty movement, and mind's emptiness is its self-appearance.

Having determined with arising, remaining, and departing that objectively mind is without an underlying basis or root, then the real introduction that determines the nature of the actual subjective mind, that it possesses threefold essential nature, compassion, and wisdom, is taught. Following this, from whichever aspect we discuss it: ground, path, or result, we are taught that mind does not pass beyond the basic space and rigpa of the three kayas, the foundational framework beyond union and separation, which possesses the three wisdoms.

> **This mind initially was not produced by causes.**
> **In the end it will not be destroyed by external conditions.**
> **It has no increase or decrease, nor does it fill or empty.**
> **Since it fully pervades samsara and nirvana, it is impartial.**
> **Not characterised as 'this', it arises as everything unobstructedly.**
> **Not existing as anything, it transcends extremes of existence and non-existence:**
> **No coming or going, birth or death, nor clarification or obscuration.**

The nature of mind, which has never been produced by causes in the first place, is self-arising wisdom. Therefore, not finding the source from which mind first arises determines the unborn dharmakaya. In the end, it cannot be destroyed by any external conditions. This is emptiness free of dissolution and destruction, which is illustrated by the symbol of a vajra, so a place where mind goes in the end cannot be found. For the mind which has no source or destination, there is even less chance of finding where it resides in the interim. Due to this, it is illustrated by the two unobstructed self-arising form bodies. Therefore, by seeing this which has no increase or decrease, does not fill up or empty, come or go, and is without birth, death, clarification, and obscuration, the signs of approaching mastery of the view which possesses the eight profound qualities beyond the extremes of existence, non-existence, and so forth, become manifest.

To teach this with examples:

> **The nature of mind is like a flawless crystal sphere:**
> **Its essence is empty, its nature is luminosity,**
> **Its compassion is unobstructed, abiding vividly.**

> **Not sullied at all by the faults of samsara,**
> **Mind itself is truly primordially enlightened.**

When we speak of examples of definitive symbols, meaning, and indications for Dzogpa Chenpo, it is represented by the symbols of Vajrasattva's mirror or crystal, an eight-faceted jewel, and so on, as we discussed during the empowerment the other day. As the object of illustration, how is actual fundamental nature indicated? A crystal sphere is unobstructedly transparent inside and out. Because there is no way to characterise it as 'this', as it is not established as the essence of anything whatsoever, empty essence represents the dharmakaya. Not nothingness or mere emptiness, its nature is luminosity, the radiance of which can arise without obstruction. This nature represents luminous sambhogakaya. When the condition of sunlight or another light source shines upon a crystal, the five colours of the spectrum can appear separately. This represents all-pervading compassion or the unobstructed nirmanakaya. This teaches that from the present time of the ground, the three kayas of the nature of mind which possess the three wisdoms, reside free of transition and change, diminishment and development.

To summarise this point:

> **This is the introduction which determines**
> **The fundamental nature of the ground aspect of mind.**

The primordially pure ground possesses the three wisdoms which abide as the ground. Empty essence is dharmakaya. The essence of the dharmakaya which is primordially pure resides as enlightened body, however, except for merely residing as the ground of arising of the trikaya unity beyond union and separation, it does not have any existent partial characteristics, such as a face or arms, in the slightest. Luminous nature is sambhogakaya. It resides exhibiting the attributes of the five-coloured lights, however it does not have any existent partial colour in the slightest. Compassionate rigpa is nirmanakaya. The knowing aspect of all-pervading rigpa wisdom which it resides as, is unobstructed, however it never exists in the manner of object or subject, action or actor. This completes the introduction which determines the nature of the view.

Teaching Day Two

Song Five
The Introduction that Determines Delusion

The following introduction determines delusion at the juncture when manifestations of the ground arise from the ground. This includes the following sub-divisions: the primordial fundamental nature of the ground; manifestations of the ground appearing from the ground; the manner of Samantabhadra's liberation; how sentient beings of the three realms are deluded; how repeated delusion is purified upon the ground, and so forth; there are many points. However, this foremost instruction is the quintessential instruction of the kusali yogi presented in the manner of a refined torrent, its full extent taught unadulterated and utterly complete, with the main purpose of mutually benefitting those of sharp, middling, and dull faculties. It does not twist words as biased sophistic commentaries do, but shows the meaning in naked clarity. It is a profound foremost instruction with the special quality of using common everyday language so it can be understood easily.

> **EMAHO!**
> Now listen once more, my fortunate heart children,
> First, this is how Dharmakaya Samantabhadra
> Was liberated without doing even a moment's meditation,
> And how the six kinds of beings wander in samsara
> Without doing even a whisker of unvirtuous action:

This is the summary.

> In the primordial beginning before everything,
> Samsara and nirvana, nameless, resided in primordial ground.
> At that time, this is how rigpa rose up from the ground:
> Like a crystal struck by the sun and its inner light becoming externally manifest,
> So rigpa wisdom, moved by the life wind,
> Broke the seal of the youthful vase body,
> And spontaneously present luminosity, like the sun rising in the sky,
> Appeared as pure realms of kayas and wisdoms.

For the yogi who realises nakedly the true face of the primordial fundamental mode of presence, it is as taught in the twelve tantric words of vajra laughter:

> O, look at the primordially complete result of vajra speech, trikaya great emptiness—how amazing it is beyond union and separation in the three times! Without training in the six transcendent perfections, the accumulations are completed in an instant—ha-ha!

Where does ground, the basis of how Dharmakaya Samantabhadra was liberated through realisation, and the basis for sentient beings of the six types and the three realms to wander in samsara, come from? As it is taught:

> A single ground, two paths, two results.

At the time of the original primordial ground, before a buddha appeared through realisation, before sentient beings appeared through non-realisation, it was great transcendence beyond description, conception, and expression, transcending all extremes of existence, non-existence, and so on. Its essence is primordially pure, and its nature is spontaneously present. Because its essence is primordially pure, it is free of the extremes of existence and permanence, and has never existed as material phenomena that can be characterised. Because its nature is spontaneously present it is free of the extremes of non-existence and nihilation, the utterly pure luminous true nature.

The single universal ground split into the two paths of the ground of liberation and the ground of confusion, the two results of samsara and nirvana, which appear while not existing in the ground. As for what is known as 'universal ground', when we divide the single basis of division of basic space, it has eight subdivisions: essence, nature, and compassion, state, quality, and quintessence, and primordial purity and spontaneous presence, thus it has eight facets.

Ground is free of any basis for expression, a primordially pure essence. Whatever appears is absolutely complete, so its nature is spontaneously present. Unobstructedly self-arising, it is all-pervading compassion. It is taught its state arises automatically, its quality is all-manifesting without fabrication, and its quintessence is infinitely pervasive, completely including all of samsara and nirvana. Timelessly and naturally pure of defilements, it is primordial purity, and issuing forth multifariously unobstructed, it is spontaneous presence. Looking at it as insubstantial rigpa, its essence of primordially pure wisdom is beyond imagination, however looking at its spontaneously present nature, it resides as deep wisdom lucidity in the manner of primordial radiance.

In the tradition of Dzogpa Chenpo, this is called the 'immaculate ground, unity of primordial purity and spontaneous presence'. From the aspect that they possess no ignorance, ground and result are designated primordially pure. From the aspect that ground and result do not abandon ignorance, they are designated spontaneously present. Moreover, actually, the view that neither ground nor result is involved with any abandonment of ignorance accords with the above teaching.

Regarding such terms and Dharma language as 'emptiness', 'beyond elaboration', 'genuine', 'primordially pure', and 'timeless liberation', these can be explained in the following way: from the aspect that something does not exist as anything, it is taught to be 'emptiness'. As an essence is unidentified, it is taught to be 'beyond elaboration'. As the nature of all phenomena resides in such a way primordially, this is taught to be 'genuine'. Never having been sullied by the faults of ordinary consciousness is referred to as 'primordially pure'. Not bound by the attachments of fleeting meditational experience, and so on, is referred to as 'timeless liberation'.

The inner luminosity of the kayas, wisdoms, and so forth, merged in the ground of arising, resides without any dullness. However, why is this not externally luminous? The internal luminosity of the inner expanse of the youthful vase body resides without its external seal being broken. Therefore, as when a crystal has its own internal essence, the externally luminous enlightened body, speech, mind, qualities, and activities, or alternatively the five wisdoms, five lights, and so forth—that which arises as many fivefold attributes—is external luminosity. Just as when sunlight strikes a crystal, the real basis is movement of the sublime knowing wind energy that makes up the life force, which breaks the seal of the youthful vase body, whereby the manifestations of the eight doors of spontaneous presence—the self-manifestation of the kayas and wisdoms, the pure and impure realms, and beings to be tamed—arise. At which time, due to awareness or ignorance, both liberation and delusion come about.

Of these, how Samantabhadra was liberated is as follows:

> At that time, Dharmakaya Samantabhadra
> Knew this to be self-manifest, so in that instant
> The outer luminosity of the kayas and wisdoms dissolved inward,
> And he was enlightened in the original ground primordial purity.

When Shabkar says 'At that time', to when does this refer? He is referring to the time when spontaneous presence arises from primordial purity, or when manifestations of the ground arise from the ground. In this regard, the extraordinary Gyalwa Lonchenpa identified a unique secret key point, a demarcation which differentiates our tradition from others. As for what this is, All-knowing Jigme Lingpa taught:

> From limpid primordial purity, like a cloudless sky,
> Spontaneous presence stirs, arising in eight ways.
> This is the threshold which connects samsara and nirvana.
> The keys of the peak vehicle Ati Yoga tantras
> And foremost instructions were turned by him alone,
> Drimed Ozer from the land of snow mountains,
> Endowed with a thousand rays of immaculate light.

The inner luminous youthful vase body, essence of the five extremely subtle wind energies of wisdom, abides as the embodiment of enlightened body essence, speech nature, and rigpa compassion. When the aspect of the life wind energy with four attributes stirs, if the manifestations of the eight doors of spontaneous presence arise in eight ways, then at the time they dissolve in eight ways, how was Samantabhadra liberated? Rising from the ground he saw his own nature, made the distinction, by means of this distinction was liberated, and so forth. These six qualities of Samantabhadra cleared delusion and expanded wisdom. The accumulated merit of knowing his own undefiled nature brought realisation of his primordially enlightened essence, so again he experienced enlightenment. Thus becoming enlightened, self-manifestations dissolved into primordial purity, ground and fruition matured, and on the level of the unity of ground and fruition, he was enlightened as the primordial protector Great Unchanging Light, who was enlightened before all else.

We just mentioned four of the six qualities of Samantabhadra: he arose from the ground, saw his own nature, made the distinction, and by means of this distinction was liberated. Added to that to complete the six are: he does not rely on any other conditions, and he abides in his own natural place. This teaches the manner in which Samantabhadra was liberated.

As for how sentient beings of the three realms became deluded:

> **Not knowing appearances of spontaneously present nature**
> **As our own manifestations,**
> **Our awareness is unconscious and oblivious.**
> **This is called 'co-emergent ignorance'.**

> Then an awareness arose that grasps dualistically
> At the luminosity of ground manifestations.
> This is called 'ignorance of all-conceptualisation'.
> It was then we entered into the confines of ignorant dualistic grasping.
>
> Then habituations gradually grew,
> And from there, all these samsaric actions arose.
> Then afflictive emotions: the three poisons, five poisons,
> Eighty-four thousand, and so on, increased.
> And so until now, we circle like a water-wheel
> In the realms of samsara, experiencing joys and sorrows.

When Shabkar says 'our' he refers to all of us sentient beings. When manifestations of the ground arose in the eight doors of spontaneous presence, we did not know them to be our own manifestations. We grasped at our own manifestations as being something other, like mistaking a heap of stones for a person, or perceiving a striped rope to be a snake, so both grasping and fixation have brought about distance and separation. We have become deluded by grasping at 'me' and 'mine'.

Just as it is taught in Samantabhadra's Aspiration:

> Vagueness without thinking anything,
> Is itself ignorance, the cause of delusion.

Looking at the way in which we do not know our own nature, the three types of ignorance arise concurrently. In the original ground there is no delusion, however, the root cause of not knowing that the manifestation of the ground itself is our own nature is the 'ignorance of same identity'. The subtle awareness that causes this to stir gets more powerful, whereby the aspect of not knowing our own nature is 'co-emergent ignorance'. Upon this, object manifestations of the five lights become more gross, many dualistic perceptions of self and other, concepts of identity of name and meaning, arise and this is called the 'ignorance of all-conceptualisation' which occurs.

As the causal condition assembles and gathers the three types of ignorance, just as when an eye, a form, and eye-consciousness assemble together, perception arises from the condition of eye-contact, likewise from the causal condition the remaining three of the four conditions arise: the referential condition, the dominant condition, and the immediate condition. Then, because their frame of reference is impure, from this the causal afflictive emotions, the three poisons and five poisons arise, up to the eighty-four thousand poisons. Due to the power of the all-pervasive arising of karma and afflictive emotions, the causes and results of the three realms of samsara are established. Like the examples of a water-wheel or a burning torch whirling in a circle, we have circled on the samsaric wheel until now without beginning, middle, or end, experiencing the suffering of the three realms and six kinds of beings.

> **For more detail, read the All-knowing One's *Treasury of the Supreme Vehicle*,**
> ***Cloud Banks of an Ocean of Profound Meaning*, and so on.**

Both samsara and nirvana are the same in the true nature of rigpa. When we get to the crucial point of liberation and delusion of the ground and manifestations of the ground, then it is very important to know the key points of how we initially become deluded, the way to practise the path, and how to be liberated in the bardo state. Therefore, if we want to learn about these in more detail, Shabkar sets us the task of reading the *Treasury of the Supreme Vehicle* from Gyalwa Longchenpa's *Seven Treasuries*, *Cloud Banks of an Ocean of Profound Meaning* from the *Cloud Banks Trilogy*, and others, so that we may understand.

If we do not know the mode of presence of the ground, then there is no need for us to explain Dzogpa Chenpo any further. Moreover, the three aspects of primordial purity, the three facets of spontaneous presence, and so on, need to be distinguished clearly with the significance of the conclusive key points, according to the experts' individual modes of explanation.

At the stage of reaching decisive experience of the foremost instructions, elaborations of precise distinction are unnecessary:

> **Now, through the lama's profound foremost instructions,**
> **You understand all the inherent faults of delusion;**
> **You realise your mind is buddha nature;**
> **You have met the primordial protector face to face;**
> **You are equal in fortune to Samantabhadra.**
> **Rejoice deeply in this, my heart children.**

If childish ordinary people want to realise directly the meaning of the profound tantras of Secret Mantra, all the hidden secret profound meanings reside in a way that is disarrayed in the tantras, convoluted in the scriptures, and scattered in the foremost instructions. Even if you wanted to read just the names of the inconceivable tantras of Secret Mantra in the short period of human life, it would be difficult to do so.

To realise their meaning is even further beyond the scope of possibility. In that case, we should realise that the lama's foremost instructions comprise their essence. The instructions of the former and latter All-knowing Ones, such as the *Precious Wish-fulfilling Treasury*, have become our share of this profound fortune.

Above we investigated the root of our mind's delusion. We established the view of undeluded actual fundamental nature which transcends the names and meaning of delusion and non-delusion: the rigpa essence of our mind, dharmakaya wisdom nature of mind. When we see this nature that we possess, then like liberation through the six qualities of Samantabhadra, by being pure from the beginning without abandoning faults, and pure in place without abandoning delusion, the enlightened qualities of knowledge and loving wisdom which are spontaneously present in their own right, increase. Thus equal in fortune with original Samantabhadra, we are able to reach the ultimate result.

At the stage when individuals train in their own way on the path, although their faculties differ, at the level of the ultimate result—dharmakaya possessing the two purities in the precious secret sphere of primordial purity—it is the case that the manner in which the essence arises is the same. Examples of this are taught: the basic space contained inside different containers is the same, and separate rivers are ultimately inseparable with the great ocean.

To summarise the current point:

This is the introduction that determines delusion.

Teaching Day Two

Song Six
Fundamental Nature

Next follows the teaching of the actual introduction to the fundamental nature of the main practice for those whose mind state is one of self-manifest rigpa. First a summary:

> **EMAHO!**
> **Now, listen again my fortunate heart children.**
>
> **'Mind', the great sound of which is widely known,**
> **As for existing, does not exist at all.**
> **As for occurring, it is the source of the myriad joys and sorrows of samsara and nirvana.**
> **As for what it is believed to be, there are many beliefs in the enumerations of the vehicles.**
> **As for its name, it is labelled in inconceivable different ways.**

The vajra words of amazement 'EMAHO' begin each song. Again, by the power of possessing karma and fortune, previously accumulated merit and the karmic propensity of previous training, this profound Dharma instruction directly introduces the realisation of Dzogpa Chenpo primordial purity, self-abiding dharmakaya, to those 'heart children' or 'principle students' who enjoy the good fortune they possess without ever becoming sated. During the empowerment the other day, when I asked 'Who are you?' the reply you repeated was 'I am your fortunate sole heart child'. Like this, Shabkar is saying 'All you children of my heart, my principle students, attune your ears and listen without distraction'.

There are no phenomena between the sky and the earth that are not included within samsara and nirvana, and moreover, these are all based on mind. All those with minds are called 'sentient beings', and it is due to this deluded mind that we experience suffering. In the days up to now, we have always looked outwards towards distant phenomena, but rather than continuing to work hard without any end in sight, we should now look inwards and resolve the root of our mind. If we actually approach experientially what is known as 'mind', which is so ubiquitously known to all, there is nothing to be found, just as when we previously searched for the arising, abiding, and disappearance of mind. If mind does exist, there is nothing about which we can say 'It is this'. If we do not realise this point and hold something non-existent to exist, then all variety of deluded appearances appear: the joyful and sorrowful manifestations of samsara and nirvana, the myriad individual apparent phenomena that the six types of sentient beings have in their perceptions.

Different methods to determine the nature of the phenomenon which is mind are asserted in the numerous expressions of the vehicles. Again, according to the constitutions, faculties, and devotion of those to be tamed, the Victorious One taught various methods to tame in the different categories of the vehicles, and some of these also form the steps of the path. So, regarding the inconceivable amount of individual terms for mind that are given in the scriptures of the philosophical positions of the individual vehicles, it is taught:

> As long as mental engagement is not exhausted,
> There is no end to the inconceivable number of vehicles.

This is the summary. As for the detailed description:

> **Ordinary people call it 'I',**
> **Some non-Buddhists name it 'self',**
> **Shravakas call it 'selflessness of persons',**
> **The Mind Only Tradition labels it 'mind',**
> **Some call it 'Prajnaparamita',**
> **Some name it 'buddha nature',**
> **Some give it the name 'Mahamudra',**
> **Some label it 'Madhyamika',**
> **Some name it the 'single bindu',**
> **Some give it the name 'basic space of phenomena',**
> **Some label it 'alaya',**
> **Some name it 'ordinary mind'.**
> **Despite whichever inconceivable names it is given,**
> **Know that the meaning is this.**

All ordinary beings are under the sway of ignorant delusion with this mind that grasps at 'I' and 'mine', deluded from beginningless time to endless time. They have not cut the root of existence, which is grasping at an 'I'. When the thunder dragon roars in the sky, we think 'Will I get struck by lightning?' At night, in the further confusion of a dream, with our extensive habitual tendencies we think 'I'm going to fall down a steep cliff', 'I'm going to be swept away by a great river', and so on. Just as the illustrious Chandrakirti said:

> First saying 'I', beings cling to self,
> Then saying 'This is mine', attachment to things develops.
> They are helpless, circling around like a waterwheel.

Shabkar teaches that people who are not adherents of any philosophical system call mind 'I'. The term 'non-Buddhists' refers to the classifications of the three hundred and sixty wrong views, and so on, of different types of doctrines other than Buddhism, which spread from the roots of eternalism and nihilism. These are distinguished by different general and specific names, such as tirthikas, charvakas, extremists, nihilists, and so on, each with their own scriptures defining their philosophical positions. The non-Buddhists Shabkar refers to here are nihilists, except for charvakas, who believe in the permanence of the imputed notion of a self and assert a permanent, autonomous, almighty god. In short, these views are concomitant with a lack of awareness.

In terms of the various doctrines of Buddhism, there are the greater and lesser vehicles of the four classes of Buddhists. For the shravakas there are the philosophical differences of vaibhashika and sautrantika, and within the vaibhashikas there are divisions which postulate individual philosophical positions that are conflicting. However, to summarise the position of the shravakas, having eliminated the gross aspect of grasping and fixation, they assert the truth of minute particles and instantaneous moments to realise the selflessness of persons as it is.

Furthermore, by eliminating fixation upon minute particles of grasping, pratyekabuddhas realise one and a half aspects of selflessness, which can also be understood here by implication. Superior to those is the Mahayana cittamatrin tradition, whose philosophical position is that outer appearances arise from mind, and only consciousness devoid of grasped-grasping, a self-knowing inherently luminous mind exists, which is called 'mind-only'.

The Madhyamika School eliminates grasping onto the true existence of self-knowing. Realising that in the realm of objects of knowledge there is not even an iota of truly existing phenomena, relative reality is like an illusion—ultimate inexpressible emptiness, the inseparable unity of the two truths—and they master the perfection of wisdom. Thus the intermediate set of the Buddha's transmitted precepts establishes the presentation of profound emptiness with the three aspects of complete liberation. The final set of transmitted precepts clarifies the vast ultimate nature through symbols, and particularly the key enlightened intent which defines the distinction between Sutra and Tantra, which is buddha nature. As All-knowing Jigme Lingpa said:

> The Victorious One taught the three liberations in the middle
>   turning of the wheel;
> The essence of this teaching is individual, self-knowing awareness.
> In the make-up of sentient beings this buddha-nature,

Naturally present, is known as Dzogpa Chenpo.

Some people give this the name 'Mahamudra' or 'Great Seal'. Why is it called this? The manifestations of whatever phenomena arise are sealed by their true nature and taken to the unity of luminosity and emptiness free of any identification of appearances and awareness. This is the tradition of Mahamudra. In the Dakpo Kagyu subset of Mahamudra which maintains the Sutra system, it is called 'Mahamudra of fundamental nature', and in the Tantra system which holds foremost the wisdom that arises from empowerment, it is called 'Mahamudra of bliss and emptiness' according to the transmission of Lord Marpa. In short, all those which maintain Mahamudra wisdom that arises from empowerment, including the Six Yogas, the Five Stages, Path and Result, and so on, are included within this.

As for Madhyamika, there are many divisions including Prasangika and Svatantrika. However, according to unified utterly non-dwelling Madhyamika, appearance-emptiness naturally without union or separation, the basic space of phenomena free of all elaboration, is within the reach of individual self-knowing; inseparability of the two truths beyond extremes resolved in the vast expanse of phenomena. Here, when Shabkar mentions 'Madhyamika', of the two: the Madhyamika path of clear distinction and the main practice of equanimity Madhyamika, he should be understood as referring mainly to the latter.

Likewise, it is called the 'all-embracing single bindu', the 'basic space of phenomena free of all elaboration', and in some Mantra tantras it is called 'alaya causal continuum' and is referred to by the term 'alaya'. At the individual stages of Dzogchen, it is taught to be 'ordinary mind', 'fundamental mind', and 'self-arising wisdom'; there are many names. Whichever name we give it, Shabkar connects them together by teaching 'The meaning is this', which really is the actual introduction to the fundamental nature of the main practice.

Our current guidance teaching is not merely an unbroken oral transmission, a half-teaching half-transmission, or a devotional teaching. It is maturing practical guidance that we actually put into practice. Therefore, for the Dzogchen introduction to rigpa, there are different methods to make the introduction: for those with faith, introduction is made through the blessings of the lineage by symbolic means; for those with wisdom, introduction is made by establishing the view, and for those with experience in practice, introduction is made based on meditation practice.

So, according to the undiminished practice system of our tradition, for all of us to gain experience, first I am going to recite a prayer to invoke blessings of the three lineages of mind, indication, and hearing.

This is accompanied by the melodious sound of the hand drum and bell. Combining this with the sound of 'P'ET', which is the unity of method and wisdom, the great blessings of inexpressible true wisdom will be brought down into the indestructible bindu at the centre of the heart. This happens according to the recital of the words of introduction. During this time of introduction you do not need to look at the text. All of you may now assume the unchanging vajra posture: hold the palms of your hands together above the crown of your head without touching it, and bring together the soles of your feet in front of you.

[Lama Rinpoche then recites in an evocative, melodious voice:]

EMAHO!
In a pure realm without limits or extremes,
Is the original buddha Dharmakaya Samantabhadra;
The sambhogakaya, like the display of the moon in water,
    Vajrasattva;
The nirmanakaya with marks complete, Garab Dorje;
I pray: bestow blessing and empowerment.

Shri Singha, treasury of the ultimate Dharma;
Manjushrimitra, sovereign of the nine yanas;
Jnanasutra, great pundit Vimalamitra;
I pray: show us the liberating path.

Sole ornament of this world, Padmasambhava;
Supreme true heart children: lord, subject, and partner;
Longchenpa, revealer of oceanic mind treasures;
Jigme Lingpa, entrusted with the dakinis' space treasury;
I pray: bestow attainment of the result—liberation.

Lord of this Dharma, Changchub Dorje;
Siddha Jigme Gyalwe Nyugu;
Supreme emanation, the one named Migyur Namkhai Dorje;
Orgyen Tenzin Shenpen Nangwa;
Guardian of the Mandala, Lord Kunanata [Jigme Yonten Gonpo];
I pray: show me the true face of fundamental nature.

Here and now, by blessings of your enlightened body, speech,
    mind,
Qualities, and activities, may all those with fortune
Arise as the outer and inner mandalas of the magical web,
Become mature in resounding indestructible vajra space,
Reside in the original womb of primordially pure rigpa,

> Perfect the four spontaneously present manifestations of dynamic energy, and
> Achieve in one lifetime the rainbow body vajra life force.
> Achieve in one lifetime the rainbow body vajra life force!
> BANZA KAYA WAKA TSITA KARMA SARWA SIDDHA PALA HUNG AH AH AH
>
> P'ET! Which is mind?
> P'ET! Which is mind?
> P'ET! Which is mind?

At this juncture, I am going to read aloud the vajra speech verses of introduction. You need to continue to sit in the unchanging vajra posture. This posture is required at the time of empowerment.

> **Settle your mind, relaxed in its own place.**
> **When you settle, ordinary mind is laid bare.**
> **If you look, there is vividness of nothing to be seen.**
> **Rigpa is direct vivid presence.**
>
> **Not existing as anything, it is empty and limpid,**
> **Lucidity of non-dual luminosity-emptiness.**
> **Not permanent, it does not exist as anything.**
> **Not nothingness, it is vivid and stark.**
> **Not singular, it is aware and clear about much.**
> **Not plural, it is inseparable and one taste.**
>
> **There is nothing else, this is your own awareness.**
> **You now see directly the face of the primordial protector**
> **Dwelling in the centre of your heart.**
> **Never separate from this, children of my heart.**
>
> **Whoever wishes to find a better alternative elsewhere,**
> **Is like someone who finds an elephant, but searches for tracks.**
> **You may weave the entire three thousandfold universe,**
> **But it is impossible to find even the name 'buddha'.**

You may now make yourselves comfortable and look at the text. First, to 'Settle your mind, relaxed in its own place' indicates the method of settling. What is called 'mind' here is the subject that appears as mind, which perceives the proliferation and subsiding of discursive thoughts. Shabkar says 'With this mind...' Here he is not referring to the nature of mind. With this mind, do not chase after the past. Do not welcome the future. Whatever present thoughts arise, this is not about engaging in enumeration of their origination and cessation. Without correcting or modifying, settle your mind relaxed in its own place as it naturally is. By relaxing in this way, what Shabkar calls 'ordinary mind' is not ordinary confused consciousness. He is referring to unmodified ordinary natural self-abiding wisdom that is present in its place. There is no way to mix unmodified ordinary rigpa, the rigpa wisdom of your own mind, with the mind of grasping and fixation. Thus it is 'bare' or 'naked'.

> If you look, there is vividness of nothing to be seen.

Here Shabkar teaches that if you look for empty luminous unobstructed wisdom it cannot be seen, but when you settle, it becomes clear. How does this happen? By looking for an empty and limpid essence that does not exist as anything, it cannot be seen. But left to settle, because it is not nothingness, the uncompounded nature of luminosity is vividly clear.

> Rigpa is direct vivid presence.
> Not existing as anything, it is empty and limpid,
> Lucidity of non-dual luminosity-emptiness.

These three lines describe an essence which combines the three: luminosity, emptiness, and non-dual wisdom all upon a single basis, thus teaching the aspects of a single essence. The first line teaches the luminosity of the father nature: the luminosity-emptiness of the vajra of rigpa, dharmakaya Samantabhadra. The middle line teaches the empty aspect of the mother essence: empty luminosity without extremes or centre, the Samantabhadri basic space of phenomena. The last line teaches inseparable basic space and rigpa which totally pervades samsara and nirvana—the universal container and the beings contained within it, samsaric existence and nirvanic peace—which is the all-pervasive unity of true nature, all-pervading wisdom.

The words 'vivid', 'limpid', and 'lucidity' refer to the ineffable ultimate meaning. There is no way to express inexpressible ultimate wisdom with spoken words in human language, so when it is necessary to demonstrate this in mere symbols, it is necessary to use terms like 'vivid', 'limpid', and 'lucidity'. Such words merely give a rough indication.

> Not permanent, it does not exist as anything.
> Not nothingness, it is vivid and stark.
> Not singular, it is aware and clear about much.
> Not plural, it is inseparable and one taste.

These four lines teach that self-arising rigpa wisdom, which dwells within primordially, without extremes or centre, fetters or liberation, is free of all extremes of elaboration: permanence and negation, unity and multiplicity, and so forth. It is not the same as the 'self' determined by non-Buddhists as it is not permanent. Not existing as anything, it is illustrated by the sound of emptiness. It is not nothingness as its nature is luminosity. The manner in which it is luminous is as distinct and vivid inseparable rigpa emptiness. It is not singular, as it is wisdom that pervades the entire universal container and the beings contained within it, spontaneously present impartial awareness and clarity. Shabkar teaches it is also not plural but is the one taste of much inseparable knowing and objects of knowledge.

In this way, both emptiness, the ineffable basic space of wisdom, and appearances, the method of rigpa wisdom, are one taste, beyond union or separation from the very beginning; the common locus of singular basic space and rigpa which should not be misunderstood as having true existence. Non-dual, transcending all characteristic elaborations of similarity and difference, and beyond all assertions, this is called 'wisdom Dzogpa Chenpo'. This is not something that needs to be found through great hardship in some distant place.

> There is nothing else, this is your own awareness.
> You now see directly the face of the primordial protector
> Dwelling in the centre of your heart.
> Never separate from this, children of my heart.

As we mentioned above, in terms of terminological divisions, countless names are given to this according to the numerous expressions of the vehicles: unabiding wisdom, primordial freedom, superior indivisible truth, wisdom mind at the moment of death, bodhicitta of great bliss, the single bindu, rigpa dharmakaya wisdom, and so on. Whatever it is called, in fact, it is the unity of ground and result, the single bindu of the dharmakaya; suchness itself. It is the indestructible genuine essence of the aggregates, elements, and sense fields in the heart centre pavilion of the precious palace, the true face of the timelessly free primordial protector who resides atemporally without union or separation.

This is introduced today, directly and immediately by the foremost instructions of the lama, the profound and extraordinary features of the instructions, and the transmission of the blessings of the lineage. If you recognise and see it at this time, this direct introduction to your own nature is determined upon this one point. Without separating from it, by not parting from this key point upon which there is nothing to meditate or be distracted from, engage in practice. Thus you discover for yourself manifest liberation, buddhahood possessing the two purities.

Shabkar teaches his fortunate 'heart children' that we need not exhaust ourselves searching for something other than this elsewhere, and he urges us not to do so with the following instruction:

> Whoever wishes to find a better alternative elsewhere,
> Is like someone who finds an elephant, but searches for tracks.
> You may weave the entire three thousandfold universe,
> But it is impossible to find even the name 'buddha'.

Self-abiding dharmakaya wisdom, a result which does not come from a cause, transcends the mind of grasping and fixation. It is our own awareness of true ultimate wisdom that does not arise from scriptures. Having actually seen this self-arising wisdom that resides within, if we are still not satisfied and go looking elsewhere under the impression that besides this there must something even better or more beautiful, then this would be like having already found an elephant but still going to search for elephant tracks, and wandering pointlessly on a wrong path.

When a weaver weaves, they are careful with each thread of warp and weft. Even carefully searching like this through the entire three thousandfold universe for something better than self-abiding wisdom, self-settled dharmakaya which resides within primordially, other than this not even the name 'buddha' has been found up to now, can be found presently, or will be found in future.

Following this is the summary:

This is the actual introduction to the fundamental nature of the main practice.

The above completes the introduction to the nature of the view from the perspective of those whose mind state is one of self-manifest rigpa.

Song Seven
How the Five Kayas, the Five Wisdoms, and so on, are Complete in Rigpa

Following that is the introduction to how the five kayas, the five wisdoms, and so forth, represented by examples and symbols, are complete in one rigpa:

> **EMAHO!**
> **Once again, children of the family, listen well.**
>
> **In this present self-knowing self-luminosity,**
> **The three kayas: essence, nature, and compassion,**
> **The five kayas, the five wisdoms, and so on, are all complete.**

This gives a summary. As for the detailed description:

> **The essence of rigpa has no existence whatsoever,**
> **Such as colour or shape; this emptiness is dharmakaya.**
> **The luminous self-radiance of emptiness is sambhogakaya.**
> **The unobstructed basis of myriad manifestation is nirmanakaya.**

This teaches how the three kayas are complete in one rigpa. The empty essence of the nature of mind, the unborn nature of phenomena, rigpa wisdom, does not exist with any attributes of shape, colour, form, or characteristics whatsoever. There is no need to cleanse it by clearing away anything or improve it by adding something. It transcends far beyond a confirmed or refuted identity of phenomena with characteristics. This is dharmakaya free of elaboration. The unobstructed self-radiance of the inherent luminosity of this emptiness is itself sambhogakaya. From this, the unobstructed basis of myriad manifestation, spontaneously present compassion's manifestive potential, arises as anything whatsoever. This which can appear as anything is itself the myriad non-duality of nirmanakaya. These are taught using an example:

> **An example to illustrate these is as follows:**
> **A glass mirror is akin to dharmakaya.**
> **Its pristine lucid nature illustrates sambhogakaya.**

This unobstructed basis for reflections to arise symbolises nirmanakaya.

This teaches the example of the crystal-clear mirror of Vajrasattva. The unobscured luminosity of clarity symbolises dharmakaya. The luminosity of radiance that can arise symbolises sambhogakaya. That which upon encountering conditions is the unobstructed basis for reflections to arise symbolises nirmanakaya. The meaning that is signified by these examples is as follows:

> **The nature of mind of all beings abides primordially as the three kayas.**
> **If they can recognise their own nature,**
> **There is no need for them to meditate for even a moment.**
> **In an instant, they will become enlightened.**

All wandering beings are pervaded by buddha nature, therefore the nature of their mind is primordially complete with the three kayas. The way mind is complete with the kayas accords with the meaning taught in the *Tantra in Two Sections*:

> All sentient beings are buddhas.

However, when mind is obscured by adventitious defilements, these delusions without any basis, like appearances in dreams, come about. As this situation where the three kayas are inherently present has never changed from the very beginning, when we can recognise this which is our own nature, through the power of the undefiled accumulation of virtue of knowing our own nature, beings do not need to do a moment's meditation but become instantly enlightened. Just as dreams clear when we wake up, when delusions are purified we attain undeluded knowing wisdom and actualise possessing the two purities.

Although at the time of clearly pointing the finger of introduction we speak of the three kayas individually in succession, the following instruction is repeated to emphasise the truth of how, in fact, they are not separate:

> **The introduction to the three kayas teaches them separately,**
> **But, in fact, they are a single basic space. Other than that,**
> **Do not become confused holding them to be different, heart children.**

Following this, the stage of reaching a decisive experience of this rigpa wisdom, vast non-fixation of luminosity-emptiness, is taught:

> The three kayas, primordial purity empty since the beginning,
> Are a single essence of unified luminosity and emptiness.
> Understand this and conduct yourself in a state of non-grasping.
> Moreover, the three: essence, nature, and compassion
> Are analogous to dharmakaya, sambhogakaya, and nirmanakaya.
> Understand all three to be vast unified luminous emptiness,
> And conduct yourself in a state of non-grasping.

Although when differentiating the three kayas we speak of the individual aspects of emptiness, luminosity, and unobstructedness, in fact, they are inseparable and complete in a single state. Because the essence of the three kayas is empty, they are primordially pure. Because primordial purity is free of elaborations, it is the unobstructedly arising radiance of spontaneous presence. Through understanding the unity of luminosity and emptiness, in the state of non-grasping through the freedom of non-distraction, we are taught to reach the decisive experience by enhancing through conduct.

Similarly for the three wisdoms of essence, nature, and compassion, just as the three: dharmakaya, sambhogakaya, and nirmanakaya are complete in one single basis, all three wisdoms are subsumed in wisdom that apprehends the ground. Therefore, once again, in the vast unity of luminosity and emptiness, in a state of non-grasping in natural non-distraction, Shabkar teaches us to conduct ourselves in a care-free manner and come to the decisive experience.

Following this is the introduction to the five kayas and five wisdoms:

> What is more, this self-arising rigpa wisdom
> Appearing as anything is the Vairochana kaya;
> Being unchanging is the Akshobhyavajra kaya;
> Having no centre or limit is the Amitabha kaya;
> Being like a jewel that is the source of all accomplishments,
> Supreme and common, is the Ratnasambhava kaya;
> Accomplishing everything meaningful is the Amoghasiddhi kaya.
> None of these is anything except the dynamic energy of rigpa.

This teaches the five buddha families. How are the five wisdoms taught?

> The unobstructed essence of rigpa wisdom,
> Directly experiencing luminosity is mirror-like wisdom;
> Pervading everything is equalness wisdom;
> Arising from dynamic energy in myriad array is individually discriminating;
> Accomplishing all purposes is all-accomplishing wisdom;
> Subsuming the essence of all these in primordial purity
> Is the wisdom of the basic space of phenomena.
> None of these has even an iota of existence
> Apart from the dynamic energy of your own rigpa.

To elucidate carefully this introduction to the five kayas and five wisdoms, self-arising abiding rigpa has never been separate from us since the beginning even for a moment, and the five kayas and the five wisdoms exist inherently in this uncontrived true nature of mind. How is this so?

Vairochana is the family of the enlightened body of all tathagatas. Embodying the luminosity of the marks and signs of enlightened body manifesting as anything whatsoever, rigpa wisdom is All-illuminating Vairochana. Akshobhyavajra is the family of enlightened mind. From the aspect of rigpa's unelaborate primordially pure essence, it is free of good and bad, transition and change, so it is unchanging and thus the body of Immutable Vajra Akshobhyavajra. Amitabha is the basis for accomplishing unlimited boundless enlightened qualities. As the manifestations of wisdom are all-encompassing without limit or centre, rigpa is the body of Limitless Illumination Amitabha. Ratnasambhava is the family of enlightened qualities. Like a jewel, rigpa wisdom is the source of all desirable qualities and precious things, so it is the Source of Preciousness Ratnasambhava. Amoghasiddhi is the family of enlightened activity. Without endeavour or effort, self-arising spontaneously accomplished wisdom is complete within us, therefore it accomplishes everything meaningful and is the body of Accomplishment of Meaning Amoghasiddhi.

Although the five kayas are distinguished in this way, it is from a single essence that this radiance or lustre of myriad variety arises. There is nothing that exists as distinct, in addition to or aside from the dynamic energy of rigpa.

Similarly, the five wisdoms that exhibit attributes which are spontaneously present and complete are as follows: the essence of rigpa wisdom is unobscured, the unobstructed knowing aspect which illuminates all phenomena. As it distinctly and directly experiences luminosity, it is mirror-like wisdom. This vast wisdom that pervades all of samsara and nirvana, the one indivisible taste of all knowing and knowables, fully pervades the universal container and its contents, all that appears and exists, therefore it is equalness wisdom. Particularly, as it arises from dynamic energy as myriad phenomena, it is individually discriminating wisdom. As it is unsought but spontaneously present effortlessness that accomplishes all purposes of enlightened activities, it is all-accomplishing wisdom. In this way, the essence of these manifesting wisdoms is primordially empty without any basis, subsumed within the single primordially pure vast basic space. Therefore it is the wisdom of the basic space of phenomena.

Also, when Shabkar refers to the five wisdoms as 'all these' and 'these' twice in succession, this is not a shortfall in his verse. He is not adding words to fill out the syllable count of the stanzas. They are to be understood as meaning 'these five wisdoms and all the boundless wisdom of the Victorious Ones which radiates out from them'. He teaches that apart from their inner luminous lustre and outer luminous radiance which are non-dual with rigpa—how the dynamic energy and emanations which radiate out from these arise—they do not have 'Even an iota of existence' and thus their non-existence is determined.

The one kaya, the two kayas, the three, four, and five kayas, the hundred kayas, the thousand kayas, the hundred buddha families, and the thousand buddha families, manifest as numerous as the atoms in billions of pure realms. If the display of the infinite magical web, all the manifested kayas and wisdoms, are subsumed into one, they are complete within this singularity. The teaching that introduces this by directly pointing it out is as follows:

> To introduce the essence, nature, and compassion
> Of the three kayas, and the five kayas and five wisdoms,
> At once by directly pointing a finger,
> They are present awareness without any fabrication,
> Unchanged by circumstances, unspoiled by fixation:
> This very rigpa, distinct and vivid.
> All buddhas of the three times arise from this.
> This is the enlightened mind of all buddhas of the three times,
> So never separate from it, all you fortunate ones.

The ground for the unfolding of all the kayas, non-dual with the enlightened mind of all buddhas of the three times, is the dharmakaya. How does this single nature arise as the three kayas? Empty essence is the dharmakaya, luminous nature is the sambhogakaya, and all-pervading compassion is the nirmanakaya. To differentiate the four kayas, they are the three kayas plus the svabhavikakaya. Further, to differentiate the five kayas, they are counted as the three kayas of inner basic space luminosity and the two kayas of outer luminosity. The abhisambodhikaya is manifest distinct from all resultant qualities. The unchanging vajrakaya is non-dual basic space and wisdom, unchanging from the beginning. Add to these the dharmakaya and they comprise the three kayas of inner luminosity. The kayas of outer luminosity are the two form bodies, the sambhogakaya and nirmanakaya, which makes five in total. However, all these without exception are subsumed within the three kayas.

Similarly, all of the inconceivable hundred buddha families and thousand buddha families are subsumed within this. Also, the five wisdoms which we just mentioned are not only subsumed within wisdom which abides as the ground—threefold essence, nature, and compassion—they are also complete in one essence, subsumed within one wisdom. As a finger is pointed directly to indicate a form in daylight to someone fully sighted, if we are to point out all of these kayas and wisdoms, subsumed into this single self-abiding wisdom, then we should turn this present mind inward. Awareness at the very moment of turning inward without making the slightest improvement or alteration, not changed by any outer circumstances or spoiled by inner grasping and fixation, is this very rigpa nature of mind: distinct and vivid unobstructed emptiness-luminosity.

This which is directly introduced within yourself without relying on words or conceptual analysis, is the footprint left behind by all buddhas of the past, and the object of practice of all future buddhas, without which there is no way to become enlightened. It is the single path to be travelled by all current buddhas, without which there is no other path to travel. Although it is symbolically labelled 'a path', in fact, it is the enlightened mind of resultant buddhahood. This being the case, up to now we have been unaware that we already possess it. To give an example, like a prince who has abandoned his kingdom and gone wandering the lands, we have become confused. Shabkar instructs us to exercise our mastery over the undeluded actual fundamental nature, the great kingdom of buddhahood which we have within, and to 'Never separate from it, all you fortunate karmically destined ones'.

At this stage, Shabkar speaks of 'present awareness'. This is what is introduced and what we should not part from. If we think about this, what is referred to as 'present awareness' and 'ordinary mind' is taught to be the dharmakaya essence of mind itself—mind unsullied by the contrived fabrication of discursive thoughts—which at the time of self-settling resides in its own way. As beginners, the one who thinks 'I need to settle without contrivance and fabrication' is mind. The 'mind' we refer to here is 'conceptual mind', which is the object that is beguiled by conventional confusion. Maybe you are thinking 'What is this conceptual mind?' When the rational or conscious mind meditates on uncompounded emptiness, or space, and so on, an impression of its imbued aspects can arise in this conceptual mind. The impression of its imbued aspects that arises is nothing other than a mere mental impression. It does not merge together with the actual uncompounded significance. However, by holding these impressions in conceptual mind like this, just as when we apply terms to the realisation of these states, if something similar to unobstructed emptiness-luminosity free of elimination or addition arises, then although this is not true ultimate wisdom, by relying on it, when we gradually become familiar with it, then we can make the shift to ultimate wisdom.

What are we saying here? Compounded conceptual mind and uncompounded emptiness are different things, two mutually exclusive opposites which cannot be mixed together, not like, for example, water and water. So maybe you are thinking 'How then is it possible delusion can become non-delusion and sentient beings can become buddhas?' All phenomena designated as dualistic—compounded and uncompounded, delusion and non-delusion, sentient beings and buddhas—these distinct perceptions are designated as such under the influence of conceptualisation. The ultimate undeluded fundamental nature, the truth of all phenomena which is our own essence, does not exist as being established in that way.

When we realise that there is not even an iota of phenomena other than the fundamental nature of suchness, the naturally luminous basic space of phenomena, then knowing and that which is known are non-dual, perceiver and objects are inseparable. When what is known as 'the object of the basic space of phenomena' and 'the perceiver rigpa wisdom' are seen to be merged and not different, then this aspect of perception where the way things are and the way things appear are in accord, is merely given the term 'merged'. What we refer to as 'the naturally luminous basic space of phenomena' is like that from the very beginning until the very end.

When we see such basic space of phenomena which is free of the slightest movement or change, this crucial point which is unborn and unceasing, there is no separate, impure, or useless 'compounded conceptual mind of intellectual analysis' to be left behind. The ultimate fundamental nature to be realised, the naturally luminous basic space of phenomena, self-arising wisdom that abides within ourselves, suchness that is however it is, is also Dzogpa Chenpo of fundamental nature. The path of means that introduces this is called the 'Dzogchen path', which is also just a label. This is the meaning to be understood here.

In conjunction with this, the defiles of doubt are cleared as follows:

This is exactly uncontrived inherent lucidity.
Why do you say you cannot see your buddha mind?
For this, there is nothing whatsoever on which to meditate.
Why do you say meditation does not arise?

This is exactly directly manifest rigpa.
Why do you say you cannot find your mind?
This is exactly unceasing vivid clarity.
Why do you say you cannot see the nature of mind?

For this, there is not the slightest thing to do.
Why do you say you cannot make it happen?
In non-dual abiding and non-abiding,
Why do you say you are unable to abide?

In self-awareness, the three kayas are effortlessly spontaneously present.
Why do you say you cannot accomplish them through practice?
Resting freely in non-action is sufficient.
Why do you say you cannot do it?

Thoughts arise and become liberated at the same time.
Why do you say the remedy does not work?
This is exactly this present awareness.
Why do you say you do not know it?

When we rest self-settled and uncontrived, present awareness is inherent lucidity. If we modify and change it, it becomes obscured once more. Other than this present unfabricated awareness, there is no buddha to be seen from elsewhere. Beyond resting self-settled and uncontrived in this state, there is no meditation to develop. Beyond this directly manifest rigpa, there is nothing that is not found. Beyond this inexpressible luminosity-emptiness, there is nothing to see. This is not the object of activities of effort or achievement. Thoughts arising and becoming liberated at the same time are like patterns drawn in water; they are drawn and disappear at the same time. As there are no fetters from the beginning, it is unnecessary to search somewhere for freedom. Shabkar is teaching that there is no not knowing rigpa wisdom, which abides directly as it always was.

Teaching Day Two

Song Eight
Fourfold Imperturbable Presence

From here the teaching continues by way of the fourfold imperturbable presence of self-liberation upon encountering rigpa, and a summary of the four main points of samaya:

> **EMAHO!**
> **Now listen again with respect, fortunate children.**

Based upon four instructions to observe directly and rest evenly, the four stages of imperturbable presence are taught one after another as follows:

> **Your mind is insubstantial like empty space.**
> **All fortunate children, to see whether or not this is so,**
> **In a manner of not looking, upon your mind,**
> **Look directly and rest evenly, then you will know.**

This is the view of mountain-like imperturbable presence. With the view of mountain-like imperturbable presence, look at the sky-like rigpa nature of mind—empty, luminous, and unobstructed—from within a manner of not looking, with rigpa itself unwavering and resting directly. By doing this, in the non-duality of knowing and knower, Shabkar teaches we will come to realise its nature.

> **Not only merely empty purity,**
> **It is determined to be self-aware wisdom primordially luminous,**
> **Self-arising self-luminosity, like the orb of the sun.**
> **Whether or not this is so, upon mind itself,**
> **Look directly and rest evenly, then you will know.**

This is meditation of ocean-like imperturbable presence. With the meditation of ocean-like imperturbable presence, we realise mind is not mere emptiness. Without developing the fabricated trap of grasping at the sixfold group of consciousness, just as when the ocean is not agitated by waves, the clarity of awareness appears. To give an example, primordially the orb of the sun has never been covered by any obscuration, so by resting directly and remaining in that state, we are taught we will come to realise its nature.

> The stirrings of discursive thoughts are determined intangible,
> Their movements uncertain like the wind in the sky.
> Whether or not this is so, upon mind itself,
> Look directly and rest evenly, then you will know.

With the conduct of foremost instruction imperturbable presence, when we settle and relax in the immediacy of the three doors, the naked self-luminosity of wisdom appears from the covers of view and meditation. The division between abiding and movement falls away, and the intangible stirrings of discursive thoughts vanish naturally without a trace, like for example the wind in the sky. Train by resting directly in immediacy and we will come to realise our own nature as it appears nakedly.

> It is determined that whatever appears, all is self-manifest.
> Whatever appears is all like reflections in a mirror.
> Whether or not this is so, upon mind itself,
> Look directly and rest evenly, then you will know.

This is resultant uncontrived imperturbable presence. With resultant uncontrived imperturbable presence, whatever self-manifest phenomena appear, all are like a mirror's reflection. When the five sense objects are left self-settled, and when doubts are cut through from within with regard to inner naked self-luminosity free of hopes and fears from the very depths, then the nature of mind, the true face of dharmakaya, is seen directly without obscuration. Again, by looking directly and resting evenly, then we will come to realise this. This is the teaching that summarises the key point of placing self-abiding wisdom self-settled.

From here, non-existence, openness, spontaneous presence, and singleness are discussed in the framework of the four samaya commitments of Dzogchen, primordially free of upholding, transgression, and degeneration. First, holding the five commitments of view, meditation, conduct, samaya, and result is taught:

> Except for mind, there is no other Dharma,
> So there is no view to see elsewhere.
> Except for mind, there is no other Dharma,
> So there is no meditation to do elsewhere.
>
> Except for mind, there is no other Dharma,
> So there is no conduct to do elsewhere.
> Except for mind, there is no other Dharma,

> So there is no samaya to keep elsewhere.
> Except for mind, there is no other Dharma,
> So there is no result to accomplish elsewhere.

Victorious Longchenpa taught:

> This non-existence, clearly apparent illusory nature,
> Is moment by moment beyond description, conception, and expression.
> Therefore, know that all phenomena that appear to mind
> Are non-existent, even as they manifest.

Just as rays of sunlight are named the sun, the self-arising wisdom of rigpa is labelled 'mind'. Except for this empty luminosity that is without basis and primordially pure, there is no view to see, no meditation to meditate on, and so forth. When we know the manner in which the true nature of non-existence resides as it is, this crosses the abyss of samsara, good and bad are equal, and deviation and obscuration become without foundation. This is the foremost instruction which reaches a conclusion regarding the three states of existence. Thus non-existence is taught.

Second is openness:

> Look at your own mind. Look again and again.
> Send your mind into the external realm of space,
> See whether or not its nature exhibits any coming or going.
> If when observed your mind neither comes nor goes,
> Look inward at your mind inside,
> See whether or not there is a proliferating agent for unfolding thoughts.
>
> If there is no proliferating agent for unfolding thoughts,
> See whether or not mind has colour, shape, and so on.
> When you encounter emptiness devoid of colour and shape,
> See whether or not emptiness has centre or edge.
>
> When there is no centre or edge, see whether or not there is inside or outside.
> Rigpa, without inside or outside, is spacious like space,
> Unobstructed transparency free of restrictions and partiality.

This determines openness. By investigating and analysing the coming and going, proliferation and abiding, colour and shape of the mind, to reach the conclusion that it is emptiness free of centre and edge—

complete rigpa openness without outside or inside—is different from the earlier preliminary practice when we searched for the arising, abiding, and disappearance of the mind. That was investigating based on the object. Here, this is resolved based upon the subject, as we mentioned earlier.

First, this demonstration that there is no coming or going teaches ground openness, space-like freedom from partial grasping and fixation. Second, this absence of a proliferating agent of thoughts teaches path openness without effort and activity, free of grasping at concepts and thoughts. Third, as mind has no colour or shape, this determination of emptiness free of centre and edge teaches result openness. Through indicating that it is without hope and fear, transition and change, openness is taught in terms of ground, path, and result.

The conclusion of all of this, this teaching on rigpa unobstructed transparency, spacious like basic space that is without outside, inside, or between, and free of restrictions and partiality, demonstrates space openness, appearances unwavering from rigpa, the unrestricted openness nature of phenomena in which there is nothing to be done. This is taught to accord with the following scriptural reference:

> Mastering all of samsara, nirvana, and the spiritual vehicles,
> This singular effortlessness overwhelms everything with its splendour.
> There is no other context which constitutes an extreme.
> There is no wavering from the sole expanse of effortlessness.
> This itself is the expanse of Samantabhadra in which there is nothing to be done.

This completes non-existence and openness. Third is spontaneous presence:

> **Within the vast spacious expanse of all-pervasive self-knowing**
> **All phenomena of samsara and nirvana are like rainbows in the sky.**
> **Although they appear in myriad variety, they are the display of mind.**
> **Look outwards from the unwavering state of self-knowing:**
> **No phenomena, illusory like the moon in water,**
> **Can be separated out in appearance-emptiness.**

Fundamental rigpa is an all-pervasive spacious expanse, vast spontaneously present emptiness-luminosity. From this, manifestations of the ground, all phenomena of samsara and nirvana that appear and exist, are manifold and unmixed. Like rainbows in the sky, although they are variously arrayed, they are the apparent yet empty illusory display of the moon in water, the single basic space without distinctions of good or bad, the single essence of the three kayas of the ground, the miraculous display of spontaneously present sole rigpa. This completes non-existence, openness, and spontaneous presence.

As for singleness:

> In the state of rigpa, samsara and nirvana are non-dual.
> Look outwards from the unwavering state of self-knowing:
> The phenomena of samsara and nirvana are like reflections in a mirror;
> However they appear, they have never existed from the very beginning.
> Samsara and nirvana are nameless, everything is dharmakaya.
>
> All beings wandering in the three realms of samsara
> Do not realise their own wisdom nature, in which
> All samsaric and nirvanic phenomena remain primordially in evenness.
> Under the influence of dualistic delusion, they grasp individually.
> Thus grasping dualistically at the non-dual truth they are not liberated.

To give an example, due to the condition of either sunlight or moonlight shining upon it, a single vaiurya jewel appears as the source of heat or coolness respectively. Like this, from within the one rigpa, samsara and nirvana arise, which in fact, is the way the display of lone rigpa arises. Whether or not this is the case, when we look from within the unwavering state of self-knowing rigpa, although a myriad variety of reflections are apparent, they are contained within a single mirror. Likewise, all phenomena are apparent yet non-existent. Under the influence of deluded dualistic grasping, things appear like motes in the vision of someone with diseased eyes.

Samsara and nirvana are nameless and primordially empty vast evenness. When we see empty luminosity free of elaboration it is like spacious empty space, appearance-emptiness without duality of divisions or breaks, the non-dual single bindu of the basic space of phenomena free of edges and corners. Thus it is taught to be the single root. Not realising this truth and grasping at non-duality as a duality, we are not free from our own fetters.

With a brief outline of this instruction, the meaning is repeated once again and summarised:

> The nature of everyone's mind is inseparable samsara and nirvana,
> Yet engaging in rejection and acceptance, adopting and abandoning, they wander in samsara.
>
> In self-knowing, the three kayas are effortlessly and spontaneously accomplished,
> Yet all wandering beings, foolish and deluded, search for the levels and paths
> With methods that are not this, taking them elsewhere far away.
> The time to arrive at the level of buddhahood has not come.
>
> Whatever appears is determined to be all your own manifestation.
> Look outwards from the unwavering state of self-knowing:
> All that appears and exists is like a reflection,
> Apparent yet empty, audible yet empty, primordially empty nature.
>
> Likewise, look inward at the mind which is looking:
> Thoughts naturally vanish, empty like the sky,
> Unelaborate simplicity beyond description, conception, and expression.
> Whatever appears is all the miraculous display of the mind.
>
> This entire miraculous display has no basis and is empty.
> If you realise it is all your own mind,
> All apparent manifestations are empty dharmakaya.
> Appearances do not bind us, we are bound by fixation.
> Sever the delusion of fixated attachment, heart children.

Victorious Longchenpa taught:

> The sun of ultimate reality, self-arising rigpa,
> Is obscured by clouds of both virtue and non-virtue, positive and negative,
> And struck by the lightning of fixated efforts to accept and reject.

Teaching Day Two

> With the continuous downpour of confused perceptions of joy and sorrow,
> The seeds of samsara grow into the foliage of the six kinds of beings.
> Alas! The tormented six kinds of beings are worthy of compassion.

No sentient beings realise their own mind to be inseparable samsara and nirvana. Not only that, but none of the lower paths or vehicles cast off the fetters of dualistic grasping. Therefore, by engaging solely in good and bad, suppression and promotion, adopting and abandoning, we wander in samsara. We disregard our own self-abiding rigpa, which has the three kayas effortlessly complete in one essence spontaneously present. Like leaving an elephant at home but going searching for its tracks in the forest, by striving at the levels and paths we search elsewhere, far away.

When does the time come for all such wandering beings to arrive at the level of buddhahood? Because whatever appears is all our own manifestation, although what appears arises externally, the ground from which things arise is inside. When we look outwards, at the time of unwavering self-knowing rigpa, we come to realise that all that appears and exists is like its reflection.

Looking outwards, all phenomena that stretch out into the distance are without basis and rootless. Apparent forms are apparent yet empty. Sounds that resound outwards are audible yet empty. Similarly, the true nature of every feeling we experience is primordially empty. Look inward at your mind which is doing the looking and it is insubstantial like the sky, simplicity primordially free of elaborations, completely transcending all objects of description, conception, and expression. Whatever appears is all the miraculous display of the mind. This miraculous display is empty without basis. In short, we come to know that everything comes down to our own mind.

If this knowing becomes realisation, then appearances do not matter in the slightest. From the qualities of the refined essence of the senses, sublime insight and clairvoyance arise. As for that which binds, appearances are not binding. What is it that actually binds us? We are bound by fixation. When we fixate we are bound in the three realms of samsara. As Jetsun Tilopa said:

> Son, it is not appearances that bind you, it is grasping.
> Cut through grasping, Naropa.

Thus Shabkar gives us the single instruction that includes a hundred crucial points:

Sever the delusion of fixated attachment, heart children.

The above concludes the instructional guidance which teaches the introduction which is primarily for those whose mind state is one of self-manifest rigpa, together with dispelling hindrances and enhancing practice.

TEACHING DAY TWO

SUMMARY OF THE TEACHING

Generally speaking, as a matter of course, we should practise trekchö meditation on a daily basis. Even if we cannot manage to maintain four practice sessions a day without missing one, we should manage two. At the very least, however busy we are, we should start to engage in one practice session a day without fail. During and between all of our practice sessions we should never part from this meditation which is the uncontrived equipoise of non-meditation.

To attain stability, beginners need to meditate in a solitary place without distractions. First, we need to recognise this rigpa which we have ourselves. Then we need to remain in this state of recognition. Finally, we need to bring this abiding potential to perfection. When we have attained stability in this, at the time when all appearances and activities do not part from the state of naturally abiding rigpa and there is no distraction, we will have arrived at the level of engagement in the yogic discipline enhancement practice of ever-changing appearances and rigpa.

From our initial activity of seeking out the teachings and studying, which is like a bee searching for its hive, the conduct of the yogic discipline of rigpa without any fear or doubt whatsoever, which is like a lion, will finally come about. For total beginners and newcomers, it is best to start by engaging in both analytical meditation and settling meditation alternately. Actually, introduction to the nature of rigpa should be given at the stage of completing analysis of the view, however by the force of faith and devotion, it is understandable if not everyone is the sort who makes instantaneous progress. But we do consider that beings to be tamed by Dzogchen have sharp faculties, so because of this, here we have already given the introduction to the nature of rigpa. Now meditation needs to be practised in many short sessions. Keeping sessions short has the benefit of not causing hindrances. Doing many sessions has the benefit of developing steady familiarity.

For those who are old hands at practice with some experiential understanding, most important is to elicit the luminous aspect of rigpa. Do not grasp at temporary experiences of bliss, luminosity, or no-thought. Allow rigpa to emerge nakedly. Particularly, do not slip into the door-less iron fortress of no-thought lethargy that is nothing in particular. You can all know which is mind and which is rigpa by whether or not it is compounded.

To qualify to attend these teachings you have all vowed to undertake three years of sacred strict retreat, so you may engage in practising this teaching. The reason for including this requirement is not for my own sake but for the sake of attaining stability in meditation. Retreat will provide the support of conducive circumstances so that those of you who are currently listening to these teachings may set about training with perseverance, and not get lost to the influence of other conditions on the path of distraction.

Dzogpa Chenpo is non-meditation, therefore it is not the kind of meditation with deliberate fixation on a point of focus. It is a foremost instruction to come to a decisive experience in a state of total freedom without aim. Guru Rinpoche taught:

> There is nothing on which to meditate, but it can be fully fathomed.

Therefore we need to develop diligence. What is known as 'deluded mind's propensity for bad habits' is very powerful. We cannot say this long-term intense delusion is easy to overcome. Just as we discussed yesterday, we start by first contemplating our understanding of self-cherishing. Perhaps some of you will be thinking 'You don't need to teach me that! Although I may not be able to cherish others, I automatically know how to cherish myself without being taught!' Although it might be true that from one point of view it feels as if we already know how to cherish ourselves, if we look from another perspective, this statement becomes proof that we actually do not truly know how to cherish ourselves. Under the influence of confusion that grasps at an 'I' we desire happiness, but conversely, we create the causes for suffering. If this is not a misunderstanding of how to cherish ourselves, then what is?

Because of this, the Blessed Buddha taught the discourses and branches of the path of beings with lesser aptitude and pure faith, so they may attain the higher realms. This, however, does not bring liberation from the realms of samsara—the three paths of samsara without beginning, middle, or end—therefore, other than being a temporary path, a mere stepping-stone, this does not eliminate completely the three types of suffering, which are also known as compounded suffering.

For this reason, following that, the Buddha taught the excellent path of liberation, the path of beings with a middling aptitude of pure renunciation. However, because this again is not a totally pure path to avoid remaining in the one-sided peace of nirvana, the Buddha taught the serene holy Dharma of the path of beings with greater aptitude of pure bodhicitta, which combines Sutra and Mantra. Finally, all these vehicles, just like all the streams of the land flowing together into a great ocean, come to settle within the effortless resultant vehicle of Dzogpa Chenpo. Thus the Blessed Buddha taught in whichever way necessary to guide beings to be tamed, all the way from Sutra to Tantra.

Teaching Day Two

Beings with extremely sharp faculties to be tamed by Dzogpa Chenpo are carried by the strength of their previously accumulated merit and karmic connection, and their faith and devotion. Although such people do possess greater fortune than those with sharp faculties which are strengthened through training in this lifetime, there are still differences in the strength of their individual constitutions, faculties, devotion, and familiarisation, which cannot be overlooked.

When we discuss Dzogchen, it is necessary to speak according to the samadhi of lofty realisation of the view. Not to speak in this way would contradict all the teachings of the melodious lion's roar of the supreme vehicle of Dzogpa Chenpo. However, for those people from whom this experience is slightly hidden, perhaps it would be better and have other advantages to train in stages, based on the foundation of the mind trainings on the paths of beings of lesser and middling capacities, and complete them in a progressive order. Whether or not this is the case, the only way to know is to check our own mind. As for more seasoned practitioners, you need to confirm such things with the measure of your own experience. The fact that the minds and attitudes of individual people are not exactly the same is an obvious phenomenon and established through our everyday experience, so such confirmation is necessary.

Whatever the case, whether of superior or lesser mental aptitude, everyone needs to meditate. Without meditation, there is no attainment of freedom or liberation. To engage in meditation on an object of focus with characteristics is somewhat easier than on a non-referential state. There is an object to contemplate, like a basis. If, when you are told to 'Settle into a non-referential state beyond thought and expression', you think there is nothing to settle on, that is because you have not become familiar with such a state. When told to 'Settle on that which is easy and comfortable', to think that it is neither comfortable nor easy is akin to someone with a rough temperament, who feels coarse sensations are readily experienced and pleasurable. This is like, having carried a large load for a long time, you get so used to carrying it that eventually you are unable to walk without it. This is to confuse what is difficult with what is easy; to confuse suffering with pleasure.

During practice sessions, first everyone needs to assume the seven-point posture of Vairochana. There have been those with sharp faculties who became liberated just by assuming these special key points of posture. With the same words and tone, both *Expression of the Names of Manjushri* and the *Tantra of Exceptional Wonder* state:

> The vajra posture perfects buddhahood.

By the strength of these physical action bindings, which are congruent with the common completion stages of unexcelled Mantra, by binding the ten kinds of vital energy in their own place, manifest realisation of the path is perfected and buddhahood can be attained. Why is it called the 'seven-point posture of Vairochana'? The reason could be that these physical action bindings are the same as the sitting posture of Buddha Vairochana Snow Lake, or that this is the true nature of the form aggregate, or the same as the natural upright posture of Vairochana.

Alternatively, we can say that which is to be purified, the form aggregate or the attributes of the body, is purified by the seven-point posture of Vairochana. Through this, the way purification occurs is that the ten kinds of vital wind are purified in basic space, by which the result of purification is to attain the level of Vairochana, and so forth. Thus the meaning can be explained in combination with the object of purification, the purifying action, as well as the result of purification.

When we enumerate these action bindings there are seven, so they are known as the seven-point posture of Vairochana. The first of the seven points is the need to place both legs in the vajra or full lotus posture. Most of you already know this, but I mention it now for those who are new. If you cannot manage to assume the vajra posture, it is taught you need to sit without discomfort, so we are also allowed to sit in a comfortable cross-legged position. Your spine needs to be kept straight like an arrow. Your upper arms should be relaxed and extended. It is taught the neck should be inclined slightly forwards. You need to touch the tip of your tongue to your pallet and to squint your eyes, looking ahead without a focus. There is a reason for saying 'without a focus'. When we have our eyes open, of course we will see something, so when we look 'without a focus' the point is we should not follow after the objects we see and not fixate on them. The instruction 'look without a focus' means we 'should not close our eyes'. There are two ways in which to gaze with the eyes: looking at the tip of the nose and looking forward the distance of one yoke, but there is no contradiction between these.

What are the differences between the meditation posture of Dzogpa Chenpo and the general seven-point meditation posture? A few days ago during tsalong practice, we breathed through the nose. This is in accordance with the common completion stage, which describes the method for the energy in the lalana and rasana channels to enter into the central channel. Now, at this stage, practising the foremost instruction section of Longchen Nyingtik, we need to breathe through our mouths. With our teeth and lips not quite touching and our mouths neither open nor closed, we need to breathe gently so that we almost cannot feel the movement of breath. What is the reason for this? As the wind passes directly through our mouths into our lungs, it has the particular purpose for the radiance of rigpa to dissolve into mother rigpa in the heart.

Another difference at our current stage of practice is that our hands are not placed in the mudra of meditative equipoise. We need to sit with the palms of our hands covering our right and left knees correspondingly, just like the seated posture of Victorious Longchenpa. There is a custom to call this the posture of 'finding rest in the nature of mind', however in actual fact this is the posture of 'finding rest in wisdom'. Why do we need to sit like this? This posture dispels the hindrances of drowsiness, enhances luminosity, and is a method to bring forth the dynamic energy of the luminous aspect of mind. The actual posture of Avalokiteshvara finding rest in the nature of mind is the way All-knowing Jigme Lingpa is sitting when he is represented in thankas. In any case, when we practise meditation, we need to start training first with the physical sitting posture and the method of settling the mind.

What is the essential meaning of that which is to be meditated on? We have already mentioned this several times before. 'Samsara' and 'nirvana' are two single words, but within them, the entirety of established knowable phenomena is subsumed. If we are to come to a definitive understanding of this, we need to reach the root of the secret essential point of mind. Master Padmasambhava said:

> Knowing this, even a cowherd will be liberated.
> Not knowing this, even a pandita will be confused.

To reach a definitive understanding of this single point, the Victorious Perfect Buddha taught the eighty-four thousand gateways to Dharma. This uncompounded virtue within the element of mental objects is given the name 'the unattached family of noble ones' by some. Some call it 'alaya', others 'suchness'. As we mentioned before, some call it 'innate mind', others 'all-pervading vajra of space', still others call it 'bodhicitta', 'the expanse of Samantabhadri', 'wisdom of self-arising rigpa', and so on; it is given many names. Whatever name it is given, in fact, the nature of mind is ineffable, inconceivable, and inexpressible, free of all elaboration.

As it is taught:

> It does not exist; the Victorious One did not see it.
> It is not non-existent; it is the basis of all samsara and nirvana.

In the upper context of buddhahood it does not become better, in the lower context of sentient beings it does not become worse, thus it is great permanence transcending both extremes of permanence and impermanence. It transcends far beyond all phenomena with characteristics, compounded and uncompounded dualistic phenomena, and so on, described by the sound of vast uncompoundedness. In fact, it is rigpa of primordially liberated dharmakaya, unceasing emptiness-luminosity not delimited whatsoever, not subject to any extremes whatsoever, possessing the three wisdoms of empty essence, luminous nature, and ceaseless compassion residing forever. It holds the ultimate destination of the views of Madhyamika, Mahamudra, and Dzogchen, and thus must be able to essentialise into one the key points of the paths of instruction.

When we speak of 'great permanence' and 'vast uncompoundedness', do not misunderstand them as being the same as the non-Buddhist concepts of the self-identity of purity, bliss, and permanence. There are four phenomena which are beyond the realm of understanding of self-centred childish minds. These are transcendent sublime purity, bliss, self, and permanence. What is the scriptural source for this? In Lord Maitreya's *Uttaratantra* it states:

> Because of purity, self, bliss, and permanence,
> This is the result of transcendent qualities.

Also, this has the same meaning as stated in *Expression of the Names of Manjushri*:

> Natural self-ness, purified self,
> Primordially unelaborate self...

This, the ultimate destination of the instructions of Madhyamika, Mahamudra, and Dzogchen, is what was introduced in the manner we received earlier, and that which we are practising. For those with wisdom, it is introduced upon the view. For those with experience, it is introduced in meditation. For those with faith, it is introduced through the strength of transferring blessings. There are these methods of introduction. What is the root upon which all these rely? The birth of realisation depends on the auspicious circumstances of the lama's blessings, and blessings are aroused through devotion. Therefore introduction depends on this transference of the inheritance of realisation of the lineage's blessings through powerful means.

Therefore, search for a holy spiritual master who possesses the authentic qualities. First, all the scriptural traditions need to arise as instructions, and in the middle, all the key points of instruction need to be gathered together into one. Finally, by resolving the essential essence of the instructions based on a single key point, never be apart from this very heart of practice at all times, during meditation and post-meditation, during and after practice sessions. Integrate Dharma conduct with your daily conduct. Merge the instructions with your mindstream. Do not fall into the two extremes, by being neither too tight nor too loose. Thus the conclusion of the view, meditation, and conduct, the true nature of self-settled spontaneity, needs to come about.

As for someone like myself, this disparate empty talk, the distant pleasant words of someone with neither view nor meditation, is like the sound of a guitar strummed by a deaf musician. However, I do follow the footsteps of the holy masters of the past, buddhas who appeared in person, whose power of bodhicitta and aspirations was inconceivable. Through the power of the One Gone to Bliss, the sound of Dharma can resound from trees, lotus flowers, rivers, and so on. As the sun in the sky possesses powerful heat, the dry grass on the ground is close to catching fire, but still it is necessary to place a magnifying glass between the two, so perhaps I could be of some limited use for those with devotion.

As we said earlier, when it is time to meditate, first the posture of the body and the settling method of the mind are very important. Although Dzogchen meditation is unfabricated self-settling, we need to rely on fabrication in order for that which is unfabricated to become born in our mindstream. Without the methods of the physical posture and settling of the mind, there is no method not to be deliberate, so we need to do so deliberately. Even for the main practice of meditative equipoise, we start at first with deliberate mindfulness, and gradually through the power of familiarisation, this becomes effortless mindfulness. If we begin initially with the support of the physical posture, at one stage the supported wisdom develops through its own power. When this happens, whatever daily activities we engage in become the manifestation and conduct of our true nature. So we certainly need to maintain such a goal.

We have already pointed out that when we engage in practice sessions, our physical sitting posture and the way we settle our mind are important. As we just mentioned, we need to sit in the seven-point posture of Vairochana, but what do we need to do to settle the mind? This is taught in the foremost instructions of the scriptures: do not follow thoughts of the past, do not welcome thoughts of the future, and do not look into the face of thoughts of the present. Settle both body and mind loosely. Within this physical posture and this method of settling the mind, the key points of threefold motionlessness are included.

Threefold motionlessness is as follows: motionless body is like Mt. Meru. Motionless sense faculties are like a lake reflecting the stars and planets. The motionless nature of mind is like the sky without clouds. As for motionless body like Mt. Meru, when we meditate we need to keep our body straight and steady. When our body is straight, the channels are straight. When the channels are straight, the wind energies are straight.

When the wind energies are straight, then the mind is workable. As for motionless sense faculties, like a lake reflecting the stars and planets, the five sense doors do not follow after external objects and engage in analysis, but nor do they remain inwardly settled. We need to settle them clearly present. In particular, the eyes are the avenue through which luminosity arises, therefore we need to settle them without any agitation and without focusing. In meditation of the Heart Essence tradition the eyes are never closed.

In the motionless nature of mind, like a sky without clouds, we need to maintain the aspect of clarity. In what is called 'the introduction to rigpa', rigpa is the true nature of the conditioned phenomena which is mind. The wisdom that transcends mind is taught to be called 'rigpa'. That which thinks 'I need to see the nature of rigpa' is mind. When we trace mind back to its innermost nature, we come to meet with rigpa. To give an example, they are like waves and the ocean. When mind does not come under the influence of discursive thoughts, we discover the nature of mind, rigpa essence. At that stage, there is nothing negative called 'mind' that remains separate. When the wind does not agitate the ocean and waves have merged with the ocean, they do not remain somewhere on the sidelines. Mind is the same.

In this way, having just turned inwards, while thinking 'I need to maintain the rigpa essence' the unimpeded perceptions of the sixfold group of consciousness are ordinary awareness. When we differentiate this awareness, there are three kinds of discursive thoughts: virtuous, unvirtuous, and indeterminate. But, when we allow unaltered mind to self-settle it is different; it is uncontrived and free of distortion. That which is empty limpidity, distinct luminosity, naked lucidity, unobstructed transparency, and ineffable is rigpa.

Because rigpa transcends mind, mind cannot see rigpa. In that case, who sees rigpa? Rigpa is self-aware of itself. When we say this, intellectuals are sure to bring to mind two polar concepts and think, 'Isn't this like a sword cutting itself with its own blade, similar to that which the Cittamatrins speak of?' However, this narrow approach of reasoning will not get us very far here. The capacity of the wisdom aspect of the dynamic energy of rigpa that arises, sees its own essence in the manner of merging with the ground or merging inwardly. In other words, the basic space of the essence of dynamic energy, and the single taste of the fully evident manner in which it appears, are said to be 'seen', which is a symbolic term but one we can comprehend.

Generally, there are two distinctions of rigpa: 'rigpa essence of the ground', and 'rigpa dynamic energy of compassion', but whichever one we refer to—rigpa of the ground or rigpa of the manifestation of the ground—it is endowed with the threefold wisdom of essence, nature, and compassion. However, this does not mean that there is only rigpa of the ground and rigpa of the manifestation of the ground. There is also 'spontaneously present rigpa of the state of liberation'. This is neither ground nor manifestation of the ground. It is rigpa of complete dissolution of the manifestations of the ground. When we speak generally about this rigpa at the stage of Dzogchen, it is that which ensures that ignorance together with habitual tendencies to be exhausted are abandoned. Alternatively, it is the single basis for accomplishment of the twofold result of abandonment.

When we speak of the characteristics of rigpa's attributes, rigpa whose essence is empty and which does not waver from the ground, is emptiness with an essence of rigpa. This has a nature of the unity of emptiness and luminosity. Rigpa whose nature is luminosity and whose lustre is inwardly luminous is luminosity with an essence of rigpa, and is the unity of luminosity and emptiness. Rigpa whose compassion is all-pervading and whose radiance is outwardly luminous is rigpa with an essence of emptiness, and is the unity of rigpa and emptiness.

As for the current topic, the nature of rigpa which is known by itself is the rigpa compassion of the wisdom aspect of the dynamic energy of rigpa that arises. First, when manifestations of the ground move from the ground, extremely subtle energy known as 'the five wind energies of wisdom that become the life force' arouses outward luminosity and thus awakens it. Also now this forms the path. When we settle in rigpa's own self-nature, this is the knowing aspect which primordial self-nature has had spontaneously from the very beginning. What are known as 'the five wind energies of wisdom that become the life force' are, in the Dharma language of the unexcelled common completion stage, the fivefold rays of light of the wind energies, which stirred from deep within and radiated forth. For this reason, to re-enter now into this essence, the basic space of no-thought, is not only easy, but the strength to do so is especially strong.

In this case, what is the difference between the compassionate dynamic energy of rigpa and the discursive thoughts of mind? Mind is that which follows after objects. If there is no object, thoughts are unable to arise. There is no way to say 'I conceived of something that can't be imagined'. Such a thing cannot be conceived. The compassionate dynamic energy of rigpa does not look outward and follow after grasping and fixation. Although myriad appearances are perceived, it does not arise by following after whichever objects are perceived or whatever arises. Like the reflections that arise on the surface of a mirror, they arise as pervasive evenness upon the expanse of rigpa. Therefore, rigpa has never resided in the confusion that grasps self-manifestation to be the appearance of something other. Thus in the immediacy of the basic space of its essence, the samadhi of vipashyana or wisdom, arises particularly clear in appearance and stable. To give an example, it is like the flame of a lamp that is not buffeted by the wind.

As for such a clear manifest appearance, this luminosity is not one which has a referential focus. Because rigpa is self-abiding meditative concentration, it is ineffable unobstructed transparency without referential focus. This basic space of rigpa is particularly easy to merge with, and the strength to merge with it is great. We said the essence of rigpa is uncontrived, free of distortion, empty limpidity, distinct luminosity, naked lucidity, unobstructed transparency, and ineffable. We also said it is that which is present at the very moment of turning inward. Because the essence of rigpa is not established as anything whatsoever, in order to communicate this, we say it is 'empty limpidity', with the thought that this is somewhat close to the true meaning.

Also, to avoid any possible misunderstanding that this is nothingness, we say that rigpa is not dull or dark. From the aspect that it is inherently luminous in all of samsara and nirvana, we say that it is 'distinct luminosity'. When mercury falls onto the ground, it does not become covered by dust. Likewise, the nature of rigpa is not covered by elaborations of characteristics, therefore we say it is 'naked'. Within the state of rigpa, no discursive thoughts or afflictive emotions whatsoever form. As there is no place for them to catch or settle onto, rigpa is known as 'unobstructed transparency'. If we wanted to say that rigpa is like such and such, there is nothing that can be said. As rigpa transcends the realm of speech, we say it is 'ineffable'. This ineffable meaning is surely also something inconceivable.

In this case, when settled upon rigpa, it is correct not to identify an essence about which we can say 'meditate on this'. Regarding this ineffable luminosity-emptiness, the feeling that arises 'If this isn't it, then what is..?!' which resolves doubt from within, is rigpa. To rest within this state of ineffable luminosity-emptiness and not to lose this state is enough. However, to think 'Am I meditating well?' with fixated attachment is not correct. We should not have such thoughts. Because this is not appropriate, the example of becoming obscured by both white and black clouds refers to this situation. This knowing of our own nature is such that there is no duality between what is known and the one who knows.

What is called 'mind' can either be something that resides or something that proliferates. There are methods to introduce rigpa based on both of these states. The reason this is possible is, regardless of the circumstances, rigpa is present without any separation. However, it is slightly easier to introduce rigpa to a beginner between stillness and movement. If introduction is made at that point, then the abiding aspect has awoken from the lethargy of no-thought, but the moving aspect of subtle and gross discursive thoughts has not yet arisen. This awareness is self-settled and remains in its natural state. From the aspect that it does not follow after objects, it is not cognitive mind. Like reflections arising on the surface of a mirror, the sixfold group of consciousness arises upon it unimpededly. Free of the fixation of grasping at a self, from the aspect that it is self-arising unimpeded emptiness-luminosity, it still resembles a state of awareness. Although apparent objects are unimpeded, arising like the reflection of the moon in water, that which is not cognitive mind but mind itself, ungrasping empty and luminous, uncontrived and free of distortion, is called by the name 'rigpa'.

Such rigpa, emptiness-luminosity without grasping, is complete with the four kayas. All the key points of threefold view, meditation, and conduct, and the ground, path, and result of Dzogpa Chenpo are subsumed within it. The essence of rigpa, empty limpidity not existing in any way, is ineffable and beyond being an object of mind or speech, indescribable, inconceivable, and inexpressible. This empty essence is dharmakaya, as we should already know. Not mere nothingness, the unimpeded nature inherently luminous in all of samsara and nirvana, is the luminous nature of sambhogakaya. The unceasing arising of rigpa emptiness, the magical display of rigpa which arises as anything whatsoever, is the all-embracing compassion of nirmanakaya. The inseparable essence of these three, beyond being an object of words or thoughts, is the svabhavikakaya. That which is self-knowing, not existing in any way, pure like space, the basic space of inseparable rigpa-emptiness, is the single bindu of dharmakaya.

As mentioned earlier, like a fully-sighted person seeing a form in daylight, recognising the true nature of rigpa is the view. Staying self-settled within this without losing it is meditation. For the sake of enhancing this, engaging in further cultivation without attachment or fixation is conduct. To embrace the equal taste of our own natural condition without hope or fear, positivity or negativity, is taught to be the result. To recognise the self-arising wisdom of rigpa, uncontrived and free of distortion in all its immediacy, is direct introduction to our true nature. To know and determine this is dharmakaya that does not waver from realisation beyond conceptual mind, is the singular decisive experience. When settled within the state of innate limpidity without elaboration, all acceptance and rejection is like the trace of a bird in the sky and becomes free from grasping and effort. This is to gain confidence in liberation.

At the time of entering meditative equipoise, limpid and unwavering like an ocean undisturbed by waves, the aspect of mind pacified from the elaborations of discursive thoughts is shamatha. The aspect of rigpa with an intensity of luminosity and radiance, arising as unimpeded emptiness-luminosity is vipashyana. Maintaining this nature of rigpa, the unity of shamatha and vipashyana, we need to meditate without engaging in fixation or grasping onto whatever meditative experiences of bliss, luminosity, or no-thought arise.

Moreover, in this rigpa, ground, path, and result are also complete. Ground rigpa abides within primordially. When we meditate on the path with our lama's foremost instructions and remain unwavering within this state of rigpa, the result is the equalness of samsara and nirvana primordially liberated upon rigpa; re-liberation which can manifest possessing the two purities. In this way, threefold ground, path, and result are complete.

In short, without engaging in fixation or grasping, when we have reached naked self-liberation, naked rigpa is not covered by the husks of repeated fabricated elaboration of fixation on meditative experiences. There are no other potential points of going astray or error. We need to decide upon this point. Otherwise, if you think 'Is there anything better than this? Is there something more attractive? Who knows if I even have this rigpa? Even if I do have it, surely I'll not be able to find it that easily' this is like, as we mentioned earlier, leaving an elephant at home and going to search for elephant tracks in the forest. The following quotation is pertinent here:

> See the secret of mind, too simple to believe,
> Through the power of the lama's foremost instructions.

Upon such an expansive and free joyful mind, without exaggerating prematurely with empty words of the lofty view, with the refined conduct of extremely subtle cause and effect, engage in adopting and abandoning, acceptance and rejection. According to the common Dharma language of the Mahayana, at first sky-like meditative equipoise and illusion-like post-meditation occur in alternation. However, once they have become more familiar, they should arise in unity. In summary, without separating from threefold mindfulness, attentiveness, and carefulness, our body sits on our cushion, our mind resides in our body, and relaxation stays in our mind.

Whatever manifests, we need to incorporate it onto the path of the view. Whatever arises, we need to make it become enhancement of conduct. Strong fixated grasping is a hindrance to the view. Strong distractions are a hindrance to meditation. Disregard for discipline is a hindrance to conduct. Free from these hindrances, if we make complete our inner conditions, then hindrances and harms of external circumstances become supportive conditions. Our mind goes towards the Dharma. Dharma becomes the path. The path clears confusion. Confusion arises as wisdom, and we accomplish all our aspirations. Thus yogic discipline is perfected and victorious in all directions!

There may be many people in these degenerate times who only enjoy pursuing flattery and fame, and so are more easily impressed by someone who says they can see gods or demons than by one who teaches a single key point of greatly secret foremost instruction. However, those who do teach according to meaning and nurture beings to be tamed according to the Dharma, should make aspirations in the manner of a true spiritual practitioner and teacher of the Dharma. In this case, for the sake of the spread of the teachings and the stable life of the holders of the teachings, if we dedicate to the cause of provisional and ultimate happiness for ourselves and all other sentient beings, then I believe the root of merit of this valuable dedication is very powerful, not only for Tibet but for the entire world.

Teaching Day Three

Opening Words
Samsaric Suffering and Renunciation

The Sakya *Separation from the Four Attachments* teaches:

> To fixate on this life is not Dharma.
> To fixate on samsara is not renunciation.

By practising the holy sublime Dharma, to pursue the goal of everlasting happiness for both ourselves and others, what can we never be without from the very beginning? We must have both faith and devotion. Faith is the door through which we can perceive the Dharma. Having entered the door of the Buddha Dharma of inner beings and taken refuge in the Three Jewels, then faith and fear need to form the foundation of our practice. If, at the beginning, we do not have any faith based on trust in karmic cause and effect, then we cannot accept the existence of future lives or the existence of a level of liberation. Then there would be no reason to have any foundation for renunciation to develop.

For those of us from the Buddhist land of Tibet, we are born in a central region of Dharma, and from an early age the first words we spoke were likely to be 'mama' and 'mani'. In particular, the excellent yogis in this Dharma gathering understand how the teachings of the Buddha are undeceiving, and they realise the truth of past and future lives and karmic cause and effect. Such fundamentals do not need to be debated by providing endless proof.

Based on this foundation of utterly pure convinced faith in cause and effect, what do we need next? It is now necessary for genuine renunciation to grow. If genuine renunciation does not develop in our mindstream, we do not understand that the suffering of samsara is suffering, and we fixate on this life. We learn from the scriptural quotation above that if we fixate on this life we are not Buddhist. If we have great attachment to this life, we will seek earnestly the level of gods and humans in the next. Whatever joyful and pleasurable experiences there are in those higher realms of gods and humans, they are only a temporary mode of manifestation which does not transcend samsara. Therefore we are taught:

> To fixate on samsara is not renunciation.

Based upon renunciation, first we need to engage in purifying our own mindstream. What is known as 'renunciation' is not just getting fed up sometimes when some samsaric suffering befalls us, and thinking miserably 'What's the point?' This is called 'mere revulsion'. To feel revulsion for samsara, and then to think 'I need to escape from here and accomplish liberation' is the actual desire for liberation.

In that case, through the guidance on the difficulty of finding the freedoms and endowments, we learn that this physical basis with the complete freedoms and endowments is difficult to find again, like an udumbara flower, and is very meaningful when found, like a wish-fulfilling jewel. Based upon this understanding, through the guidance on the impermanence of life, we understand that with birth comes death. Moreover, we also understand that there is no certainty as to when death will come. Based on this understanding, and relying on the guidance which contemplates the suffering of samsara, we need to give birth to genuine renunciation.

Some other teaching traditions cover the aspiration of beings of lesser capacity who turn their minds away from the three lower realms and strive for the higher realms. They also teach the aspiration of beings of middling capacity who turn their minds away from samsara, nirvana, and the six kinds of beings in their entirety, and strive for liberation. But, except for those two, they teach nothing more. In contrast, in our tradition which was expounded by the all-knowing father and son, we are taught that turning our minds away from self-centred preoccupations is considered the most crucial point. This is given the term 'great renunciation that does not reside in either extreme'. Thus we can determine that not everything called 'renunciation' is the same. The first kind of renunciation is the motivation of beings of lesser capacity who strive for the higher realms, and is called 'mere renunciation'. Then there are the two kinds of renunciation of shravakas and pratyekabuddhas, and 'great renunciation' is the fourth.

Alternatively, we can distinguish three particular kinds of renunciation as follows: there are the two types of renunciation of shravakas and pratyekabuddhas who turn away from samsara and focus on attaining peace and happiness for personal benefit, and then there is the renunciation of bodhisattvas, which is great renunciation that does not reside in either extreme.

When we contemplate that which we develop renunciation against: all the multitudinous categories of samsaric suffering, then we know that these cannot be enumerated or measured. Generally speaking, the numbers of sentient beings who experience suffering cannot be calculated in figures, so the karma and karmic results of suffering that they experience are similarly inconceivable. Therefore, when we summarise beings into types, there are taught to be six kinds. However, in actual fact, the amount of suffering which is experienced and the numbers of sentient beings who experience it, can only be said to be 'unable to be measured'.

Wherever space pervades, so sentient beings pervade. Wherever sentient beings pervade, so in turn they are pervaded by karma and afflictive emotions. This being the case, to speak of their numbers and to come to a general summary of them all, is obviously very difficult. When we think about observable phenomena, we can see there are so many disparate kinds of suffering for each and every individual human and animal, and the beings who experience these sufferings are also similarly diverse. The variety of different kinds of animal are inconceivable, and also in terms of human beings, even the residents of one town or the members of one family all have widely varying dispositions. Similarly, the impetus of karma and afflictive emotions can be very different. With all these variations, the manner in which suffering is experienced also varies, which is something we can observe ourselves.

When we consider the general suffering that humans experience, everyone who is born has a nature of death, as if we were born in order to die. Not only do we experience so much meaningless difficulty and suffering during life, but everyone with a physical body is similarly bound from birth at the beginning to death at the end. The first thing we experience in this life is the suffering of being born. In the interim, there is the suffering of ageing, accompanied by the suffering of sickness, and in the end comes the inevitable suffering of dying. Life is filled with so much suffering that we cannot discuss it all.

What is more, when we must take rebirth in a future life, even if it were possible to continue to have a human body in the higher realms, there is still no way to avoid experiencing such suffering, from the beginning of life all the way to the end. If we have to experience these sufferings from the start over and over again, we will of course feel total disgust and certainly not any enthusiasm. Not only that, but when we begin to consider the suffering of dying, we also evoke the suffering of the terrifying bardo. After death we have to experience all the suffering of the intermediate state, which only serves to lead us on to further suffering in the next life.

At the time when someone dies, the amount of suffering they experience at the point of death varies depending on the strength of their individual karma. Against our wishes, the propelling force of this life is exhausted. We are powerless to remain any longer with loved ones and friends, and we cannot retain any of our wealth and possessions. When the time comes, we have no choice but to go to the unpredictable and unfamiliar land of the bardo. Like a hair plucked out from butter we are plucked from life never to return. At this moment, there are few without dread in their hearts. However, this is not only terrifying for the person who is dying. Those who are left behind also experience suffering somewhat akin to physical death. Parting forever, never to see their loved ones again, both the dying and the living experience such suffering.

After death we do not just disappear, like water evaporating or a flame becoming extinguished. The dead must experience the suffering of the bardo intermediate state. What is that like? There 'four terrifying sounds' resound forth from the elements: the thunderous sound is like a great landmass quaking all at once, and the blazing sound is like the fire of the three thousandfold universe burning simultaneously. Likewise, there is howling like the buffeting of the wind and roaring like destructive floodwater. Moreover, there are experiences which develop from the three poisons. Wherever you look appears as dull reddishness like the gloom of dusk, which develops from attachment. An insipid greyness develops from aversion, and a murky blackness develops from ignorance, which is frightening and terrible to be engulfed in. Following this, when the three impassable defiles which develop from the three poisons arise, how much more suffering is experienced!

Having obtained a human body in this life and met with the holy Dharma, while we are in charge of our own independence, if we do not realise the potential of this opportunity, when we depart empty-handed having let the freedoms and advantages go to waste, even if we were to grow regretful at that time, it is too late. We will have already arrived at the place where regret is of no use. In particular, those who spend their lives engaging entirely in unvirtuous actions have impure perceptions. Therefore, chased by impure karmic wind, if someone has the karma to be reborn, for example, in hell, during the second half of the bardo of becoming the appearances of their upcoming rebirth in hell begin to arise, and subsequently they are born in hell. In comparison, those who accumulate the negative karma of terrible sins—the actions with immediate consequence, and so forth—do not experience any intermediate state, but descend directly to be reborn in the hell of unending torment.

Generally, it is the sufferings of the hot and cold hells that are spoken about predominately. Just like the endless enumerations of accumulated karma, the categories of suffering experienced in the hell realms are just illustrations, so we must examine them through reasoning to understand correctly. In the same way, the thirst and hunger of the pretas, and the stupidity and foolishness of the animals, how they are exploited and suffer from preying upon one another, are all relatable experiences. Of course, there is also human birth, ageing, sickness, and death. Among the samsaric universe and every inhabitant subsumed within the truth of suffering, all forms that are seen are entirely the embodiment of suffering experiences. All sounds which are heard are cries of misery and suffering. This we can understand when we think carefully. Similarly, the fighting of the demi-gods, the death and fall of the gods, the human suffering of birth, ageing, sickness, and death, and so on, all of these are clearly related in the *Sutra of a Hundred Actions*, the *Realisation Stories of Purna*, and the *Close Application of Mindfulness*. Thus inconceivable suffering occurs in samsara.

These teachings on the mind trainings need to be truly taken on board and contemplated. When we meditate on the sufferings of the lower realms, we should be driven by the four factors of place, physical support, suffering, and lifespan. We need to direct our focus intensely, as if we were actually reborn in those places right now. It is not suitable to contemplate the suffering of samsara as if we were being told a story or listening to a fable. We should begin with the suffering of death and the terror of the bardo and actually meditate. Cover your mouth and nose with your hands for a few moments, and get an idea of the kind of terror you will experience when you finally exhale but can no longer inhale. Contemplate the suffering of separating from family and friends forever. Think how much you miss your loved ones now when you do not see them for a month or two. How much more suffering will we feel when we actually become separated from them permanently at the end of this life?

Throughout our succession of past lives up until now, how many fully ripened results of the accumulated ten non-virtues must still remain having not yet been purified? All those that we have not confessed and purified individually have been multiplying constantly, so if we calculate the volume of unvirtuous negativities and their increase, just think of the weight of suffering we are due to bear in future. All this can be understood by engaging in the mind trainings in connection with the detailed classifications of karmic results.

Teaching Day Three

Main Teaching

The time has come for us to continue teaching and listening to the songs of Shabkar Tsokdruk Rangdrol, and his well-known *Flight of the Garuda*. This excellent foremost instruction text teaches how to determine the view, meditation, and conduct of the ground, path, and result of Dzogchen trekchö primordial purity. It teaches fortunate ordinary and extraordinary beings to be tamed how to practise in a multitude of ways, gradually and non-sequentially, by studying our extraordinary tradition of this Dharma lineage, in connection with the practical guidance of practice training. During the last two days of teaching, we discussed the goodness of the beginning. From the goodness of the middle, we have already completed the preliminary practices of the threefold arising, abiding, and disappearance of the mind, and also the main topic of introduction to the nature of the mind.

Song Nine
The Ordinary Introduction

Although, in general, all those to be tamed by Dzogchen have sharp faculties, we make two divisions, and today we begin by teaching the ordinary introduction, mainly for the sake of those whose mind state is one of objective appearances. We begin with the synopsis and then continue with the detailed explanation:

> **EMAHO!**
> **Fortunate and exceptional heart children,**
> **Without applying the whip, a horse will not gallop.**
> **Without much churning, milk will not turn into butter.**
> **Without detailed explanation, a definitive conclusion is not reached.**
> **So do not feel bored by the many words of this song,**
> **But listen with a joyful mind.**

With these examples, those of the fortunate family are exhorted to awaken to their spiritual birthright, not to fall asleep at the time of confusion, but to awaken from this delusory perception of wandering in samsara. This is the instruction to see ultimate wisdom of non-delusion, and for sentient beings to become buddhas. We are told not to become bored by this meaningful song, which is unrivalled even by the melodies of hundreds or thousands of gandharva flutes, but to listen with great enthusiasm while it is sung.

Here appearances are introduced as mind, which is summarised as follows:

> **If you do not know that all appearances are mind,**
> **You will never realise the meaning of emptiness.**
> **From where do these appearances initially arise?**
> **In the interim where do they remain? Finally, where do they go?**
> **All fortunate children, consider and analyse well.**
>
> **When examined, they are for example, like mist in the sky,**
> **Which arises from the sky and returns again to the sky.**
> **Similarly appearances, the magical illusions of mind,**
> **Arise in your mind and return to mind.**
>
> **For example, someone whose sight faculty is impaired**
> **Will see aberrations when looking into the sky,**
> **Appearing as if something is present.**
> **However there is nothing, it is a trick of the eye.**

At this stage, when Shabkar refers to 'appearances', according to our tradition, which is the extraordinary viewpoint of Victorious Longchenpa, the father and the son, we need to distinguish between sensory appearances in general and individual perception of these as apparent sense objects. Jigme Lingpa taught the following example in *Yeshe Lama*: in the first moment of seeing a mountain, those who do not think 'It is a mountain' are not on the path of ordinary people. In the second instant, the potential of awareness of the clear appearance of the non-existent nature of the mountain is complete, and the thought of the mountain vanishes naturally without a trace. At that time, without fixation on the appearance, one remains in one's true nature.

All wandering beings with the same kind of perception of apparent sense objects are established as having the same common experience. However, appearances that are apparent in front of us arise in our mind. They are apparent in our mind and vanish in our mind. Thus, we are taught that by considering and analysing the arising, abiding, and disappearance of appearances, we will come to understand them. The examples for this are mist in the sky, and someone with diseased or impaired eyesight. Just as aberrations may appear in the sky to someone who has impaired eyesight, appearances are taught to be the mind.

The teaching that mind is empty is as follows:

> Similarly, due to bad habits of reifying reality,
> And the power of a distorted mental faculty,
> All relative phenomena seen and heard
> Appear as if they do truly exist.
>
> However, primordially there is not even an iota of substantial existence.
> They are magical illusions of our mind.
> All these illusions are groundless and empty,
> Non-existent yet clearly apparent, like a mirage or the moon in water.
> Enter into equipoise in the truth of inseparable appearance-emptiness.
>
> Now, in our dreams while we sleep,
> Our homeland, house, relatives, and so on,
> Appear distinctly, and we experience joy and sorrow.
> However, at that time, not one of our relatives is present.
> We have not moved even an inch from our beds,
> Yet we experience them just as they are, plain as day.
>
> Similarly, all appearances of this life
> Are like the experiences of last night's dream.
> Our mind labels and grasps at things,
> And they are seen in that way, experienced by mind.
> Dreams during sleep are devoid of self-nature,
> Likewise, no matter what you perceive, it is empty.

Dense mist in the sky has no basis and vanishes naturally. Likewise, the appearances of what are known as 'visual aberrations' or 'vitreous floaters' do not exist, but arise from the impaired eyes of someone with faulty eyesight. Similarly, fixated grasping at things as truly existing, ascribing them with a concrete nature, is mind having become distorted by negative habituation. Due to the fault of this distortion, all relative false and deceptive phenomena that are seen and heard arise. Without close examination, we perceive these things as enjoyable and completely real. However, despite being apparent, from the very beginning they do not have even an iota of true existence. The reason for this is that they are mind's own illusory manifestations.

Because appearances are an illusory display, everything is baseless and empty, as shown in the examples of a mirage and the reflection of the moon in water. The reason that myriad appearances arise is because they are empty. Thus, enter into equipoise in the truth of inseparable appearance and emptiness, or emptiness and interdependent origination, apparent yet empty, empty while being apparent. As shown in the above example, although during sleep dreams appear as truly existing, while they are apparent, they have no self-nature. Similarly, although appearances are seen to be truly existing in relation to their conventional appearance, they lack any truly existing nature. Thus this teaches that appearances themselves do not transcend the nature of ultimate emptiness, but have the same essence.

Teaching Day Three

Song Ten
Introduction to Appearances as Mind and Mind as Empty

Once again, we are taught the reasoning for the introduction that demonstrates appearances are mind and mind is empty, together with logical examples. First, the detailed teaching to demonstrate that appearances are mind is as follows:

> **EMAHO!**
> **Fortunate and only heart children,**
> **All appearances are non-definitive.**

Shabkar makes this assertion, and then explains briefly how appearances are not definitive with one example:

> **What for some is light, is darkness for others.**

What is night-time for us, appears as clear as day for an owl. A more detailed explanation with examples is as follows:

> **Moreover, for some sentient beings, regarding the earth:**
> **There are sentient beings who perceive earth as earth.**
> **There are sentient beings who perceive earth as fire.**
> **There are sentient beings who perceive earth as enjoyment.**
> **There are sentient beings who perceive earth as suffering.**

With reference to this last sentence, it is not only the earth but the entire samsaric universe and its contents that is subsumed within the truth of suffering. However, here we need to understand that this refers specifically to the apparent perception of some sentient beings who suffer from being crushed by earth. This thus indicates how all beings have dissimilar apparent perception. Likewise:

> **There are sentient beings who perceive water as water.**
> **There are sentient beings who perceive water as fire.**
> **There are sentient beings who perceive water as nectar.**
> **There are sentient beings who perceive water as an abode.**
> **There are sentient beings who perceive water as earth.**

Again, likewise:

> There are sentient beings who perceive fire as fire.
> There are sentient beings who perceive fire as enjoyment.
> There are sentient beings who perceive fire as an abode.
> There are sentient beings who perceive fire as food.

Also:

> There are sentient beings who perceive space as space.
> There are sentient beings who perceive space as an abode.
> There are sentient beings who perceive space as earth.

These are the same kind of examples as a cup of water appearing differently in the perception of the six kinds of sentient being.

> Thus appearances are not definitive,
> Because they appear as they do through the power of habitual tendencies.
> Similarly, to perceive the four elements
> As being separate is the perception of humans.

This teaches that human perception perceives the four elements individually.

> Moreover, other beings perceive this earth
> As fiery hell, farmers as a resource to enjoy,
> Or for those with a depressed mind, as suffering.
> Similarly, fire is enjoyable for the fire gods.
> For pretas with a body of fire it is an abode,
> And fire beings perceive it as food.
>
> Likewise, for hell beings, water is fire.
> For preta beings it is pus and blood.
> For elephants it is earth, and for gods, nectar.
> For the Gods who Control Other's Emanations it is jewels
> And rains of flowers. For nagas it is an abode.
> In the same way, space is also an abode
> Which all the gods perceive as the ground.

Because appearances are the manifest perception of the mind, appearances are taught to be the mind, which in turn is taught to be empty as follows:

Teaching Day Three

> That being so, everything appears
> According to how one labels it.

This is the brief explanation, which teaches one aspect of the summarised meaning. The details of how this occurs are related through the following legends, which appear in ancient texts:

> Moreover, when Devaputra asked the Buddha,
> 'Who made Mt. Meru, the sun, the moon, and so on?'
> The Buddha replied,
> 'They have no other creator at all.
> The concretisation of habitual tendencies of one's thoughts
> Labels things, grasps at things, and they appear as such.
> Everything is made by one's mind.'
>
> When Devaputra again enquired of the Buddha,
> 'However concrete one's thoughts,
> Where does such solidity and firmness
> Of Mt. Meru, the sun, moon, and so on, come from?'
> The Buddha replied,
> 'In Varanasi, an old woman visualised her body
> To be a tiger, and seeing a tiger
> The city was emptied.
> If, in a short time, she could make that appear,
> The mind of habitual tendencies, accustomed from
>   beginningless rebirths,
> Indeed creates such appearances.' So said the Sage.
> Thus everything is made by mind.

These are examples of appearances made by mind. Because appearances are made by mind, it follows that they are established as empty, which is taught as follows:

> Furthermore, it is said that a non-Buddhist,
> In order to prevent distractions of worldly excitement,
> Visualised a place of solitude. Thereby, a quiet place
> Was actually manifested, and could also be seen by others.
>
> Another visualised space to be rock,
> And having become rock, it trapped his body.
> Thus everything is created by mind's thoughts,
> So is the self-manifestation of mind,
> And in fact, all self-manifestation is empty.

> Moreover, the sentient beings in the Ephemeral Hells
> Perceive their forms to be doors or pillars, stoves or ropes,
> And so on, thus experiencing suffering.

This highlights the experience of suffering which springs from our own perception of our body or form.

> Therefore, however mind's thoughts label things,
> That is how they are perceived.

Thus, having taught this point in detail with examples given in everyday language, the meaning is summarised as follows:

> All the joys and suffering of the six kinds of sentient beings
> Are created solely by their own minds.
> Thus everything is the illusion of our own mind,
> The non-existent yet apparent inherent form of emptiness.
> Decide this with resolute confidence and rest evenly.

The above introduces appearances as mind, and mind as empty. Among the many introductions which adorn the tantras, these are one part of various different introductions for those with sharp and dull faculties, in the manner of an introduction for those whose mind state is one of objective appearances. Why is this required? This introduction to appearances as mind is not the same as asserting apparent objects inherently endowed with characteristics to be mind, in the manner asserted by the Mind Only True Aspectarians. In order to guide people whose mind state is one of objective appearances gradually on the path, first grasped apparent objects are taught to have no basis. Secondly, we are made aware that objects upon which grasping mind fixates, lack actual substance. Thirdly, the unity of rigpa and emptiness beyond extremes is determined. Thus the stages of the path, the manner of guidance of the main practice, are passed through.

If everything that is apparent or unapparent is grasped by mind's discursive thought, the mind that appraises the initial object is the mind that will grasp at an appearance. What arises following this is the subsequently arising distinct mental event of analysis, the mind of grasping, which we ascertain. Recognising this focus for liberation on arising, self-disappearing, and self-settling, the sign that the root of something to be discarded and its remedy has been cut is taught to be the purpose of the introduction to appearances as mind. When mind looks at the nature of the mental event which arises upon an object, without recognition of it being something or any reference point, a nature of emptiness that does not exist as anything arises, whereby this introduction to mind as empty cuts the root of dualistic grasped-grasping.

However, what is called 'empty' is not nothingness, or a nihilistic extreme of empty voidness. The nature of emptiness arises as an unceasing self-luminosity of empty radiance, inseparable basic space and wisdom, indivisible limpidity which transcends all grasped-grasping. From the aspect of rigpa, it has never ceased. From the aspect of essence, it does not abide in permanence. Free of all extremes of elaboration, the introduction to emptiness as rigpa is like this.

As mind is empty, it can appear as anything whatsoever. Rigpa emptiness, primordially pure and spontaneously present, arises unceasingly as anything. The reason for this is taught as follows:

> Moreover, it is taught the Capable One Great Snow Lake
> Has upon a single anther of the lotus in his hand
> The three thousandfold universe of Endurance.
>
> When tögal rigpa reaches full measure,
> It is taught in each pore of one's body
> Immeasurable buddha realms are seen,
> And also countless places of the six kinds of sentient beings
>   are seen.
> Emanations are sent forth to tame these beings,
> Bringing them benefit as if in a dream.

Capable One Great Snow Lake refers to the buddha who is mentioned in the 'Pure Realm of the Five Families of Great Snow Lake', which is explained to be represented as such due to the reflections of five great snow mountains that arise in five great lakes.

Having thus arranged the rationale with quantified examples and causal factors, the meaning is summarised as follows:

> Therefore, the phenomena of samsara and nirvana are self-manifest.
> Everything self-manifest is groundless and empty.
> Form confidence in the state of ungrasping emptiness-luminosity.

Having taught a part of the instruction with these intermediate verses, more follow:

> Furthermore, it is taught that upon one atom

> There are immeasurable buddha realms, as many as there are atoms,
> And countless places of the six kinds of beings.
> The Victorious One taught all these are distinct,
> Without disturbance or bringing harm.

Thinking in this way, in the realm of knowable objects, there is nothing that is not included within the two which we call 'samsara' and 'nirvana'. When we investigate from where these two unfold, the ground from which they proliferate, it is as Glorious Saraha said:

> From where existence and nirvana proliferate...

Thus there is no phenomenon which does not arise from mind. In which case, when we need to cut the root of samsaric delusory appearances it is necessary to uproot the ground of confusion, the illusionist of the mind. If we tame the mind, which is like a magician, then the delusory appearances made by mind naturally become eliminated. If we destroy the principal linchpin of the mechanisms of delusion, then it is as if all the other parts naturally run out of steam. The Bhagavan said:

> O son of the Victorious Ones, these three realms are merely mind.

Also, Bodhisattva Shantideva taught:

> By taming this mind alone,
> They all become subdued.

The teaching that the way in which things appear is produced by mind continues as follows:

> Moreover, it is taught inside each insect
> There are countless cities of insects.
> It is taught in the realm of space
> There are countless cities,
> Many are formed facing downwards,
> And similarly, they exist facing sideways and upwards.

The extent of the arrayed realms of beings to be tamed by the dharmakaya, sambhogakaya, and nirmanakaya is beyond the scope of ordinary beings' conceptual minds. Even just a part of this, the nirmanakaya pure realm of the billion universes of Endurance, is inconceivable. However, it exists in the collective perception of everyone currently alive.

Take for instance this planet which is present in our immediate perception, when we look at the movement of the globe and its continuous orbit, there does not exist anything which can be called a top or bottom, or any cardinal or intermediate directions. Similarly, in something huge, there are many minute aspects. However, the very subtle extreme of a huge aspect that can be seen in something minute remains exclusive to the realm of all-knowing wisdom, therefore other than the wisdom of individual self-knowing, this is established as being immeasurable. As this is the case:

> **If you wonder who made these things in such a way,**
> **The Victorious One taught everything is made by mind.**

How this is explained was already presented above, and if we realise the nature of mind, it is enlightened. Therefore it is taught:

> Cultivate well the notion that buddhahood is not to be searched for elsewhere.
>
> **The nature of mind is primordially like space.**
> **Know that all phenomena are likewise.**

When we settle in the sky-like state of the nature of mind free of proliferation and subsiding, not engaging in grasping however apparent objects may appear, then all engagement in cognitive acts and mental events dissolve into basic space, and non-dual liberation occurs in their own place.

> **All sights and sounds of relative phenomena**
> **Are solely the self-manifestation of one's mind.**
> **At the time of death one's mindstream changes,**
> **So the outer world does not change, but self-manifestations change.**

The arising of the manifestations of countless pure lands of the Sugatas is the apparent perception of the pure mind of a yogi. Similarly, neither does the perception of a wicked person being born in hell entail arriving in a place called 'hell' separated by a great distance. As it is taught:

> The Sage taught that all such things
> Are the mind of non-virtue.

> Thus everything is the self-manifestation of mind.
> All self-manifestation is groundless and empty,
> Non-existent yet clearly apparent, like a reflection, the moon in water.
> Maintain the experience of the state of non-dual luminosity-emptiness rigpa.

In this way, having entered ineffable rigpa-emptiness, it is luminous yet empty and empty yet luminous. While maintaining this state of sky-like wisdom, however things appear, if we realise the grasped apparent object to be like an illusion, then the nature of non-engagement in grasping that fixates on things is pure, like space. Therefore, free of all elaborations of assertion, the non-dual origination and cessation of self-arising wisdom arises from within.

To summarise these points:

> All apparent perceptions are the self-manifestation of mind.
> The appearance of an inanimate universal container is mind.
> The appearance of six classes of beings contained within is also mind.
> The appearance of happiness of the higher realms of gods and humans is also mind.
> The appearance of suffering of the three lower realms is also mind.
>
> The appearance of five poisons of ignorant afflictive emotions is also mind.
> The appearance of self-arising wisdom rigpa is also mind.
> The appearance of negative thoughts of samsaric habitual tendencies is also mind.
> The appearance of positive thoughts of pure buddha realms is also mind.
>
> The appearance of obstacles caused by negative forces and demons is also mind.
> The appearance of positive deities and spiritual attainments is also mind.
> The appearance of myriad discursive thoughts is also mind.
> The appearance of no-thought one-pointed meditation is also mind.

> The appearance of things, characteristics, and colours is also mind.
> The absence of characteristics and elaboration is also mind.
> The appearance of non-duality of one and many is also mind.
> The appearance of no establishment of existence and non-existence whatsoever is also mind.

This teaching, that all apparent appearances of samsara and nirvana, positive and negative, joyful and miserable, arise in this way from the mind, establishes the connection that although the rigpa essence of mind itself is not subject to samsara or nirvana, neither does it fall into partiality. Samsara and nirvana arise from rigpa's own dynamic energy. The nature of mind, inseparable rigpa-emptiness, is the suchness seen by individual self-knowing. This is not only the nature of mind, but is established as the suchness of all phenomena. How is this so? All phenomena arise from the mind, and the nature of mind is thusness, therefore that which is the single taste of multiplicity, non-dual knowing and objects of knowledge, is the all-pervading wisdom of everything. This is established as transcending phenomena characterised by grasped-grasping.

Again, to conclude the point with examples:

> Except for what comes from mind, there are no appearances whatsoever.
> Mind is, for example, like an artist.
> One's body is made by mind.
> Three thousandfold universes, as many as there are,
> They are all drawn by mind.
>
> This picture drawn by one's thoughts
> Deceives all beings with childish minds.
> Therefore, it is important to develop decisive certainty
> That everything is the illusion of mind.
>
> This is the introduction to discursive thoughts as mind.

By introducing discursive thoughts as mind, when the suchness of mind is seen, it is summed up by seeing it. If the true nature of mind was mere empty nothingness, nothing whatsoever like an empty space, then myriad appearances, the appearances of samsara and nirvana, would not be able to occur. As this is not the case, as it is the nature of empty luminosity, self-arising wisdom and the spontaneously existing appearances of samsara and nirvana arise unceasingly. Although they arise, as everything is the true nature of realisation, there is nothing at all that is not liberated in the expanse of true nature. Therefore, possessing the most supreme of all methods, it is called 'emptiness that is endowed with the most sublime of all qualities'.

At the time when, from the fundamental true nature which transcends both liberation and delusion of the timeless primordial ground, manifestations of the ground were displayed, due to the differences of realisation and non-realisation, the designations of liberation and delusion occurred. Because both sentient beings and buddhas appeared at that moment, the term 'a single ground, two paths' arises from there. Although this is the moment sentient beings became deluded, it is impossible that the ground does not have the nature of fundamental true nature. However, those who do not eliminate even the slightest delusion do not realise it, like a pauper under whose house treasure is buried. When understanding, experience, and realisation develop a little, although it was always like that, we come to see this place which we did not recognise before.

Teaching Day Three

Song Eleven
Self-Liberation of Non-dual
Appearances and Emptiness

Next we arrive at the introduction to the self-liberation of non-dual appearances and emptiness. This is taught in three stages: introduction to the nature of mind as empty, introduction to emptiness as appearances, and introduction to the non-duality of appearances and emptiness.

EMAHO!
Now listen again, all exceptional heart children.

At the stage of the extraordinary introduction to Dzogpa Chenpo, fortunate exceptional children of enlightened mind who hold the Dharma lineage are here called 'heart children'. This is an even more exalted term of address than 'children of enlightened body', or 'children of enlightened speech'. Those who are vessels for the profound foremost instructions of Dzogpa Chenpo are strengthened by previously accumulated merit, and the karmic propensity of former spiritual practice. If such people become familiar with this teaching, not only can they attain the level of supreme liberation in this life or the next, but if they merely establish a connection to these teachings with faith and devotion, gradually rebirth in the higher realms and liberation is within their reach. Accordingly, this warm address indicates that we may develop enthusiasm and joy for what we are about to hear.

Having just sung about how all appearances of samsara and nirvana are the illusion of mind and made by mind, Shabkar continues:

> **Even the Buddha did not teach that**
> **Our mind, which creates in this way,**
> **Has an identifiable essence of shape, colour, and so on.**
> **Primordially empty and non-grasping like space,**
> **Mind itself is determined to be empty and groundless.**
>
> **Although mind itself is illustrated by the example of space,**
> **This temporarily illustrates merely the aspect of emptiness.**
> **Mind itself has awareness, an emptiness that arises as**
>   **anything.**
> **Space has no awareness, a blank empty void.**

Therefore, the meaning of mind cannot be illustrated by space.

The creator of myriad dualistic appearances of samsara and nirvana, happiness and sorrow, positive and negative, and so on, is established to be our mind itself. It is established in this way, but if we examine and analyse carefully, we cannot identify anything to say 'this is its essence' and we cannot find any shape or colour to indicate 'this is its appearance'. This applies not only to us ordinary people, but even the Buddha had nothing to demonstrate in this respect. This is because mind's essence cannot be defined. Considering the manner in which it is primordially empty, from the aspect that there is nothing to grasp or seize onto, its basis of designation is 'space', like an empty sky. Hence mind itself is empty, and this emptiness is determined to be groundless.

At the stage of teaching, to represent the meaning of the suchness of mind, the example of space is given. Of course, what is called an 'example' is something that represents just an aspect of something, with a meaning that is partially similar. If every aspect was identical then it would no longer be an example, but would become the actual meaning. If it were necessary to give an example of every quality of mind, then there would be nothing else to say except 'Mind is just as mind itself is'. Therefore, saying 'Mind is like space' merely gives us a rough example of something that it somewhat resembles.

To explain this further, mind itself is emptiness with awareness and luminosity that arises as anything whatsoever. Space is the emptiness of blank void without any qualities of awareness or luminosity. Therefore, from this perspective, they are not the same. But at the stage of Dzogpa Chenpo, we do use examples that are still partially representative such as: empty like space, luminous like the sun and moon, and unwavering like an ocean undisturbed by wind.

This is the introduction to mind as empty.

This is the summary. Second, the introduction to emptiness as appearances is as follows:

> **From the innate dynamic energy of this luminous and empty mind,**
> **Myriad appearances arise as anything whatsoever.**
> **Although these arise, like reflections in a mirror,**
> **There is no duality, one in the state of emptiness.**

Mind itself is not mere empty nothingness. From mind's innate dynamic energy, or its own potential of luminosity-emptiness of empty luminosity, the myriad appearances of samsara and nirvana, joy and sorrow, and positive and negative arise. Although these arise as such, in all their variety:

> At the time of arising, appearances arise equally, without positive or negative.

Although things arise, as when reflections arise in a mirror, the mirror does not become the reflection, reflections do not become the mirror, and reflections do not come out from the mirror. This arising is unceasing, its groundlessness is emptiness, and the mirror is unchanging as it was before, non-dual appearance-emptiness. Luminosity does not separate away from emptiness. In the state of emptiness free of elaboration, or within basic space, they are one.

In summary:

> **This is the introduction to emptiness as appearances.**

Third, the introduction to non-dual appearances and emptiness is as follows:

> **Primordially, appearances and emptiness are non-dual.**
> **As one's mind is empty, appearances are ceaseless,**
> **And from the state of emptiness, appearances are arrayed without grasping.**
> **Appearances do not obstruct emptiness,**
> **And although they appear, their nature is primordially empty.**
>
> **Like a rainbow in the sky or a reflection of the moon in water,**
> **To the yogi who realises the non-duality of appearances and emptiness,**
> **The phenomena of samsara and nirvana are like an illusory spectacle.**
> **When observing this non-dual apparent yet empty spectacle,**
> **The yogi whose mind is unchanging is at ease.**
>
> **All fortunate children, can your mind be separated**
> **Into two, emptiness and appearances, individually?**
> **Look whether or not this is so, and then you will know,**
> **Primordially appearances and emptiness are non-dual.**

This teaching, that from the very beginning appearances and emptiness are non-dual, indicates the basic space of the unity of rigpa-emptiness. The inseparable truth of the ground is established, and the path of inseparable samsara and nirvana is practised. As that which is to be attained: inseparable ground and result, needs to be discussed, non-dual appearances and emptiness, or the essence of inseparable rigpa and emptiness, are illustrated by space. This nature, which does not reside in any extreme whatsoever and transcends all elaborations, indicates the empty aspect. Illustrated by the essence of the sun, the aspect of lucidity of luminous rigpa free of obscurations is indicated. The uncompounded nature of the unity of these two, the identity of the spontaneously present knowing aspect, is established as the two: appearances and emptiness unseparated from one another.

By giving examples of inseparable appearances and emptiness, such as a rainbow in the sky and the reflection of the moon's form in water, what Shabkar refers to as the 'illusory spectacle of samsara and nirvana' is as follows: while never departing or changing from the basic space of phenomena, appearances of illusory karmic appearances and wisdom's illusory manifestation arise from within that state. Therefore, except for all appearances of the self-manifestation of conditioned existence and the state of peace, which occur through the interdependent connection of causes and conditions, no phenomena whatsoever of the basic space of phenomena are made by a generated cause.

Not only that, but due to this being the accommodating aspect of the sky-like basic space of phenomena, from within this basic space of phenomena, liberation and delusion arise. Even as liberation and delusion are arising, they reside in the basic space of phenomena. And finally, because they subside into the basic space of phenomena, the yogi who reaches mind which is unchanging, where how things are and how things appear accord in the spectacle of the unity of appearances and emptiness of the unchanging basic space of phenomena—this inseparable basic space and rigpa—is taught to be 'at ease'.

One who arrives at what is simply the mind of the genuine truth of the nature of phenomena is the definition of a yogi. However, this term can also be used for someone who is on that path. Similarly, even before having arrived in Lhasa, someone who has just embarked on the journey is already given the name 'traveller to Central Tibet'. These truths, which are difficult to indicate precisely in words, need to be distinguished through the true state of a yogi's realisation. Thus, Shabkar teaches us to see whether or not this is so, and then we will come to understand. This introduction is not merely an outward indication. Our true nature is introduced inwardly, which is the ultimate introduction.

In summary:

This is the introduction to non-dual appearance-emptiness.

The following introduction to non-dual liberation in its own place summarises all the key points of the above introductions as follows:

> **Thus self-arising rigpa, inherently luminous, distinct, and vivid,**
> **In which appearances and emptiness are non-dual,**
> **Is the spontaneously accomplished enlightened intent of the three kayas.**
> **Maintain this practice at all times heart children,**
> **Day and night, during and between practice sessions.**

Thus, not falling into partiality of appearances or emptiness, existing primordially as inseparable emptiness-luminosity, uncompounded spontaneously accomplished luminosity is not created by anyone. This self-arising rigpa, apparent in and of itself, is clearly distinct and inherently luminous. It is unchanging empty limpidity, vividness that has never altered. The single wisdom of empty essence, luminous nature, and unceasing compassion of the three kayas possesses the three wisdoms. This enlightened intent, which has not been newly compounded by a contrived conscious mind, is called the 'spontaneously accomplished enlightened intent of the three kayas'. Within this spontaneously accomplished enlightened intent of the three kayas, without differentiating practice sessions from the intervals between practice sessions, Shabkar gives his heart children the heartfelt instruction to 'Maintain this practice at all times, day and night'.

The self-arising wisdom of rigpa is the ultimate wisdom kaya of all buddhas of the three times: past, future, and present. Similarly, because enlightened speech, mind, qualities, and activities are all complete, it is called the 'wisdom kaya'. Having recognised this, while abiding in this state, however things appear everything arises from its dynamic energy. Therefore in this apparent mode, whatever features of purity or impurity, positive or negative, arise, they are non-dual from this essence. Thus, samsara and nirvana abide purely from the very beginning. To a yogi who has actualised the spontaneously accomplished enlightened intent of the three kayas, these ordinary appearances, without changing their fur or adjusting their colour, abide in enlightenment. As this is actually realised, it is also the ultimate destination of the enlightened intent of all paths.

There is no difference in the manner in which discursive thoughts arise to a practitioner of Dzogchen and an ordinary worldly person, because both are likewise human. However, the way we take control of discursive thoughts is different. Worldly people follow after confused discursive thoughts, and wander endlessly and uninterruptedly in samsara. A practitioner severs the underlying basis of whatever arises upon itself, and without any adulteration of faults or qualities whatsoever practises present naked rigpa, without ever engaging in any contrivance or contamination. When one is never separate from this, without any distinction of day or night, during and between practice sessions, enlightened mind is fully realised and one arrives at the level of nirvana.

In order to be able to bring about this transformation, develop renunciation of mundane samsaric activities. Direct your innermost mind towards the lama and the Precious Jewels. Following in the footsteps of the holy masters of the past, give up concern with possessions and wealth, food and clothes. Do not exchange what is meaningful for something trivial. Bear negative conditions as friends. Purify desirable things as illusions. Having established the understanding and certainty that things are impermanent like last night's dreams, we need to engage in practice for accomplishment with irreversible dedicated determination. In doing so, even if we are unable to exhaust the perception of unrelenting birth and death, at least when we arrive at the brink of death we will have no regrets, which is the real point of engaging in the Dzogchen path, the pinnacle of all Dharma vehicles.

The ultimate view, meditation, and conduct of the practice of the three greats: Mahamadhyamika, Mahamudra, and Mahasandhi are of course one and not different. If we do not know how to essentialise the teachings into a single key point, then we do not know how to practise Dharma in general. From the aspect of their features, there are differences in terms of how to engage in Madhyamika, Mahamudra, and Dzogchen practice. Former generations of Tibetan proponents of Madhyamika would first establish an impression of the view by means of detailed analysis. At the time of meditation, they would prioritise resting meditation. Among them, if we take those of Mount Ganden as an example, they would prioritise vipashyana and analytical meditation of learning and contemplation.

In terms of engaging in the separate stages of the Sutra tradition and Mantra tradition of Mahamudra, the Sutra tradition takes the foremost instructions of *Uttaratantra* as its basis and meditates on Mahamudra of fundamental nature, which is somewhat similar to Madhyamika. As for the Mantra tradition, it primarily concerns empowerment. Relying on the foremost instructions of the fourth empowerment, wisdom is brought to rain down through the blessings of the lama and yidam, the key points of the action bindings, and so on. As for practitioners of Dzogchen, generally when we refer to the 'mind section of Dzogchen', it teaches all phenomena are subsumed within the display of mind.

In terms of establishing objects as rigpa-emptiness, what differences are there between Mahamudra and Dzogchen? In Mahamudra the view places a seal upon objects, and primarily luminosity-emptiness is determined. In Dzogchen we are taught that all phenomena are subsumed within the display of mind, and primarily rigpa-emptiness is determined.

However, in the inner categories of Dzogchen, there are the three sections of Mind, Space, and Foremost Instruction. The Mind Section maintains all phenomena to be the ineffable wisdom of self-arising bodhicitta. The Space Section maintains mind itself and the appearances of its dynamic energy to be primordially liberated and naturally pure in the true nature of the expanse of Samantabhadri. As for the Foremost Instruction Section, by self-settled uncontrived self-resting in the primordial unity of self-arising wisdom that transcends mind and involves no effort or achievement, one is taken to the true nature of reality with nothing to be removed or added. This also has the distinction that the primordially pure wisdom of emptiness and the wisdom of tögal appearances are united in the key point of the unity of luminous rigpa emptiness.

This introduction to the self-liberation of non-dual appearances and emptiness is thus concluded:

This is the introduction to non-dual self-liberation.

Teaching Day Three

Song Twelve
The Three Kayas of Ground, Path, and Result

The introduction to the three kayas of ground, path, and result is as follows:

> EMAHO!
> Now listen once more to the song of this renunciant.
>
> By understanding well the two distinctions
> How the three kayas are complete in rigpa of the ground
> And how at the time of ground manifestation the three kayas are complete,
> Samsara and nirvana will be realised to be the realm of the three kayas.

Beginning with this synopsis, more detailed explanations then follow for the three kayas in each of the ground, path, and result. First, how the three kayas are present in the ground:

> Regarding how the three kayas are complete in rigpa of the ground,
> Although it was mentioned earlier, I will explain it here again.

As this is an important point, it warrants repeating.

> The self-knowing ground is like a crystal sphere.
> Its emptiness is the nature of dharmakaya,
> Its natural radiance of luminosity is sambhogakaya,
> And its unobstructed basis for manifestation is nirmanakaya.
> This is how the three kayas are complete in rigpa of the ground.
> In this there is never any joining or separating.

Shabkar gives this teaching in everyday language, so there is really nothing that cannot be understood directly from these words. In the case of the teachings of All-knowing Gyalwa Longchenpa, the father and the son, when the broad generality of the meaning is covered thoroughly, even if we do not become entirely convinced that we understand, the sensation of combined faith and pure vision, or the joyful feeling that we experience when reading through these teachings, is due to the power of the blessings and the strength of these masters' bodhicitta.

Generally speaking, the lower causal vehicles which base the path on cognitive divisions of ground, path, and result of view, meditation, and conduct, those philosophical standpoints of individual tenets which can be expressed in specialised terminology, are very difficult to understand. So when we come to the profound meaning of Dzogchen, which transcends sounds, words, thoughts, and expressions, of course it is not going to get any easier. Although we cannot assume that no one can transfer inexpressible realisation directly to another practitioner through powerful means, if someone is not a suitable vessel with karmic affinity, the profound meaning of Dzogchen is not something that can be understood by sharp scientific sophistry alone.

Here, when Shabkar presents how the three kayas are present in the ground, that which is epitomised as compassionate ground, essence, and nature is illustrated by a crystal sphere. If we think about the simplicity of this teaching, there is no need to repeat it. However, if we concentrate on the more complicated final line, it is not only meaningful but profound. Actually one could write a whole volume of commentary on this meaning and still not exhaust the topic:

> In this, there is never any joining or separation.

We need to understand what is called 'ground' to be the ground of both liberation and confusion. Moreover, when we hear of the ground in 'manifestations of the ground which arise from the ground' there are many meanings to be understood, such as the ground of ultimate inseparable ground and result, primordial ground, temporal ground, and so forth. Similarly, there is not just 'self-knowing rigpa'. There are many differences and distinctions for rigpa.

Although the details of these can be understood from the broad scope covered in the textual tradition of the all-knowing father and son, if we discuss them just briefly, what is called the 'primordial fundamental nature of the ground' is taught to be the ground before sentient beings existed as 'sentient beings' and buddhas existed as 'buddhas'. In order for those who follow the tenets not to fall into partial extreme views, the six grounds are revealed to be flawed, and those who follow this path are taught flawless primordial purity according to our tradition, as a way of being guided on the path.

The 'primordial purity of the timeless ground' is indescribable, inconceivable, and inexpressible, transcending the extremes of both existence and non-existence. As its essence is primordially pure it transcends the extreme of existing permanence. As its nature is spontaneously present it transcends the extreme of non-existing nihilation. This luminous empty nature is the unchanging enlightened mind of dharmakaya, self-arising wisdom which does not exist anywhere in samsara or nirvana, and thus from the very beginning abides as such like space.

> Its very essence is primordial purity,
> Thus its nature is spontaneously present.

The vast emptiness of primordial purity and spontaneous presence which knows no separation is inherently present in this way. The essence of this basis upon which the differentiation of primordial purity is made does not exist whatsoever as samsara or nirvana, happiness or sorrow, knowledge or ignorance, and so forth. Liberation and confusion are no different because primordial purity is the state that transcends liberation and confusion. Its nature is one that possesses twofold and threefold wisdom.

As for the ground, it needs to be differentiated into two: the ground of basic space and temporal ground. At the time when manifestations of the ground arise from the ground, the ground still possesses threefold wisdom. In the Mahayoga tantras and so forth, as set forth at the stage of Dzogchen Maha'i Ati, the 'ground' which is spoken of should be understood to be this ground. The ground at the time present rigpa resides in the body is when rigpa resides in the house of light. Not only that, at the current time, even regarding rigpa at the time its dynamic energy arises upon objects, the separate aspects of its essence know no separation.

In terms of what is most important, we speak about the rigpa of dynamic energy. In this case, the ground that is distinguished between ground and ground manifestations is essence rigpa. But there is no certainty that essence rigpa must be this ground. If it is this ground, then it is determined not to be rigpa of ground manifestation. In this way, rigpa can also be differentiated into three: rigpa of essence, nature, and compassion. When we do this, although generally the three know no separation, rigpa prior to ground manifestation arising is emptiness with an essence of rigpa, which is given the name empty essence, as I mentioned yesterday. At the time radiance becomes outwardly luminous, it is luminosity with an essence of rigpa. This is called luminous nature. When dynamic energy arises upon grasped-grasping, this is the rigpa-emptiness compassionate aspect of rigpa. This is taught to be all-pervading compassion. Actually, this should be referred to as rigpa dynamic energy of compassion.

Not obstructing inner luminosity and based on the presence of outer luminosity, if one encounters the foremost instructions of the lama it is easy to introduce the nature of rigpa. Based on this, as the rigpa aspect appears nakedly, if one is able to maintain its continuity, the rigpa aspect can be awakened. In short, at whatever stage of ground, path, or result, the way the three kayas are complete in rigpa and never separate is like this.

The teaching on how the three kayas are complete in rigpa of the path is as follows:

> For example, as five-coloured lights shine from crystal,
> At the time of ground manifestations arising from this,
> All pure manifestations of the Victorious Ones' pure realms
> And impure manifestations of the universal container and its contents,
> Whatever appears, its essence is empty, the dharmakaya.
> The nature of appearance is sambhogakaya.
> Myriad unobstructed arising is nirmanakaya.
> Thus at the time of ground manifestation the three kayas are complete.

This is the same as the above teaching on how the three kayas are always complete in rigpa, and the reason that essence, nature, and compassion pervade all rigpa.

At this juncture, some key points difficult to unravel are elucidated, taught in a manner of an incidental clarification:

> This distinction rarely made elsewhere,
> Is a key point that needs to be well realised,
> That I learned through the kindness of the All-knowing One's excellent explanations.
>
> When known like that, all appearance and existence
> Is primordially the spontaneously present mandala of the three kayas;
> There is no pure realm of the three kayas to be sought elsewhere.
> Moreover, the six kinds of sentient beings abide
> As the three kayas. If they can recognise their own nature,
> They do not need to do the slightest bit of meditation;
> All wandering beings will become enlightened.
>
> What is more, in fact, the three kayas of the ground

> Are also dharmakaya, so do not hold them to be separate.
> At the time of ground manifestation, the three kayas
> Are also rupakaya, so do not hold them to be separate.
> Moreover, in fact, dharmakaya and rupakaya are not separate,
> They are one taste in the state of empty dharmakaya.

These important key points can be understood fundamentally by relying on the writings of the founder of the Dzogchen chariot in the Land of Snows, Victorious Longchenpa. Although the six kinds of beings experience delusion, they do not pass beyond the three kayas. And although the three kayas are comprised of dharmakaya and rupakaya, in fact, they are subsumed in dharmakaya. Moreover, although wisdom is differentiated into three, they are subsumed in the essence of empty dharmakaya.

Thirdly, how the three kayas are complete in rigpa of the result is as follows:

> Ultimately, as ground manifestations dissolve of themselves into ground,
> When enlightened dharmakaya mind of the ground becomes actualised,
> That is manifestation of the ultimate result.
> Thereafter, while not moving from dharmakaya space,
> Both form kayas manifest like rainbows
> And benefit wandering beings continuously.

The ultimate resultant state of liberation at the time manifestations of the ground arise from the ground, through the six qualities of Samantabhadra knowing his own nature, or the three spontaneously arising qualities, is the primordially pure ground original state of liberation, not the basis of delusion. Just like extracting poison from mercury, liberated from manifestations of the ground which dissolve into the ground, enlightenment occurs in the inseparable essence of ground and result. From sky-like dharmakaya, without striving or effort, the two form bodies of sambhogakaya and nirmanakaya appear to beings to be tamed with pure or impure karma. This teaches how the three kayas are complete in the ground, path, and result.

Teaching Day Three

Song Thirteen
Self-Liberation of the Five Poisons

The introduction to the self-liberation of the five poisons is as follows:

EMAHO!
Now listen once more to the song of this renunciant.

Here, each of the five poisons is shown to be self-liberated in connection with the five wisdoms. First, how aversion unabandoned is liberated in mirror-like wisdom is as follows:

> **In the past, you all have been harmed,**
> **Castigated, struck and beaten,**
> **Humiliated, and had your feelings hurt.**
> **By contemplating how it was in your heart,**
> **All the ways in which others have done this,**
> **Allow anger to grow. When it arises,**
> **Look directly at its essence, the agent of anger.**
> **First, where did it come from? Currently,**
> **Where does it reside? Finally, where does it go?**
> **Look. Does it have shape, colour, and so on?**
> **When observed, it is primordially empty and ungraspable.**

The worldly deluded appearances referred to here are the objects of attachment and aversion called 'loved ones' and 'enemies', which when analysed generally, are merely conceptual labels within conceptual labels. The object of last year's attachment and fixation becomes this year's enemy, and similarly, there are hated enemies who end up becoming friends. Due to this, they cannot be permanent, which is the nature of the world.

All these changes of thoughts, in fact, do not go beyond the innate dynamic energy of wisdom. Therefore it is taught that the five poisons are the innate dynamic energy of the five wisdoms. In this case, in terms of a discursive thought that gives rise to aversion towards an enemy, a yogi who takes whatever they encounter onto the path does not need to engage in a battle between something to be discarded and its antidote, leading one to victory and the other to defeat. There is no need for a method to transform afflictive emotions into wisdom.

When we look directly at aversion's own essence, generally speaking, aversion has the characteristic of rejection or separation away from a discordant object. This kind of dynamic energy is in the mind. At the time of the path, having searched for the arising, abiding, and disappearance of the mind, when aversion is seen to be primordially pure, at the time of the result, as the defilements of delusion are cleared away from this nature just as it is, the fundamental nature of ultimate wisdom shines forth. Thus, liberation in the luminous empty mirror-like wisdom nature is summarised as follows:

> **Without abandoning anger, it is mirror-like wisdom.**

Second, the teaching that attachment unabandoned is discriminating wisdom is as follows:

> **All of you, bring to mind an attractive woman,**
> **Whatever you desire to eat: meat, and so forth,**
> **Whatever you desire to wear: clothes, and so forth,**
> **Whatever you want, such as horses and your livestock, just as they are.**
> **Allow desire to grow. When it arises,**
> **Look directly at its essence, the agent of desire.**
> **First, where did it come from? Currently,**
> **Where does it reside? Finally, where does it go?**
> **Look. Does it have shape, colour, and so on?**
> **When observed it is primordially empty and ungraspable.**

The objects towards which attachment develops are women and men, and similarly our relatives and offspring, food, clothing, horses, wealth, and so on; whatever kinds of material belongings to which you are most attached. When attachment to these things grows rampant, look directly at the essence of attachment. Attachment is mind desiring an object, and takes the form of grasping. At the time of the path, this dynamic energy takes the form of supreme longing for the Dharma of the path and result. At the time of the result, similarly, one does not turn one's back on all phenomena, but embraces it as having the nature of supreme bliss. Thus, this teaches liberation in the bliss-emptiness of discriminating wisdom, which is summarised as follows:

> **Without abandoning desire, it is discriminating wisdom.**

Third, the teaching that ignorance unabandoned is wisdom of the basic space of phenomena is as follows:

> **All of you, allow the ignorance of sleep,**

> Drowsiness, dullness, and so on, to grow. When it arises
> Look directly at its essence, the agent of ignorance.
> First, where did it come from? Currently,
> Where does it reside? Finally, where does it go?
> Look. Does it have shape, colour, and so on?
> When observed it is primordially empty and ungraspable.

Once again, regarding the affliction called 'ignorance', especially while engaging in sessions of spiritual practice, when we come under the influence of sleepiness, drowsiness, and dullness, we should look directly at the essence of this ignorance. At that time, not only is there no source from which it came, no place where it resides, and no destination to which it departs, there are no characteristics to show shape, colour, and so forth, of which we can say 'this is ignorance'.

When we look at its nature, ignorance has the characteristics of being non-conceptual as an object and remaining in equanimity. So, because mind has this dynamic energy, at the time of the path, mind cannot be conceived of in terms of characteristics. And similarly, at the time of the result, all spheres of elaborated activity are free of conceptual thinking, and mind is liberated in emptiness without grasping, the thought-emptiness of wisdom of the basic space of phenomena. Thus, this is summarised as follows:

> Ignorance unabandoned is wisdom of the basic space of phenomena.

Four, the teaching that pride unabandoned is liberated as equalness wisdom is as follows:

> All of you, contemplate your social class, family line, power, and wealth,
> Your fine body and face, and the melodious tone of your voice,
> Your learning, contemplation, and meditation, writing and reading,
> Your expert knowledge, village rites, students, and so on.
> Considering the extent of your qualities,
> Allow the pride that thinks 'I am a little better than others'
> To grow. When it arises,
> Look directly at its essence, the agent of pride.
> First, where did it come from? Currently,
> Where does it reside? Finally, where does it go?
> Look. Does it have shape, colour, and so on?

When observed it is primordially empty and ungraspable.

In every respect, pride is the arrogant thought that oneself is better than others. In terms of greatness of power, wealth, or qualities, someone who belongs to the family of sublime beings does not have any pride. As Shantideva said:

> May the lowly attain prominence
> And pride be purified and overcome.

When those who are ignoble find themselves in a position of superiority they often become very proud. Regardless, when pride grows if we look directly at its essence, where did the pride come from? Where does it go? Not only does it have no source or destination, but neither can we find any shape or colour of which we can say 'this is pride'. Because pride is the aspect that engages in the desire for status and greatness, at the time of the path it is unwavering engagement in practice. At the time of the result, without the aspect of discouragement, free of the sorrow of being unequal, pride is liberated in the thought-emptiness of equalness wisdom. This is summarised as follows:

Pride unabandoned is equalness wisdom.

Five, the teaching that jealousy unabandoned is liberated as activity-accomplishing wisdom is as follows:

> **Contemplate the power and wealth of others greater than your own,**
> **Those who have good qualities, many students,**
> **Expert knowledge, fine voices, and who excel at recitation,**
> **Understand the Dharma and worldly discourse, and so on.**
> **Considering all the good qualities of others,**
> **Allow the mind of jealousy, anxious about those superior to oneself,**
> **To grow. When it arises,**
> **Look directly at its essence, the agent of jealousy.**
> **First, where did it come from? Currently,**
> **Where does it reside? Finally, where does it go?**
> **Look. Does it have shape, colour, and so on?**
> **When observed, it is primordially empty and ungraspable.**

Again, envious of the power, wealth, qualities, and so forth, of others, you do not need to be afraid when you think jealousy is appearing. Allow it to arise. When it has grown, look clearly and directly at its essence. Can you find where it came from? Where it remains? Where it went to? That which is unfound is confirmed to be unfindable primordially empty essence.

When Shabkar says 'Look directly' he means 'look at the nature of its essence', not 'follow discursive thoughts and get caught by the demon of infinite delusion'. Jealousy is a mental state that through focusing on others establishes unevenness. As mind has this kind of dynamic energy, at the time of the path, jealousy brings about engagement in abiding and disengagement in non-abiding. At the time of the result, it accomplishes benefit for beings to be tamed and abandons harm, being naturally liberated in sensation-emptiness activity-accomplishing wisdom. Thus to summarise the teaching concerning jealousy:

Jealousy unabandoned is activity-accomplishing wisdom.

Then follows a general summary:

If you realise in this way, afflictive emotions are wisdom.

The teaching that this is not just introduction, but also training the potential, is as follows:

**Conversely, to abandon afflictive emotional thought
And search for the wisdom of emptiness is ridiculous.
How pitiful to search but not to find.**

**In this way, knowing that the five poisons are empty,
In future, whatever thoughts of the five poisons arise,
There is no need to analyse according to this introduction,
The place they arise, dwell, or go, their shape or colour,
Because the five poisons are already understood to be empty.**

**As soon as they arise, do not follow after them.
Allow yourself to relax within the natural state of mind.
There is no doubt they will come to vanish of themselves.**

At the stage of practising Dzogpa Chenpo we do not need to block discursive thoughts, preventing them from arising. Even if someone wanted to block discursive thoughts, they cannot be stopped. By failing to understand this, not knowing how to meditate, meditation can become faulty, and subtle wind energy can enter the life channel causing madness. Such madness is not caused by meditation, but occurs because of not knowing how to meditate correctly. Although at the stage of unrealised delusion, the five poisons of afflictive emotions create samsara, at the stage of realisation and non-delusion, they cause all the activities of nirvana. Just like the effectiveness of medicine and the intrinsic glow of a jewel, according to such reasoning, because the mind has the innate dynamic energy of these five primordially, when they are not contrived by delusion their essences are established to be liberated as the five wisdoms.

It is because of this, in the *Sutra Taught by Vimalakirti* the Blessed Buddha said:

> The afflictive emotions are the family of the Tathagata.

If uncompounded abandonment of the afflictive emotions is accomplished, this is the same accomplishment as that of shravakas who reside in quietude, and in fact, this is not able to reach complete buddhahood. Through this understanding, we can infer the excellence of the swift path of Vajrayana. At the stage of practising Dzogchen, we do not welcome or follow after whatever discursive thoughts arise, but we look at the nature of the one to whom they arise. Just by looking upon this, discursive thoughts become self-liberated, which is their true nature. This is taught to be 'realisation of mental stirring purified in place'. At that time, the essence of ungraspable awareness-insight of clear luminosity, empty and pristine non-grasping which becomes manifest, is rigpa. Therefore, Shabkar teaches that to do the opposite, to abandon afflictive emotions and discursive thoughts, and consider finding something called 'wisdom of emptiness' is merely laughable, and those who strive to do so are worthy of compassion. As it is said:

> As self-arising wisdom is free of effort and accomplishment,
> The dualistic view of cause and effect is tiresome.

From a situation of being emotionally afflicted in dualistic effort and accomplishment, we arrive at letting go in the self-arising effortless expanse. From the state of the way things are, which has no self-nature, how things appear arising as conditions—that which can become anything whatsoever—is understood through the examples of a magical display in the sky and illusory manifestations. All samsaric phenomena that appear in grasping and fixation, the perception of mistaken understanding of objects like a dream or a mirage, are engaged with by our mistaken understanding, so are perceptions based on delusion. Although they are apparent, in fact, that which does not waver from the suchness of mind itself, the fundamental nature of rigpa wisdom, is like the transition and change of the four elements which do not waver from the state of space. Thus, whatever suppressed or encouraged discursive thoughts arise, none waver from the state of wisdom mind itself.

Here, having understood the five poisons to be empty, Shabkar tells us to settle directly in this understanding. Having realised the essence of rigpa, when we settle in the immediacy of this realisation uncontrived and uncorrupted, free of drowsiness and agitation, from this unelaborate state, that which is radiant luminosity-emptiness not moved by thoughts, consciousness which is aware and luminous, free of grasped objects and fixating mind, is the non-dual meditative equipoise of Dzogpa Chenpo of fundamental nature. This kind of realisation which abides in primordial purity is called the 'meditation unity of day and night'. This is also the essence of samsara and nirvana not subject to division or exclusion.

Moreover, what is called 'searching for your own nature' is mainly discussed at the time of distinguishing the ground of delusion and deluded appearances. Then, after the nature of rigpa has been introduced, at the occasion of knowing the suchness of vipashyana, whether appearances arise, remain, or liberate, when one does not stray from recognising the nature of rigpa, these are a single actuality whose mere expression is of opposing characteristics, like water and waves, or a mirror and reflections that are seen. Seeing this, the continuity of thoughts of the three times is cut, and this is taught to be the fundamental nature of self-abiding dharmakaya, individual self-knowing wisdom.

To summarise:

This is both introduction and training.

By practising in this way, the teaching on arising and liberation occurring simultaneously is as follows:

Thus, if training has been done previously,
In future, whenever the five poisonous afflictive emotions arise,
Due to already knowing the faults of afflictive emotions,
Both emptiness and wisdom will arise together, whereby
Arising and liberation are simultaneous, arising and liberation are simultaneous!

Here 'simultaneous' is repeated twice. This may be a printing error rather than emphasis of the point, as in *Self-liberation through Naked Perception* it states:

> Arising and liberation are simultaneous, arising and liberation are equally sublime!

In the past I did not pay much attention to this point, but I now notice that in both the tantras and the teachings of Longchenpa it states:

> Samaya commitments are primordially liberated, liberated in vast ultimate nature.

So perhaps this is the way to understand it. Whatever the case, by training in this, when one has mastered familiarity, by saying 'Both emptiness and wisdom will arise together', Shabkar teaches that non-dual basic space and wisdom, or basic space and rigpa, are liberated upon arising.

Here a secret and difficult key point of Dzogchen is revealed. All these phenomena that manifest in samsara and nirvana—compounded, uncompounded, and so forth—which appear as separate due to conceptualisation, appear in this way as dualistic to someone with dualistic perception, labelled as 'this' and 'that'. However, in fact, in terms of their own essence, they do not exist in that way. The basic space of phenomena of inseparable appearances and emptiness, which abides as seen by individual self-knowing itself, is demonstrated to be the fundamental nature of suchness. At the time of realising directly that there is not even one atom of phenomena other than this, dualistic phenomena do not exist.

Thus this non-existence, the non-dual and inseparable true nature of the uncompounded basic space of phenomena and the subjective agent of rigpa wisdom, is called 'inseparable basic space and rigpa mixed in one taste'. The apparent aspect of the harmony between appearance and existence is merely a mode of expression as they have not become newly merged together. As such, that which is to be realised: ultimate fundamental nature, this luminosity of the nature of the basic space of phenomena itself, is self-arising wisdom or Dzogpa Chenpo of fundamental nature.

At that time, how are arising and liberation simultaneous? The details of liberation through the key points, liberation through time, liberation without effort, and liberation through confidence, through the five kinds of liberation: primordial liberation, self-liberation, direct liberation, liberation from extremes, and liberation in oneness, can be understood by studying the section in the *Treasury of Word Meanings* which embraces the theme of total freedom in great evenness.

Regarding this essence of naked rigpa primordially without fetter or liberation, 'liberation' is merely a term used to convey meaning. In fact, no fetters have ever existed. Thus for something that has never been bound, it also has no features of becoming loose or free.

> **In the oral tradition of the life stories of past masters it is said:**
> **'The more afflictive emotions and thoughts, the more dharmakaya'.**
> **Understand this is how it is.**

However many afflictive emotions or discursive thought arise, by maintaining the state of the true nature of liberation upon arising, first the manner of liberation is as old friends meeting. Following that, the manner of freedom is like drawing a picture on water or like a knot in a snake disappearing into space. At one intermediate stage, it is like a thief entering an empty house. Eventually, with the manner of liberation which is like arriving at an isle of gold, where no ordinary earth or stone can be found, liberation occurs whereby whatever discursive thoughts or afflictive emotions arise, they are liberated in the realisation of rigpa-emptiness dharmakaya. At that time, if one hundred thoughts arise, one hundred are liberated in dharmakaya rigpa expanse. If one thousand thoughts arise, one thousand are liberated in dharmakaya rigpa expanse. This is demonstrated by the example that however much firewood there is, that much brighter the flames burn.

When the garuda soars through the sky there is no danger of it deviating or straying from its path. Likewise, according to the realisation of the seven or eight great expressions of amazement:

> A yogi on the actionless path equal to space is at ease.

However, for those whose minds have not realised in this way:

> **For beginners, when a mind of emotional affliction**
> **Arises intensely, it is good to analyse and rest.**
> **This is the oral instruction, so keep it in mind.**

For the person with a sharp sense of conceptualisation and analysis, if rigpa nature becomes recognised at the juncture when analysis has been completed, then that is its culmination. However, whether or not rigpa nature is recognised by engaging in alternation between analytical and resting meditating, is for us ourselves to see. Shabkar teaches that this is the lamas' way of explanation, their oral instruction.

During post-meditation conduct, to not engage in non-separation from the main meditation practice by not embracing the key point of self-liberation of conduct, is to get lost in ordinary attachments and aversions. Then the view gets kicked out by conduct, meditation gets kicked out by distractions, and although an old monk may pretend to demonstrate having the nature of a great renunciant meditator which transcends normal human beings, their own hidden faults will be copiously apparent every day to the eyes and ears of others.

This is the introduction to the self-liberation of the five poisons.

Teaching Day Three

Summary of the Teaching

Generally speaking, at the stage of Mantra, what is known as 'realising the view' is different from the view that is established by learning and contemplation at the stage of the vehicle of characteristics. It needs to be understood as mastery of the view of experiential samadhi. In the Mantra outer tantras and so forth, it is taught that at the level of perfect buddhahood, the single essence of the single basic space of phenomena is maintained to be different from the wisdom of practice, just like logs are distinct from a bonfire. However at this stage of Dzogchen, in the expanse of single self-arising wisdom, all phenomena of samsara and nirvana are spontaneously complete. Thus sameness and difference, and so on, all elaborations of dualistic phenomena, subside within basic space. Thus the specific feature of Dzogchen is determined by this distinct absolute completeness.

At the stage of meditative equipoise, just as all rivers on land flow into the expanse of the great ocean, all appearances of phenomenal entities are perceived in the rigpa-emptiness expanse of true nature, without rejection and primordially liberated. Having arisen from that meditative equipoise in post-meditation, just as all streams on land spread out from the expanse of the ocean, from the state of the unity of rigpa emptiness with rigpa dynamic energy of wisdom that realises selflessness, one understands the hidden faults and characteristics of all appearances of substantial phenomenal entities. Knowing this, fundamental nature just as it is, is realised.

If self-arising wisdom is like the sky, the accumulation of all-pervasive karma and afflictions is like clouds. If self-arising wisdom is like the sun, the accumulation of all-pervasive karma and afflicted emotions is like the sun's rays. If self-arising wisdom is like an ocean, the accumulation of all-pervasive karma and afflictions is like waves. If self-arising wisdom is analogous to a mirror, the entire accumulation of all-pervasive karma and afflictions is like a reflection.

At this stage of Mantra, methods are not concealed but clearly taught, but at the level of ordinary beings, the self-characterised nature of phenomena cannot actually be seen. As it is said:

> In the yogi's rigpa or direct perception,
> The only discussion is the scope of their perception of appearances.

But obviously, the capacity of practitioners differs depending on their karmic fortune. Some with sharp faculties are introduced at the stage of empowerment, and a few become realised just by teaching logical reasoning. Some with middling faculties gradually become realised as their branch channels are liberated, and others need to go through much accumulation and purification before becoming realised. However, realisation mainly depends on utterly pure faith and samaya commitments. Generally speaking, Secret Mantra is the path of pure vision. Moreover, the vows of Mantra are gained through empowerment and maintained by the samaya commitments. If a yogi's samaya commitments are pure, spiritual attainments will naturally become accomplished, and even without beating the ritual drum, Dharma protectors will naturally gather around them.

Why do Dharma protectors gather around true practitioners? The general name for oath-bound guardians who have accepted the vow to protect those who maintain samaya and behave in accordance with the Dharma is 'Dharma protector'. When entering into practice sessions of meditation, even if yogis with pure vows cannot resolve the vast extent of what can be known through thorough investigation, based on the foundation of pristine samaya commitments, if they relax with utterly pure faith and devotion combined with unwavering self-settled meditation into one essence, this seizes the marrow of the key point. Therefore faith, samaya commitments, and devotion are most important.

The Kadampa masters taught that devotion is the beginning of meditation, and that in order to meditate, first it is necessary to have devotion. Lord Maitreya taught:

> The ultimate truth of the Self-arising Ones
> Is that which is realised by faith alone.

Both faith and devotion are a single practice. When we engage in a practice session, we start with guru yoga, and because we already have the ground empowerment we take the path empowerment ourselves. Then, in order to actually engage with the final result empowerment, we merge inseparably with the lama's enlightened mind, and this needs to be founded on the practice of a session. Having established this, the lama within whom enlightened mind and our mind merge is the representative symbolic lama appearing in the form of a human in the end times, and this is where we direct our faith and devotion. The object of representation that they represent—the ultimate lama—is uncontrived self-knowing free of elaboration: empty, luminous, unceasing self-arising wisdom, which, having previously been introduced is subsequently recognised. As this is non-dual with no-thought dharmakaya realisation, we need to rest self-settled within this, unaltered and just as it is. Such kind of resting is the main meditation practice of Dzogchen as well as the essential meaning of guru yoga meditation.

Having meditated in this way by merging our mind with enlightened mind, what is it like when they fully merge? What is the method of merging them? The representative symbolic lama who appears in the form of a human represents no-thought dharmakaya realisation, empty luminosity free of elaboration, as we just mentioned. Therefore the ultimate lama who is thus represented is the realisation of all buddhas of the three times. Referring to these as 'having no duality' or 'having no separation' are different ways to say that they are, in fact, one. All buddhas of the three times in the expanse of the basic space of phenomena are a single enlightened mind. This is the same as the wisdom that is attained in the fourth empowerment, the self-abiding wisdom nature of mind, and primordially pure fundamental nature, which is what was introduced in the introduction to the nature of mind a few days ago.

Because of this, bound by the physical enclosure of our current coarse body of flesh and blood, we are deluded within the manifestations of the dynamic energy of ground manifestation. However, in fact, we reside in the unchanging true nature. Therefore, when this becomes manifest it is like the space inside a vase merges with the vast space outside to become a single space, inseparable and of one taste. Our own mind, ultimate wisdom essence of dharmakaya, which merges with the enlightened expanse of dharmakaya, the enlightened mind of all the Victorious Ones represented by the mind of the lama, ultimately becomes enlightened possessing the twofold purity. Thus the merging of mind and enlightened mind is like this.

To explain how merging occurs, just now we used the example of the sky to represent with words this ineffable meaning. But if we consider another example, the rain in the sky and the rivers on the land both have a single essence, a nature of water that is liquid and moist. Therefore they are easy to mix, they can merge together, and having merged they can develop the same essence. To express this in simple everyday language, by training in the enlightened mind of perfect buddhahod, one becomes fully trained in buddha mind and thus becomes enlightened. To illustrate this the example of a prince wandering the land is given. If the enlightened mind of perfect buddhahood did not exist in the nature of our own mind, there would be no way to develop familiarisation through training, just like squeezing a stone produces no juice. A prince, while being heir to the throne, may go wandering the land and develop the demeanour of a vagrant. But upon recognising his status, if he makes an effort to reach the kingdom, royal sovereignty is within his power.

Is it really that easy to attain buddhahood? In the fundamental unity of the two truths, is it not necessary to rely on the unity of the two accumulations of the path to actualise the resultant two kayas? The ultimate goal to be accomplished in both Sutra and Tantra is the same, otherwise it could not be united within the structure of the single doctrine. But, just as we discussed before, like plodding cattle, running elephants, or the swift coursing of the sun and moon, from the aspect of the difference in their speed, the various stages of vehicles were taught in accordance with the mind and attitude of beings to be tamed. Due to the difference in these methods, there is a greater or lesser potential of completing the accumulations. Because of this, on the extremely swift path of Dzogpa Chenpo it is established logically that liberation is attained in mere months and years. This is the method to actualise all contaminated compounded virtuous accumulations as uncompounded wisdom not subject to contamination. On this path, the uncontaminated virtuous accumulation of knowing one's own nature fully completes the accumulation of wisdom, whereby in a single instant of making the distinction, perfect buddhahood is instantaneous.

In the tradition of All-knowing Rongzompa, when precise definitions of Dzogchen are explained, there is the explanation that because the two accumulations are completed at the same time, Dzogchen is called 'Great Completion'. As for what is here called 'instantaneous buddhahood', there is no need for the question: 'Is this the instant of the completed action or the instant of ultimate time?' Although it is an instant, that does not necessitate it to be one of these two. For all such things, they cannot be forced: *a thump on the nose does not move a yak.* Thus I think this is to be understood as the instant of complete liberation and the instant of true nature.

Regarding liberation through the six qualities of Samantabhadra and how discursive thoughts are liberated for a yogi training on the path, I do not think these two are dissimilar, different paths or a dissimilar mode of cause and effect. When Samantabhadra was liberated, he arose from the ground, made the distinction, and through this distinction was liberated. When, from the dynamic energy of ground rigpa's true nature, its manifestation becomes apparent, I do not think it is necessary to think 'My meditative equipoise has been spoiled by a discursive thought' and to get startled or flustered. Of course, every living person has thoughts. If thoughts arise, let them; allow the potential of their arising to complete.

If the potential of their arising does not complete, then how do we make any distinction? Upon this distinction, when we settle relaxed in primordially liberated enlightened mind, whatever discursive thoughts arise in the self-resting expanse of true nature, they are liberated like the flight of a bird, leaving no trace. Although they are liberated, due to the habitual tendencies of ordinary peoples' negative habits of mental confusion, if you think you will continue to chase after confusion again, maintain the watchman of mindfulness. Also, if you become familiar with

Teaching Day Three

the single essence of non-dual mindfulness and objects of mindfulness, when you master familiarisation, objects of distraction become purified in their true nature.

As mentioned before, at the stage of primordial original ground, before buddhas appeared through realisation and samsara appeared through non-realisation, there is no conditioned existence or state of peace which has become positive or negative. However, the mere manifestations of rigpa awareness and non-rigpa unawareness, known as 'buddhas' and 'sentient beings', are individually apparent. In order for those sentient beings who do not realise this suchness to reverse this false delusory perception, which is like the further confusion of a dream, we followed this guidance text, and on day one learnt that mind is chief of the three doors of body, speech, and mind. We also learnt that all external and internal phenomena arise merely as the self-radiance of mind. By relying on arising, abiding, and disappearance, we trained in causing the false core of the mind to collapse, whereby confused thoughts naturally disappear.

On our second day of teaching, in the introduction that determines delusion for those whose mind state is one of self-manifest rigpa, the fundamental nature of the main practice was actually introduced. If at that time we thought that the manner in which true nature is fundamentally present was not understood fully in this way, for those who consider the luminous emptiness of mind—this intangible unobstructedness—to be the true nature of mind, today's third day of teaching introduced appearances as mind, mind itself was introduced as emptiness, and emptiness was introduced as rigpa. This is in accordance with the intention of the tantra *Direct Introduction*, and thus we engaged in the methods which guide on the path.

What is the purpose of doing this? By introducing appearances as mind and engaging in the method of seeing that which currently arises to us as external apparent objects as merely the yogi's internal manifest aspect of the mind, grasping which fixates on external objects as having inherent characteristics is reversed. Following that, by introducing mind itself as empty, there is not even the slightest ultimately existent thing in mind-apparent phenomena which is apparent and arises in this way, whereby grasping which seizes onto inherent characteristics is reversed. Then, by introducing emptiness as rigpa, all appearances of grasping and fixation are introduced to be the unborn and unceasing emanations of rigpa emptiness, and we are taught the need to come to a decisive experience within this state.

This is one entranceway of method to establish people of lesser mental capacity onto the authentic path. However, because fixation on true existence has still not been eradicated, the all-knowing father and son have refuted it as a method to connect with the ultimate definitive meaning. In their refutation, because discordant distinctions between grasping at true existence of knowing and objects of knowledge are not logically consistent, ultimately the fettered aspect that grasps is not observable at all. Thus they determine that the basic space of luminosity-emptiness is seen by individual self-knowing. If you are wondering why we are discussing this, as we just mentioned, upon the foundation of an ordinary student of Dzogchen who is taught this ordinary introduction—upon this carpet that is laid out—the true key point of the extraordinary natural supreme vehicle path of the Victorious One still needs to be taught.

Vastly transcending the mode of dualistic delusion of grasped-grasping, we need to maintain the state of present instantaneous rigpa, the nature of which is introduced. At the time of resting in the state of ordinary self-settling without any modification whatsoever, free of mental analysis and movement of the thinking mind, what is the fundamental mode of presence that surpasses the intellect like? Free of applying labels such as 'it is this... it is not that...' not an iota of any fetter is observable in its nature. It is taught to be wisdom that is all-pervasive like space. Relax loosely upon this freedom from acceptance and rejection, proliferation and subsiding. Beyond settling upon mindfulness of uncontrived true nature that does not lose its stability, there is no other view or meditation of which to speak.

However, due to previous familiarisation and habituation, the habitual patterning of delusion is extremely powerful. Therefore, lost to the delusional perspective of biased solidity and manifestations of grasping and fixation, if you think that delusion cannot be purified or you cannot reach the key point of practice, what you most need to do is become skilled at distinguishing clearly the key points of the method of liberation as they appear in the teachings of the all-knowing father and son.

How should we maintain the continuity of mindfulness of the essence of wisdom that was introduced as rigpa nature? To summarise and express this in a way that is easy to understand for beginners new to meditation, establish rigpa which was previously introduced by the lama as an alternative to the ordinary discursive thoughts which were present. Then, based on not forgetting for an instant this essence, we need to maintain the continuity of mindfulness.

When we mention 'mindfulness' it is classified in many ways in both Mahamudra and Dzogchen. Although the extraordinary and specific presentation of the six types of mindfulness that Victorious Longchenpa taught is extremely important, we may speak in more simple terms that are easier for beginners to understand: to maintain mindfulness, both the object of mindfulness and that which is mindful are not two things, like an arrow and a target or that which is aimed and the point which it is aimed at. Within a spacious and carefree state of mind, merely by not losing the true face of uncontrived genuine nature we need to be able to destroy directly the delusion of grasping and fixation.

Actualisation of the self-characterised nature of reality however it is, occurs at the time of attaining the bodhisattva levels. However, at the stage of accumulation and application, meditation on this general notion is not something that cannot be present, or is unsuitable to engage in. This is because the essence of true nature has the characteristics of freedom from elaboration transcending dualistic appearances, and is therefore not something that has newly occurred or newly appeared. Because it abides primordially as the true nature of mind, presently at the stage of ordinary people this general notion can be apparent in mind. I think what is taught at the Sutra stage to be emptiness realised in a general notional manner, and what is called 'similitude wisdom' at the Mantra stage, both have a similar significance.

Of course, there are differences in the stages and specifics of threefold understanding, experience, and realisation, as illustrated by the examples of the moon in the sky, a reflection of the moon in water, and a drawing of the moon. In this case, there is no need to mention that it is actual genuine wisdom that corresponds with the way things are. Alternatively, by relying on the analysis of extraordinary similitude wisdom, delusion can be reversed, so through being seen, unknowing is overcome. Even just to hear about the characteristics of the unity of suchness wisdom and for them merely to arise in the mind, is due to the power of previously gathering a vast accumulation of merit. In Aryadeva's *Four Hundred Verses* it states:

> Those with little merit
> Will not even doubt these phenomena.
> But to merely entertain doubts
> About samsara will make it fall into shreds.

In the teachings of Guru Rinpoche, he says that if one can merge one's mind with the enlightened mind of the lama for as long as it takes a bead of sweat to fall from the tip of a hair onto one's lap, then many aeons of accumulations will be completed. Thus, it is suitable to think that the fortune we come to possess through engaging in sessions of meditative equipoise is truly unrivalled by ordinary roots of merit. While I mention this, all three thousand of us here have taken the vow to remain in strict retreat for three years, to practise these teachings of Dzogchen. The merit of such an undertaking is further magnified by the transformative power of the blessings of such a large gathering of spiritual practitioners, so much so that it must be beyond the bounds of measurement even for the Victorious Ones and bodhisattvas.

CLOSING WORDS

Yesterday, I slightly reduced the time for group practice of our trekchö meditation sessions, during which we maintain rigpa nature. This was necessary for the beginners, so their meditation does not become lost in weariness. As it is said about diligence:

> Diligence is that which delights in virtue.

We need to wish to engage in virtue with delight without ever becoming satisfied, like a hungry yak grazing on grass. Therefore, when we engage in practice sessions of equipoise meditation, we should be full of anticipation for the chance to meditate together with the Sangha, and hope that the time for practice will never come to an end. It is not suitable to go in with a negative and gloomy attitude that thinks 'It's group practice time again... I can't not attend, but my knees and back are so sore, and I always get so sleepy. It feels like it goes on forever...' Generally speaking, it is taught that a good place for meditation is cool in summer and elevated, like snowy mountain retreats, and so on. This valley where we are now is usually quite warm, and it is particularly hot at the moment, so I think our practice sessions do not need to be extremely long.

As for meditation, there are two kinds named 'positive development' and 'negative development'. What is positive development? When we are meditating well, we become rested and develop the wish to meditate in future. The opposite is to become burdened with weariness. Even during practice sessions, we need to engage in many short periods of meditation. It is said:

> Disrupting a yogi's meditation is good.
> Obstructing a strong valley torrent is good.

Particularly for very new practitioners who wish to engage in the guidance tradition of the shamatha entrance, if they think they should search first for the abiding aspect, when they feel they can remain for a moment in the no-thought state free of thinking and objects of thought, they need to stop and rest within that state. Then again they should settle into that state, and once again they should disrupt it and rest. By doing this, at one stage they will develop familiarisation and come to attain the steady aspect.

No-thought unwavering shamatha and the luminous radiance with intensity of vipashyana need to be integrated. Terms that seem to be the same, such as 'shamatha' and 'vipashyana', also appear in the Sutra system. Not only are these terms used, but from the perspective of practice, these trainings are taught even in the sutras, albeit just broadly. However, unconcealed and fully developed teachings are not found in the sutras. That being said, whatever is taught in Mantra is also mentioned in Sutra but only briefly, as if to leave a place holder. We can say that sutras are summarised teachings and tantras are detailed explanations, or the meaning hidden in Sutra is disclosed in Mantra. Similarly in Mantra, what is earlier only a hidden meaning later becomes clearly and completely disclosed in synopsis. This is as mentioned in *Ornament of the Sutras*:

> In dependence on the former, the latter arises.
> As they are present as inferior and superior,
> And because they are coarse and subtle,
> They are taught in stages.

When we speak about Dzogchen, although we do not go into dialectic reasoning, it is not the case that followers of the Dharma with sharp faculties never need to engage in analysis. For this reason, if rigpa nature is recognised at the juncture when analysis has been completed, it is taught that upon directly recognising our own nature, deciding upon this one point and gaining confidence in liberation occur at the same time. In the meantime, there is no need to invoke the sevenfold reasoning of a chariot and re-establish a foundation. Thus, at our present stage of study and contemplation, we need to refine a definite understanding of the crucial points of meditation. Particularly in these end times, if one is not extremely learned, with swift intelligence and the capacity for fine analysis, then as All-knowing Jigme Lingpa taught in *Yeshe Lama*, one will not grasp the teachings of Secret Heart Essence.

Now, we have just been saying 'the essence of discursive thoughts is wisdom'. So let us ask, are things which are apparent to discursive thought also apparent to rigpa? We might think we better say they are not apparent in rigpa, but actually, there is no way not to say they are apparent in rigpa, because we can still observe them. In saying that they are apparent like this, we are also affirming that earth, stones, mountains, and crags are all manifest to the nature of rigpa. If we were to try to distinguish some differences in the way things appear and say that to discursive thought, earth, stone, and so forth, appear as ordinary, and to wisdom mind the self-manifestation of earth, stone, and so on, is apparent, then this would imply that the objects of the six senses do not really have the essence of rigpa, and we could not justify what we said earlier.

So what should we say? At this point, as we mentioned earlier, this needs to be explained based on the meaning of appearances and apparent objects. Apparent objects remain the same, but appearances, either to mind and rigpa, do differ. To say that this is like a white conch seen in different ways, depending on whether or not someone's vision is accurate or faulty, is the answer that hits the key point. To explain this further requires knowing how to establish all-pervading purity, without which further questions will only leave us lacking answers.

So if we wish to maintain our tradition of Nyingma Secret Mantra purely, then the unimpaired flow of the four rivers of transmission of the main tantras of the Early Translations: Sutra, Illusion, and Mind together with Kama, Terma, and Pure Vision of the undiminishing practice lineage tradition of authentic continuity, needs to be spread by unified study, contemplation, and meditation. What is more, the lineage needs to be spread purely without having any taints of impurities or impaired and broken samaya commitments.

In particular, it is important that all yogis young and old need to know the five main features of a tantra, the five arrangements of scripture, the five great nails of the foremost instructions, and so on, which the root tantras have in common. The five main features of a tantra include the feature of the main essential meaning, the feature of the chapter groups, the feature of the foremost instructions for practice, and so forth. In terms of the five combinations of the sutras they are: combining Tantra with Sutra, combining Sutra with sadhana, combining sadhana with activities, combining activities with application, and combining application with experience.

Especially, among the three: upholding, protecting, and spreading the teachings, in terms of the groups of yogi upholders of rigpa who sport white robes and braided hair, and have the responsibility to protect the doctrine, it is absolutely necessary for you all to understand fully the five great nails of activities. What are the five great nails of activities? 'Threefold protection, prevention, and elimination' refers to the nail of protection which relies on mandala, the nail of prevention which relies on torma offerings, and the nail of elimination which relies on power substances. 'Twofold suppression and burning' refers to the nail of burning which relies on effigies, and the nail of suppression which relies on skull cups.

Among all of you in attendance, I am sure there are one or two senior yogis who, when you whip down your long matted hair, indeed cause sparks to fly. I am not sure such power could be matched by tens or even hundreds of younger yogis. Whatever the case, all these yogis are going to engage in three years of Dzogchen practice retreat. Having completed three years of genuine practice retreat, even if someone were to tell you to abandon your practice, you would not agree. Thus, in the foremost instructions of the four nails to bind the life-force, the nail of unchanging intention is like the life-force of all the nails. Without this life, the other nails become lifeless like corpses. Particularly lacking this force, how can one direct the aim of the arrow of the four activities of pacifying, enriching, magnetising, and destroying by means of the nail of emanating and absorbing activity? It would not be possible.

Thus, at the ultimate of all the completion stages, the practice of Dzogpa Chenpo, when the nail of unchanging intention of the life-force of enlightened mind has been established firmly in your mindstream, all of the other nails appear automatically as its branches. In this case, all you young yogis, having completed the full measure of recitals of the Heart Essence roots, on top of completing a full measure of the root sadhana recitals of the eight classes of Heruka, you should strive at the practice of approach and accomplishment of whichever of the four classes of the blood-drinker Heruka to whom it is your allotted fortune to have devotion.

It is excellent to make a promise to accumulate one hundred thousand approach recitations of Kilaya, Hayagriva, Yangdak, or Yama, whichever one of these four is most suitable. Among the few thousand groups of yogis here, if one thousand nine hundred of you can each complete the full number of one hundred thousand approach recitations of whichever of these deities is suitable, then it goes without saying that you will be the ones who seize the kingdom of enlightenment of the famed one thousand nine hundred yogis of ancient times.

Teaching Day Four

Opening Words
Karma

While we practise the Dharma of the mind trainings, regardless of whether we repeat them a hundred or a thousand times, if this is like pouring water into a bottomless container, then we will know through evaluating our mind whether or not even one single rare point has become established in our mindstream. But without these mind trainings, we have no hope whatsoever of embracing the path to freedom. So we should not give in to a defeatist attitude that abandons the trainings, but continue to reiterate them every day. Of course, when the karmically-fortunate meet with the mind trainings, indeed they bring great benefit. If they could benefit a hundred people in a thousand, there is no need to express how wonderful that would be. If genuine renunciation can be born in the mindstreams of even one percent of people, and their mindstreams can merge with the Dharma whereby they arrive at the result of accomplishment, then, of course, that would be satisfactory.

As we discuss the Dharma here in the land of Amdo, we may consider that among all of us who requested teachings this year, there are perhaps about one or two hundred who are genuine practitioners. Among those, probably around ten apply themselves strictly to one-pointed practice. If this is actually so, then we may consider that in this degenerate time an enlightened action of the Victorious One has indeed been accomplished. With this in mind, each day I have been repeating the topics of the mind trainings. We know how truly difficult it is to find the endowments that we currently possess. Without considering anything else, just looking at obtaining a physical human basis, among the seven billion people on this small planet, those with faith in the holy Dharma are few, and those who are true Buddhists with the complete freedoms and advantages are fewer still.

Life is impermanent. What we had yesterday is gone today. We cannot say definitively 'I will surely be alive tomorrow'. After tomorrow there are many more tomorrows, so we are certain to depart from this life on one of those tomorrows. Although we depart we do not disappear. We must follow our karma. It is said:

To see where you will be reborn, look at your current actions.

Wherever we are born in samsara, it is a place of suffering. Wherever we are born, we do not escape the three sufferings. If we look at our current actions, to gain the result of a positive physical form without good cause is, of course, difficult. When we consider the way in which sentient beings in samsara are under the control of karma, then people seem powerless. But if we consider this carefully, we are not truly powerless. Whatever virtuous or non-virtuous actions we perform is entirely up to us. Although we believe we have our own karmic destiny, what is called 'karma' is something that we create through our own actions, and indeed in the Tibetan language 'actions' and 'karma' are referred to by the same word. Thus someone's karma is not loaded upon anyone else. The karma we create ripens exclusively upon us ourselves. So I firmly believe the happiness or sorrow we experience is not at all out of our control.

While we stand at the current threshold of progress, whether upwards or downwards, while we grasp the reins to steer our horse, the choice of where we turn and the actual moment we have control over our body, is right now. Grasping onto suffering, and entering into a miserable way of life, is the path travelled by most sentient beings in samsara.

If there was anything positive to be gained from samsara, the average worldly layperson, weathered and seasoned, must have already fought to attain it, so who knows if anything remains as our share? To follow such self-centred people is to end up just the same as them. If someone engages solely in unvirtuous actions, then the later part of life is worse than the earlier part, the bardo is worse than the later part of life, and the next life is even worse than that, in the suffering of the lower realms. We can all observe such misery in our everyday experience.

Now, if we wish to enter onto the path that embraces happiness, we should read the biographies of ancient holy masters, those Victorious Ones and their spiritual children who followed after the Buddha Bhagavan. Read the life stories of the former lamas of our lineage and follow in their footsteps. As we learn from their example, at first while we are still unaccustomed to practice, our strength to bear hardship patiently for the sake of the Dharma is weak. Moreover, while we do not have the tough armour of the diligence of devoted and constant application, we will experience occasional minor difficulties and suffering. However, when we do become well accustomed, we should find the joyful sun of inner happiness within our own mind.

Through practising virtuous activities and abandoning unvirtuous ones, the way to grasp the essence of the freedoms and endowments is by means of the paths of the three types of beings: lesser, middling, and great. In terms of the path of great beings, it comprises the long path of the vehicle of characteristics and the close path of the vajra vehicle. These two paths are further divided into subcategories: the long paths of the three sections from Kriya to Yoga, the close paths of Maha and Anu, as well as the swift path of Ati Dzogpa Chenpo. Moreover, within that swift path is the extremely swift most secret path of foremost instruction. Upon this path, in the short period of a few months and years, the rainbow body of great transference can be attained, whereby buddhahood is attained in this very lifetime without abandoning this body. This is enlightenment without needing to leave this body.

Not only is the beginning of the path which brings about benefit for limitless sentient beings within our hands, but also the time of manifest good fortune when the oral instructions are delivered to our door has come upon us. At the time our teacher turned the first wheel of Dharma, he taught the four truths elaborated in sixteen topics. The meaning of the teaching 'know suffering' is to allow us to understand samsaric suffering. When the Sage taught 'abandon its source', this definitive presentation of karmic cause and effect, and the sequence of the four truths which form the foundational framework of his doctrine, are consistent and like the progression of the rungs of a ladder. These four seals which signify the view are summed up in the teaching of the *Essence of Interdependence*:

YE DHARMA HETU DRABHAVA HETUN TEKAN
TATAGATO IIYAVADAT TEKANTZAYO NIRODHA
EVAM VADI MAHASHRAMANA

When translated, what does this mean?

> The Tathagata graciously taught
> All phenomena arise from causes,
> What these causes are, and what brings about their cessation.
> This is the teaching of the Great Shramana.

Thus, all phenomena of the objects of knowledge of samsara, nirvana, and the three paths which are subsumed within interdependent origination, all arise from causes. Cause is the truth of source, and effect is the truth of suffering. These two are the cause and effect of samsara. Cause is the truth of the path, and effect is the truth of cessation. These two are the cause and effect of nirvana. We do not desire suffering, but as suffering is a result, it cannot be stopped by preventing a result. We need to search for the cause of suffering and prevent it. For example, if someone consumes poison this results in sickness. In this case, it is not prudent merely to aim to combat the resulting sickness. Only by preventing the original consumption of poison is the basis of the sickness severed. By preventing the cause of the source: karma, afflictive emotions, and habituations, their results: the subtle and gross suffering of the three realms of samsara, obscurations of every kind that are to be removed, are rejected entirely. Thus wisdom that does not dwell in duality is attained and enlightenment becomes manifest.

Initially, when entering onto the path of lesser beings, the suffering of the three lower realms is recognised. To escape from this for the sake of striving towards the higher realms of gods and humans, the ten non-virtues are rejected and the ten virtues are practised. Based on this, by meditating on the non-transferring actions, the meditative concentration of samadhi of the eight formlessnesses, the level of gods and humans is attained. However, other than merely blocking unvirtuous karma with virtuous, the cause of afflictive emotions is unable to be prevented. Therefore, that which is like the root of lingering poison is not cut, so the actual sickness remains uncured and is certain to recur once more.

As for both middling and superior beings, having turned their minds away from the three realms of existence—the six states of samsaric beings—they renounce both samsaric cause and effect, and engage in the accomplishment of nirvana. What is the difference between this path and the path of lesser beings? It is taught that either the four truths are yet to be done, or there is nothing yet to be done. This is said to be the difference between all actions being fully complete or incomplete.

Because neither shravakas and pratyekabuddhas know the subtle suffering of interdependent connection, the co-emergent aspect of non-afflictive ignorance, the body which is the nature of the mind, karma without defilement, inconceivable death and transference, and so forth, so knowing suffering is yet to be done, and remnants of karma still remain.

In terms of abandonment of the all-pervasive origin of suffering, although karma and obscurations of afflictions may have been abandoned, without completely abandoning obscurations to the knowable, abandonment of the all-pervasive origin of suffering is also yet to be done. Still residual karmic cause remains.

Then there is cessation and the path. In terms of relying on the continuum of the path, although the non-existence of a personal self is realised, because the non-existence of a self of phenomena is not fully realised, the path is yet to be done. In terms of actualising cessation, although the level of shravaka or arhat is accomplished, they still need to arise from the meditative equipoise of cessation, which is triggered through the power of the light rays of the buddhas. At that point, they must arouse bodhicitta on the Mahayana and accomplish the level of buddhahood. Thus it is taught that cessation is also yet to be done.

So, which is the fully complete path which leaves nothing yet to be done? The path of superior beings turns one's mind away from the entirety of samsara, as well as the individual union with peace and happiness of shravakas and pratyekabuddhas. Thus, knowing suffering is not something that is yet to be done. As the all-pervasive origin of suffering, karma, afflictions, the two obscurations, and habituations are seized upon as objects to be abandoned, then abandonment of the all-pervasive origin of suffering is not something yet to be done. To rely on the truth of the path, the wisdom which realises non-existence of a personal self, the fundamental nature of all phenomena that is the nature of the ultimate truth of the continuum of the path, is also not something yet to be done. In terms of actualising cessation, as there is nothing else to be attained beyond the attainment of the result of the two: the enlightened dharmakaya and rupakaya, actualising cessation is also not something yet to be done.

To distinguish further the differences between the paths, with the motivation of great renunciation which turns the mind away from both extremes of samsaric existence and nirvanic peace, one's mindstream is bound by the vows of the long path of the vehicle of characteristics and the lower vehicles of the close path of the Mantra vehicle. In terms of the higher meditations, all meditations of the eight thoughts and forms, and the generation and completion stages of Mantra, are merely branches of meditative concentration. Based on this, realisation of the three great views is wisdom.

As the eight vehicles are these paths which are labelled by conceptual thought, all of them are elaborated. By maintaining the very essence of the single unelaborate primordially pure view of Ati Dzogpa Chenpo, all positive and negative thoughts are liberated in the single expanse of great wisdom. Having conquered all obscurations of karma, afflictions, knowables, and habituations, subtle and gross, the enlightened dharmakaya is attained. When dharmakaya is attained, from it the unceasing rupakaya—both sambhogakaya and nirmanakaya—engage in benefitting wandering beings, taming them in any way necessary. This is the general structure of a presentation of the four truths.

Thus, unvirtuous activities which are to be abandoned: the three poisons that motivate all actions of inherent non-virtue, and concomitant non-virtues which come to be motivated by them, are abandoned entirely. Virtuous activities are those which are to be accomplished: the ten virtues unattached, unaverse, and without ignorance, ethical discipline that abandons the ten non-virtues, and so forth. These countless enumerations of activities arise according to the scriptures and foremost instructions. In short, they all have a karmic nature.

What is karmically uncreated is not encountered. What is created does not go to waste. What is created by one person does not ripen upon someone else. It ripens solely upon the mind-body aggregates held by the one who created it, occurring through interdependent connection which is the nature of emptiness, emptiness-interdependence without division or exclusion. In this way, the four truths are also interdependent.

From where does interdependence arise? It arises from ultimate truth. From the truth of the primordially pure essence of the nature of phenomena, in what way do all relative phenomena of infallible cause and effect occur? They arise like clouds from the sky. As all relative phenomena arise in this way, except for a result which does not arise because it has no cause, nothing else can be genuine causation of something being produced and something producing it.

Concerning such wisdom of the two truths, the view is loftier than the sky, but karmic cause and effect is finer than flour. Without separating from threefold mindfulness, attentiveness, and carefulness of completely authentic method and knowledge, by means of the unity of the two truths, the unity of the two kayas is attained. Thus this presentation, which merely touches on karmic causality, should serve as a brief reminder and encouragement.

Teaching Day Four

Main Teaching

Now we reach the stage of teaching and listening to *Flight of the Garuda, Songs of the Trekchö View of Luminous Dzogpa Chenpo, Capable of Swiftly Traversing the Paths and Levels without Exception*. Having become depressed by samsaric suffering, we are either searching for the path or we are already on the path, and long to establish ourselves and others on this supreme path to the permanent happiness of holy liberation. In this case, there are the different levels of the long path, the short path, the swift path, and the extremely swift path upon which to seek the result of perfect buddhahood. Among these many levels, entering onto the extremely swift path of luminous Dzogpa Chenpo, and based on this body of this single lifetime, we wish to attain the capacity to be able to establish all mother-like sentient beings into perfect enlightenment.

When we enter onto the extremely swift path of Dzogchen, it is a mistake to think that we can abandon the lower paths, believing we have no connection with them whatsoever. Particularly, as the Mantra path is the swift path and the Sutra path is slower to traverse, to think that the paths of Sutra and Mantra are different in direction and essence is a mistake. Because of this, the title of *Flight of the Garuda* states that it is a guide to '*Swiftly Traverse the Paths and Levels without Exception*'. Here the words 'without exception' are clear and meaningful. Both Sutra and Mantra are the paths of a single journey, the essential meaning accomplished by the ultimate single vehicle. With the conduct of the six transcendent perfections and the four means of positive influence, the purpose of all the paths to benefit self and others by completion, maturation, and cultivation to reach consummation is the same.

The path which uses particular skilful means is that of Mantra, thus all the key points from the stages of the lower vehicle of shravakas to the path of Sutra and Mantra are entirely complete and subsumed into one, in what is known as 'Great Completion' or 'Dzogpa Chenpo'. Although this practice can be taught in many profound and extensive ways, here we learn that Dzogpa Chenpo is not the blank view of void nothingness. This unity of luminosity and emptiness, inseparable basic space and wisdom that subsumes all the key points of ground, path, and result is taught mainly by emphasising introduction to the nature of the view. This is taught in verses recounting the yogi's experience which spring forth, arising as vajra songs of spiritual realisation.

In that case, maybe you are wondering: except for the view, is meditation not also taught? As it is said:

Look and the feet will follow.

When someone takes a step forward wanting to travel where they wish to go, they should progress by watching where they step and treading firmly. Similarly, based on the foundation of the view, through meditation and conduct, the result is pursued. When the unexcelled common path is taught, then view, meditation, conduct, empowerments, mandalas, and so forth are all discussed. Based upon gaining certainty in the view, there are the stages of meditation, conduct, mandalas, empowerments, samaya commitments, sadhana practice, offerings, activities, mantras, and mudras, which are the ten attributes of Mantra. In short, we are discussing this foremost instruction that summarises completely all the stages of the Buddha's doctrine, which are like the steps of a ladder.

We have already covered the goodness of the beginning, the introduction. And from the goodness of the middle, the meaning of the text, having completed the introduction to the self-liberation of the five poisons yesterday, today we arrive at the introduction to the self-liberation of the sixfold group of consciousness.

Song Fourteen
Self-Liberation of the Sixfold Group of Consciousness

To the six sense avenues of the eyes, ears, nose, tongue, body, and mind, whatever objects of the sixfold group of consciousness arise—form, sound, smell, taste, touch, or phenomena—whether good or bad, joyful or sorrowful, attractive or unattractive, the following teaching introduces and determines them all to have a nature of emptiness.

EMAHO!
Now, listen again my heart-like children.

The six consciousnesses are discussed individually, beginning with objects of touch:

> **Wrap your body in something smooth like cloth,**
> **Look at your mind that thinks 'How smooth!'**
> **Wrap your body in something rough like yak wool,**
> **Look at your mind that thinks 'How rough!'**
> **When observed, both are of equal taste in being empty.**

Imagine cloth, and so forth, that is either smooth or rough, balanced in warmth or coolness, or too hot or too cold. Alternatively, to use more extreme examples, meditate that your right side is being massaged with fragrant oil, and the flesh on your left side is being cut with a knife. When you look at mind—the one who is experiencing the essence of these sensations, whether smooth or rough, pleasurable or painful—to see that both of these are of equal taste in being empty is the introduction to the self-liberation of empty tactile perceptions.

Second is form:

> **Look at a beautiful form such as a golden statue,**
> **Observe your mind that thinks 'How beautiful!'**
> **Look at an ugly form such as a toad,**
> **Observe your mind that thinks 'How ugly!'**
> **When observed, both are of equal taste in being empty.**

As these appearances of beauty and ugliness are also labelled by thought, there is no certainty that if something appears beautiful to one person, it will be seen as beautiful by everyone. That which labels and evaluates things as beautiful or ugly is again the mind, so look at the essence of mind that experiences things in this way. Both experiences of beauty and ugliness are empty and of equal taste. This, integrated into a single liberation, is taught to be the introduction to the self-liberation of empty yet apparent forms.

Third is flavour:

> **Eat something delicious such as muscovado,**
> **Observe your mind that thinks 'How sweet!'**
> **Taste something like ginger,**
> **Observe your mind that thinks 'How bitter!'**
> **When observed, both are of equal taste in being empty.**

Among the six tastes—sweet, sour, bitter, salty, and so on—whichever appears to you as delicious may be considered by others as revolting. When we observe the essence of these experiences and compare them, both are baseless and empty, like grey clouds in the sky. Just as they arise from the state of emptiness, they disappear back into the state of emptiness. Whichever we observe, at that moment this emptiness of equal taste is taught to be the introduction to empty yet apparent tastes.

Four is smell and five is sound:

> **Smell something fragrant such as sandalwood incense,**
> **Observe your mind that thinks 'How fragrant!'**
> **Smell something foul such as asafoetida or garlic,**
> **Observe your mind that thinks 'How foul!'**

> When observed, both are of equal taste in being empty.
>
> Listen to the sounds of a bell, sitar, or flute,
> Observe your mind that thinks 'How melodious!'
> Listen to the sounds of stones or hands clapping,
> Observe your mind that thinks 'How jarring!'
> When observed, both are of equal taste in being empty.

Whether fragrant or foul, melodious or jarring, there is no certainty that these feelings are the same for everyone. They are the perceived perspective of the mind. When we look directly at the essence of mind at the time it thinks something is melodious, and at the time it thinks something is jarring, the sound itself is baseless and empty. The arising of thoughts such as 'melodious' and 'jarring' is also insubstantial, like the form of a rainbow in the sky. As the principal basis of everything is empty, then whatever is apparent and whatever arises, arises as anything whatsoever. As this is apparent as anything whatsoever, this itself establishes emptiness. This is introduction to the self-liberation of empty yet apparent sound in which appearances and emptiness know no separation.

Following this, phenomena which are an object of the mind are taught one after another, based upon mental feelings of both joy and misery:

> Imagine you are born a universal monarch,
> Ruling a kingdom of the four continents,
> Surrounded by an entourage of many queens and ministers,
> Partaking in food of a hundred flavours,
> In a palace made of the five precious substances.
> When such appearances arise in mind,
> Observe your mind that thinks 'How joyful!'

For some what is joyful, is misery for others, so there is no certainty that these are the same. However, for an ordinary person, even if they are not a universal monarch, when they are free from illness with a comfortable body and easy mind, and according to their own appraisal, have an abundance of power, wealth, and enjoyment, then of course joyful feelings arise. At that time, when feelings of happiness and joy arise in your mind, look directly at the essence of mind. This introduces the self-liberation of empty joyful appearances in which joyful appearances lack self-nature.

Also, similarly:

Teaching Day Four

> Imagine you are impoverished, without a single friend or helper,
> Lying in a crumbling earthen yard,
> Rain dripping from above and the earth damp below.
> Your body is struck with various diseases such as leprosy.
> Feet and hands gone, you are tormented,
> Experiencing so much suffering.
> When such feelings arise in mind,
> Observe your mind that thinks 'How miserable!'
> When observed, both joy and misery are of equal taste in being empty.

This is the opposite of the above joyful feeling of abundant wealth. Without any family or friends, cast away by relatives and helpers, you live in a shack or tent in the corner of a yard with crumbling earthen walls, which you share with only a few wretched stray dogs. There is no roof over your head to protect you from the cold and heat, or from the wind and rain. There is nothing below to insulate you from the wet ground, no carpet or bed. Moreover, bereft of food and clothing, you are sick and in pain. Leprosy, a disease caused by nagas, was often mentioned in the past because it could not be cured. Similarly, in modern times there are newly identified diseases with no known cure. By imagining we have contracted one of these terrible diseases, we are instructed to let ourselves experience the torment of terrible mental and physical suffering.

It is not enough to sit there with the vague thought 'There are these kinds of meditation... That's how I should be thinking...' We need to bring to mind actually having such experiences ourselves, exactly as they would be. Based upon such a change of mind, a change in body and speech can be achieved, whereby we need to manifest the three doors as the timeless nature of the three vajras. The example that we usually mention is that although the essence of ice is water, it is frozen by the delusory appearance of freezing wind. If we want water to become its natural liquid state, we must rely on warm air to thaw the cold temperature. Although you may not usually have any terrible physical feelings of suffering, when you experience serious mental pain, look at your mind that thinks 'How miserable!' Thereby a nature of empty essence, self-liberation of empty miserable appearances, will come to be introduced directly. This completes the introduction to the emptiness of the six consciousnesses individually.

Following that, the meaning is summarised as follows:

> **Thus, having understood the sixfold group to be empty,**

> Henceforth, however the six consciousnesses arise, good or bad,
> At that time it is not necessary to analyse according to this introduction.
> As they are groundless, primordially liberated, and empty,
> The moment they arise, do not follow after them.
> Settle into the state of mind itself, relaxed in its own place.
> Without a doubt, they will become self-liberated themselves.

According to what is taught above, when we have understood, one by one, that the six consciousnesses are empty, in the future we do not need to engage in alternating analytical and resting meditation all the time. When we know that whatever arises, nothing transcends the groundless, primordially liberated, and empty true nature, then whatever arises is liberated the moment it arises as the shifting array of the mind. The truth of simultaneous arising and liberation that does not stray from the enlightened mind of self-liberated dharmakaya becomes actualised.

In summary:

> **This is the introduction to the self-liberation of the sixfold group of consciousness.**

Teaching Day Four

Song Fifteen
Non-duality of Proliferation and Abiding

Now we come to introduction to the non-duality of proliferation and abiding. We should understand that the above introduction refers principally to sense objects, and this introduction now refers principally to the subjective perceiver.

> **EMAHO!**
> **Once again, children of the family, listen well.**

This introduction reminds us once again of the necessity to listen carefully to the following important point, and to keep it in mind. The following instruction includes three sub-sections: introduction to abiding as mind, introduction to proliferation as the display of mind, and introduction to proliferation and abiding as non-dual.

The first of these, introduction to abiding as mind, is as follows:

> **Leave your mind relaxed and self-settled.**
> **Observe the way in which it abides.**
> **When you look, as it abides in the state of rigpa,**
> **It is the abiding yet empty state of rigpa.**
> **So understand this, fortunate heart children.**

Having let yourself relax and self-settle, when you observe the nature of abiding it should possess the clear aspect, or the intense aspect, of luminous radiant rigpa. Indeterminate mere emptiness, shamatha which grasps at luminosity, and mentally conceived vipashyana—none of these three is close to the Dzogchen position.

In summary:

> **This is the introduction to abiding as the ornament of the mind.**

The introduction to proliferation as the display of mind is as follows:

> **Observe the way in which elaborate discursive thoughts proliferate.**
> **As there is not the slightest deviation away**
> **From the very state of empty luminous rigpa,**
> **It is the proliferating yet empty state of rigpa,**

So understand this, fortunate heart children.

Proliferating mind, or the nature of mind, is the display of rigpa wisdom. Regardless of how the ornament, display, or dynamic energy, and so forth, arise, they do not deviate from single rigpa. However thought patterns arise, without good or bad, acceptance or rejection, settle in the naked state of the rigpa aspect, unceasing rigpa emptiness-luminosity.

In summary:

> **This is the introduction to proliferation as the display of mind.**

The terms 'ornament' and 'display' are Dharma terminology from the Dzogchen Mind Section. Here the key points of the enlightened intent of the Three Sections of Dzogchen are taught unified into one.

The introduction to proliferation and abiding as non-dual is as follows:

> For example, whatever waves rise upon the ocean,
> They do not deviate in the slightest from the ocean itself.
> Likewise, whether mind abides or stirs,
> It does not waver in the slightest from the state of rigpa emptiness.
> Thus, however it abides, settle in the state of rigpa.
> However it arises, settle in the radiance of rigpa.
>
> The belief that if mind abides it is meditation,
> And if mind proliferates it is not meditation,
> Is to misunderstand the nature of both abiding and stirring,
> The sign that threefold abiding, stirring, and rigpa have not been merged into one.
>
> Thus, all you fortunate and excellent heart children,
> As abiding or stirring is the state of rigpa regardless,
> Having already realised these points,
> Practise threefold abiding, stirring, and rigpa as one.

Generally, what is called 'threefold abiding, stirring, and awareness' or 'rigpa' is the Dharma language of Mahamudra, which is also suitable to be used in connection with Dzogchen. Both abiding and stirring are illustrated by the presence or absence of waves stirred up by wind on the ocean, neither of which stray from the ocean. Thus, we need to understand that at the time of both abiding and stirring, mind is pervaded by the one rigpa. When this is not certain, practice becomes divided into two aspects. If someone who is a great meditator during practice sessions becomes the lowest of ordinary people between practice sessions, this is an inappropriate way to meditate.

However much we abide in a state of no-thought mere emptiness, it is pointless. Without the intensity of luminosity-emptiness rigpa, it is taught:

> There are those among the animals that abide for long periods.

This introduction of threefold abiding, stirring, and rigpa in the immediacy of our true nature is the important foremost instruction of discursive thoughts arising as wisdom.

In summary:

> **This is the introduction to non-dual proliferation and abiding.**

Teaching Day Four

Song Sixteen
The Single Emptiness of the View

Now, reaching the decisive experience of the single emptiness of the view is taught in a summary of the key points of introduction to the view:

> **EMAHO!**
> **Fortunate and sole heart children,**
> **Listen with undistracted and attentive ears.**
> **Keep in your snow mountain minds this melodious song**
> **By me, Tsokdruk Rangdrol, the renunciant singer.**

First, there is a brief explanation to describe the main principles:

> **When all phenomena are determined to be one taste in emptiness,**
> **Samsara and nirvana are beyond rejection and acceptance,**
> **The delusion of grasping at enemies and friends is destroyed.**
> **There are no appearances of dualistic grasping at self and other,**
> **As everything is realised to be one taste in emptiness.**

Briefly stated, just as all rock-salt has the same taste, all apparent labelled phenomena of samsara and nirvana are one taste in being empty. Because of this, in samsara and nirvana, rejection and acceptance, enemies and friends, joy and sorrow, and so forth are overcome and destroyed. The detailed explanation continues as follows:

> **Here is an extensive explanation to summarise the essential points:**
> **In the pinnacle of vehicles, Dzogpa Chenpo,**
> **All of samsara and nirvana is free of ground and root,**
> **Primordially enlightened, one taste in dharmakaya.**

The way in which they are one taste in dharmakaya is as follows:

> **In the state of Dzogchen there is no duality of gods and demons.**
> **In the land of Dzogchen there are no buddhas or sentient beings.**
> **In the ground of Dzogchen there is no good or bad.**

> On the path of Dzogchen there is no near or far.
> In the result of Dzogchen there is no attaining or not attaining.
> In the Dharma of Dzogchen there is no doing or not doing.
> In the truth of Dzogchen there is no meditating or not meditating.

Without realising the truth of self-knowing dharmakaya, however much effort we make with the three doors, it is a mere semblance of Dharma conduct, nothing more than tying yet more fettered knots which bind us once again. Whether bound by fetters of golden thread or ordinary rope they are equally binding. Because they are compounded, like a vase which is subject to disintegration, if left unproduced in their own place, the indestructible unchanging true nature is seen. Thus Shabkar teaches that the threefold ground, path, and result of Dzogchen transcends the extremes of good and bad, rejection and acceptance, hope and fear. What is this like when realised?

> The majestic view of Dzogchen abides as such.
> When the Dzogchen view is realised like this,
> All the coarse and subtle thoughts of the three doors are pacified,
> Like, for example, water sprinkled onto wool.
> The three doors remain in a peaceful and tame state,
> The samadhis of bliss, luminosity, and no-thought arise,
> And for all beings wandering in samsara who have not realised as such,
> Uncontrived compassion is born,
> Like a mother's love for her only child.
> Know that these are the special features of the Dzogchen view.

By remaining in the majestic state of the Dzogchen view, at the time of realising the truth of the view, ordinary confused thoughts connected with the three doors become pacified, just as when water is sprinkled upon wool. Without any pride, ambition, cruelty, attachment, or aversion, the outer sign of this realisation is having the three doors peaceful and tame. The inner sign of this realisation is the arising of the samadhis of bliss, luminosity, and no-thought. In particular, the strength of compassion—emptiness with an essence of compassion which knows no separation, like fire and heat, water and wetness—increases. As compassion grows greater than ever before, extraordinary impartial compassion for all beings, like that of a mother for her child, is born. These are the special features of realising the Dzogchen view.

Regarding this, there are points of potential error, which are taught as follows:

> **If you, having decided that everything is emptiness,**
> **Abandon virtue and turn to engaging in non-virtue without restraint,**
> **This is the disseminated negativity of the view of demons.**
> **It is essential not to lose control to such a demonic view.**

Just as the Great One from Oddiyana said:

> Your view should be higher than the sky, and your regard for karmic cause and effect finer than flour.

Our view needs to be courageous, but our conduct needs to be timid. Just as Guru Rinpoche taught, do not lose your conduct to the perspective of the view. In short, the point Shabkar is teaching is to distinguish whether or not our faith and compassion have increased.

To summarise the current point:

> **These are the introductions to Dzogpa Chenpo.**

The general meaning of the introduction to the view is as follows:

> **These introductions are extremely important.**
> **Not realising that all external relative phenomena**
> **Of appearances and sounds are entirely empty,**
> **You think you meditate on the view, but what do you meditate on?**
>
> **Therefore, first proceed like this:**
> **Sometimes observe while praying to the lama.**
> **Sometimes observe carefully while relaxing and tightening.**

At that time, the following signs of warmth of progress in practice come to arise:

> **When observing in this way, mind is joyful,**
> **And everything arises vividly as emptiness.**
> **Deep certainty will surely be born that thinks,**
> **'I touch objects of external appearances with my hand,**

> But there is nothing to grasp onto',
> And 'This is definitely the view'.
> This is the time of finding certainty of the view.
> Do not spoil it by grasping; relax in a state of non-grasping.
>
> Having received introduction, even if you do not practise,
> At the time of death, whatever terrors arise in the bardo,
> You will know all are the self-manifest inherent form of emptiness,
> And you will become enlightened in the primordially pure ground.

This teaches both the benefits of receiving introduction and its purpose. What are the faults of not receiving introduction, the opposite of the above?

> To practise without having received introduction is like,
> For example, if someone mistakes the first of the month,
> They will be mistaken through to the fifteenth.
> Not having realised all relative phenomena to be untrue,
> To say 'I have realised emptiness' is a huge lie.
>
> Thus, according to this introduction, at first,
> Stay in the presence of the lama, and based on fundamental nature,
> Reach definite conclusion, then there are no points of straying.
> Therefore, fortunate children, keep this in your heart.

Regarding all of this, first be introduced directly to the essential nature in all its immediacy. Based on that, subsequently decide definitively upon this one point. Finally, gain confidence in liberation. Thus, take Garab Dorje's foremost instruction of *Three Phrases that Hit the Key Points* as the foundation. Following that, practise in keeping with the foremost instructions of Shri Singha, which are to reach decisive experience of the vast primordial purity of the exhaustion of phenomena, encapsulate activity-free unimpeded nakedness, and embrace the vast evenness of total liberation. Moreover, follow Jnanasutra's *Four Methods of Settling*.

That which embodies the self-abiding enlightened intent of dharmakaya endowed with three wisdoms is what Master Padmakara taught to be the incorporation of essence, nature, and compassion. This timelessly settled, self-resting fundamental nature does not cut off appearances outwardly, does not engage in inward grasping, and in between, does not arrive at the remedy that seizes upon meditation. Naturally purely present from the very beginning, if we maintain the non-grasping state of rigpa that surpasses conceptual mind, then that is taught to be the unmistaken focus of Dzogchen meditation.

When any slight qualities of experience and realisation come to be born, if you feel that you are becoming bloated with pride, recall the enlightened qualities of past masters. If you feel you are attached to this life, meditate on impermanence. If you have fixation on meditative experiences, disrupt them and meditate. If you lack love and compassion, meditate on the beings of the six realms as your parents. If you find that your practice of rigpa does not stand up to circumstances, then meditate by merging circumstances and appearances. If the arising and liberation of thoughts is too prolific, meditate again on shamatha. Also, if you feel attachment to the bliss of innate clarity is becoming too prolific, encourage appearances. By training in non-grasping liberation upon arising of multifarious discursive thoughts as they elaborate, it is taught that hindrances will become dispelled. There is also such foremost instruction for beginners that states, while certainty has not been developed, one should engage in analytical meditation, and at the stage when certainty does not decline, one may engage in resting meditation.

In short, at first it is very important to receive introduction. Having received introduction, if we remain in that state, cultivation will dawn through the power of experience, so when its luminosity is recognised, one experience surpasses a hundred explanations. If we pass through these stages of understanding, experience, and realisation, then knowledge of the gradual path: a peaceful and tame mindstream, great compassion, and so forth, will arise, just as we have learned above.

The above can be considered primarily to teach the view, and now following on from that, meditation is chiefly taught. However, in general, view, meditation, conduct, and result are connected to one another, and in particular, it is unnecessary to make definite outlined divisions in the foremost instructions of experiential guidance.

Teaching Day Four

Song Seventeen
The Key Points of Meditation

EMAHO!
Now again, fortunate children of the family, listen!

In this way, having assimilated the fundamental nature of the view,
Completely sever ties of attachment and aversion to homeland and people.

At best, those with wisdom make a definitive decision upon receiving introduction in the immediacy of the fundamental nature of the view. Those with diligence practise maintaining the state of meditation. So sever ties to the objects of samsaric delusory appearances of attachment, aversion, and hostile actions, and to those towns and cities which are prisons of negative influence. Having come to a definitive decision yourself, *you hold your own lead*. By going to live in a solitary secluded mountain hermitage, wherever the holy masters of the past attained enlightened qualities of experience and realisation, we need to meditate.

In terms of someone living at home, they are likely to have kind parents or relatives, beloved children, nephews and nieces, or at least a few friends, and so on, from whom they do not wish to separate. In terms of someone who leaves home and wanders between monasteries, they will surely also have fellow monastics, friends, siblings, and relatives from whom, in the same way, they do not wish to separate. But, without separating from such people, among distractions of attachment, aversion, and karmic connections, while experiencing a few fleeting days of misery, suddenly one day it becomes time to die. When we must travel powerless to the land of the next life, there is no one to whom we can say 'Please do not separate us!'

Better than allowing that to happen, while we are in control of our mind and we have our independence, is to practise the authentic holy Dharma for the benefit of both self and others. To do so not just merely in name, but actually to accomplish this purpose, we need an ultimate and long-term plan that aims to maintain happiness and joyfulness together without union or separation, continuously in our succession of lifetimes, either in a pure realm or alternatively in the self-manifestation of singular wisdom. This is what Rinzin Gangshar Rangdrol spoke of:

Without favouring homeland or country,

Monastic home is an unspecific hermitage,
Family is the six kinds of sentient beings.
The carefree vagrant is happy.

Although we may live in a secluded mountain hermitage, if one, two, or more friends gather together, then distractions and excitements automatically occur. Wherever we are distracted, it is still distraction. Master Awa Bodhi said:

Groups of people always become quarrelsome.

When many people live together, after some time they will inevitably come to regard each other with disdain. They will see each other's faults, and due to this, animosity and fighting will break out eventually. It is said:

A duo will become rivals.

When two lamas of equal standing, two comparable monasteries, or two similar neighbours stay together for a long period, and if there is attachment, aversion, jealousy, or something similar that does not subside, at some point they will become rivals. It is said:

Like a maiden's bracelet,
Alone, one can move completely freely.

If a girl wears two bracelets together they make a clattering, clanging sound. One single bracelet makes no noise and is totally peaceful. So a place which is merely remote does not necessarily qualify to be called 'solitary'.

Alone among the trees and mountains,
Abandon physical endeavours and remain naturally.
Cut verbal expression, and in silence,
Mind is spacious beyond the realm of thought.
Relax in that state without addition or subtraction.

Together with relying on the solitude of the three doors, we depend on the method of resting the mind. What is this method of resting, settled stable concentration meditation without fault, actually like? In summary:

When mind has no reference point, that is the view.
Remain in the state in which there is no meditating.

Teaching Day Four

Attain the result of Dzogchen non-attainment.

In that case, what is the vast expanse of enlightened intent without reference point actually like? If we remain in primordial resting free of contrivance and contamination, the meditation of Dzogchen non-meditation, then the fundamentally unattained result of Dzogchen which transcends acceptance and rejection, hope and fear, is attained. So we are instructed to attain it thus.

The meaning of this is taught in detail as follows:

> **Moreover, when you settle in equipoise in the view,**
> **Do not become caught in any web of thoughts,**
> **Thinking 'Settle in the state of rigpa like this...' or**
> **'I'm falling under the influence of drowsiness or agitation'.**
> **Without any referential focus, settle relaxed**
> **In a clear and unconfined state, unobstructed openness.**
>
> **The truth beyond rational mind cannot be seen by the attributes of rational mind.**
> **The ground of non-action cannot be reached by produced phenomena.**
> **If you wish to attain the truth of non-activity beyond rational mind,**
> **Do not contrive or tamper; settle in naked rigpa.**

When we try to settle in meditative equipoise in the view of self-arising wisdom, to mix it with view and meditation that combine conceptualisation and analysis which arise from elsewhere, is not effective meditation. Basing the path on rigpa at the stage of Dzogchen, direct rigpa free of all elaborations, suchness of non-action transcending produced phenomena, is already present as enlightenment from the very beginning. Therefore, when we settle in the state that is natural freedom from clarification and obscuration, like the essence of the sun, there is no need to search elsewhere in the web of thoughts for binding fetters involving referential focus. Therefore, without wearing myriad elaborate clothing that obscures, as unobstructed bare and naked rigpa appears vividly, settle and let go without correction or modification.

Having settled in this way:

> **Freedom from all grasping and fixation is the supreme view.**
> **Absence of acceptance and rejection is the supreme meditation.**
> **Transcendence of concerted effort is the supreme conduct.**

Self-abiding free of hope is the supreme result.

Freedom from the dualistic fetters of grasping and fixation is the supreme view. Residing in unconstrained vast evenness without positive and negative, acceptance and rejection, is the supreme meditation. Transcendence beyond mental grasping and effort of doing this and that, is the supreme conduct. Freedom from hope, doubt, and fear, unwavering in the self-abiding true nature of enlightened intent is the supreme result. Thus view, meditation, conduct, and result are identified.

Not seen by looking, lay aside further searching for the view.
Not discovered by meditation, discard referential fixated mindfulness.
Not accomplished by conduct, abandon grasping at illusions.
Not found by searching, lose hope of a result.

The view of Dzogchen is not such that it can be found by searching with the mind. It is not such that one can become familiar with it by practising with deliberate meditation. Nor is it such that it can be achieved by engaging in contrived conduct. Moreover, there is no result bound up in hope and fear that comes to be attained from somewhere. In this way, potential hazards of view, meditation, conduct, and result are eliminated. In that case, what needs to be done?

In present awareness, uncontrived and relaxed,
Do not engage in partiality, do not spoil it by grasping.

As external objects are merely apparent, however myriad appearances appear, mind should not grasp onto them in that way. Not holding onto mere non-grasping, whether appearances arise or remain, allow present awareness free of contrivance and contamination to settle directly without correction or modification, or any antidotes of renunciation. Thus, whatever appears will become the expanse of true nature. This is the instruction we are given.

The way that not spoiling present awareness with partiality is the pinnacle and supreme view, meditation, conduct, and result, is as follows:

This present rigpa, intangible luminosity,
Is exactly the pinnacle of all views.
This absence of referential pervasive conceptualisation,
Is exactly the pinnacle of all meditations.
This uncontrived non-grasping relaxed resting,
Is exactly the pinnacle of all conduct.

> This unsought primordial spontaneous presence,
> Is exactly the pinnacle of all results.
>
> Look at the essence of the view, luminosity without grasping.
> Maintain the essence of meditation, self-liberation without grasping.
> Settle in the essence of conduct, the sixfold group relaxed.
> The essence of the result is the collapse of hope and fear.
>
> When you are free of limitations, that is the supreme king of views.
> When you are free of reference points, that is the supreme king of meditation.
> When you are free of acceptance and rejection, that is the supreme king of conduct.
> When you are free of hope and fear, that is the supreme king of results.

Although in ordinary mind or direct wisdom—present rigpa free of grasping to emptiness-luminosity without restrictions or falling into extremes—from the apparent aspect, illusion-like emanations arise, from the empty aspect, it is free of all extremes of elaboration. To give an example, it is sky-like true nature.

Recognising the essence of the fundamental nature of enlightened mind is the pinnacle and supreme king of views. Residing in great transcendence of pervasive conceptualisation—self-liberated non-grasping, innate radiance of primordially pure enlightened mind—is the supreme meditation. Uncontrived non-grasping gone beyond the sixfold group, non-dual total freedom, is the supreme conduct. Uncontrived spontaneous presence that eliminates hope and fear directly, unwavering from the vast evenness, perfection, and unobstructedness of the enlightened intent, is the supreme or pinnacle of results, taught to be epitomised as the king.

> As there is nothing to see, discard referential focus of the view.
> As there is nothing to meditate on, leave whatever arises as it is.
> As there is nothing to engage in, set free suppression and encouragement, rejection and acceptance.
> As there is nothing to be attained, lose hope of a result.
> As whatever is, is, do not engage in deliberate grasping.

> As there is no 'it is this', do not engage in suppression or encouragement.
> As there is no point of reference, do not engage in partiality.

In unobservable rigpa, Dharma that transcends conceptual mind, discard engaging in tiring effort and achievement of the three doors, referential focus of the view that thinks it necessary to look at something. Similarly in non-meditation, do not fabricate having an object of meditation. In the conduct of nothing to engage in, leave behind suppression and encouragement, acceptance and rejection. Abandon grasping at, and fixation onto, the hope of an ultimate result of something to be attained. Whatever is, let it be as it is. Whatever is not, let it be as such, and leave it. Having cast away partiality and bias of suppression and encouragement, contrivance and contamination with a fixated reference point, within the state of vast non-action yoga, settle without an object of settling and the action of settling. Thus, enlightened intent in which there is nothing to be done is encapsulated.

Following this, the ultimate essence to incorporate onto the path is taught as follows:

> In primordially pure self-knowing self-luminosity,
> There is nothing to see, as it transcends conceptual objects of thought.
> There is nothing to meditate on, as its essence is free of basis.
> There is nothing to engage in, as self-liberation transcends extremes.
> There is no result, it is beyond fixated effort and achievement.
>
> As essence is emptiness, there is no abandonment or attainment.
> As nature is luminosity-emptiness, effort and achievement collapse.
> As compassion is unobstructed, there is no partiality.
> However things arise, do not grasp at them in that way.
>
> A yogi's awareness is like the path of a bird in the sky;
> A bird's earlier trace has ceased and cannot be seen.
> Similarly, past thoughts, having ceased, cannot be seen,
> So do not continue fixating on following after them.
>
> Just as a bird's future trace is un-manifest,
> Do not welcome thoughts of the future.

> Just as a bird's present trace has no colour or shape,
> For present thoughts left unto themselves as they are,
> Do not contrive or contaminate them with particular remedies.
> However things arise, do not grasp at them in that way.
> This is the ultimate essence to incorporate onto the path.

Pure from the very beginning, rigpa emptiness-luminosity transcending conceptual mind, free of ground and root, self-liberation beyond effort and accomplishment, is in essence emptiness, therefore whatever appears is free of abandonment and attainment. In nature it is luminous emptiness, therefore whatever arises, there is no need to engage in effort or accomplishment. Being free of anything to be done, it is not appropriate to do anything. In unobstructed compassion, whatever arises is naked rigpa emptiness, so there is not a single object of partiality. Therefore, however things arise, there is nothing to grasp onto in that way.

This is illustrated by the path of a bird in the sky. A bird's past, future, and present path is similar to our past, future, and present recollections and thoughts. If a yogi's space-like enlightened mind, free of anything to be done, is likened to the surrounding sky, then nothing appears following the sudden manifestation of a bird's trace. Similarly, having settled into uncontrived vast evenness, the single line of teaching: 'However things arise, do not grasp at them in that way' indicates the absolute encapsulation of the essence, the ultimate foremost instruction to incorporate onto the path.

The teaching regarding the instruction on direct manifestation of view, meditation, conduct, and result without meditation is as follows:

> However things arise, if you do not grasp at them in that way,
> Afflictive emotions vanishing by themselves is great wisdom.
>
> The view is unborn primordial liberation transcending thought,
> So if you endeavour, there is nothing to see.
> Meditation is self-settled loosely-set self-abiding,
> So if you endeavour, there is nothing on which to meditate.
> Conduct is illusory non-dual rejection and acceptance,
> So if you endeavour, there is nothing to engage in.
> The nature of the result is non-dual hope and fear,
> So if you endeavour, there is no result.

Afflictive emotions and discursive thoughts vanish of themselves in unborn great primordial liberation beyond the realm of thought, like the path of a bird in the sky that does not leave a trace. With concerted effort of produced phenomena, whatever endeavours you make to see thoughts or emotions, in complete immersion in the view of unobservable rigpa there is nothing visible to see and no apparent result to be seen. Beyond self-settling relaxed within the unobservable view in continuous resting, there is nothing to endeavour towards in meditation. Even if we endeavour to engage in conduct that is free of rejection and acceptance, suppression and encouragement, and a result that transcends dualistic hope and fear, we are like children building castles in sand. Reaching a decisive experience concerning vast non-action yoga is taught in this way.

Following that, extolling the serene mind of self-abiding which perceives directly the wondrous enlightened mind of the Victorious One, is as follows:

> **This nature of mind, free of root in the three times,**
> **Is directly perceived without meditation—how delightful!**
> **From beginning to end, phenomena are by nature pure,**
> **Primordially liberated and totally free, with effort**
>   **eliminated—how wonderful!**
> **This ordinary mind, unfabricated and relaxed,**
> **Is the limitless spacious expanse of the Victorious One's**
>   **mind.**

The nature of mind, free of the foundations of the three times, transcends time of the three times, and is called 'instantaneous rigpa of four aspects without the three'. It is basic freedom of vast spaciousness. The meaning of such basic freedom of vast spaciousness is said to be totally complete without abandonment. Enlightened mind of 'four aspects without the three' is taught to be the fourth aspect of time, which transcends the other three aspects of time. Vast baselessness, or basic freedom of vast spaciousness, is totally complete liberation of non-abandonment, which seen directly in non-meditation is the fundamental delight of the yogi, through which they are always serene.

Without beginning, end, or middle, all phenomena are naturally pure. Primordially liberated without bondage or freedom, total freedom without the need for any effort is taught to be wondrous. This ordinary mind, without changing its appearance or altering its colour, sufficient to be left unfabricated in its own place, is the definitive truth of the Victorious One's enlightened mind. As it is without limits, it does not fall into partiality. As it is a spacious expanse, it is not subject to restrictions. Thus its nature is summarised in terms of these essential points.

Following this, a summary of accomplishment through the continuous yoga of settling in the state of undistracted non-meditation is as follows:

> **Moreover, through efforts of analysis and meditation,**
> **You will not come to see the genuine fundamental nature of mind itself.**
> **In uncontemplated and unanalysed ordinary true nature,**
> **There is no meditating or non-meditating, distraction or non-distraction.**
> **Through non-meditating relaxation, many are liberated.**
> **Liberation and non-liberation are in fact non-dual.**
> **If you know fundamental nature, mind is effortlessly at ease.**
>
> **If you become ensnared in thoughts wanting no thought,**
> **Having arisen, discursive thoughts will pursue the ten directions.**
> **Upon the nature of rigpa without coming or going,**
> **If you let loose and rest freely,**
> **You will remain firm like an immovable mountain.**
> **Children, understand the mode of this paradox.**

When all phenomena subsumed by samsara and nirvana are examined in terms of the mode of presence of their fundamental unconditioned nature, all are without distinctions of good or bad, already liberated in primordially empty basic space that transcends thought and expression. However much we strive in meditation with the conceptual analytical mind, we will only move further away from seeing the ultimate fundamental nature of mind itself, our genuine nature. Regarding this, Victorious Longchenpa said:

> Don't do it! Don't do it! Do not strive or practise!
> Don't look! Don't look! Do not look at mental objects!
> Don't meditate! Don't meditate! Do not meditate on conceptual phenomena!
> Don't analyse! Don't analyse! Do not analyse following objects or mind!

The truth of inconceivable true nature is not conceived of by mind. This would be like following the trace of a bird in the sky. The unanalysable phenomena of primordially pure rigpa emptiness are not something that can be evaluated by conceptual analysis. This would be like measuring the sky in arm spans. The truth of genuine true nature is without meditation or distraction, therefore we are taught that by remaining in self-resting many practitioners have already become liberated, so settle in such a state of self-resting.

The non-dual truth of the meaning of liberation and non-liberation is the absence of an observer and something that is observed. So, if we have understood the key point of the nature of the way things are, free of deliberate effort, with effortless self-resting inherently so, this is finding the confidence of delightful spontaneously accomplished effort. Not only that, but in the place where the exertion of proliferation and subsiding of discursive thoughts does not reach, when we chase after the beautiful images of conceptual analysis of rational mind with desirous thought, they do not remain for a moment. Like swirling clouds, myriad discursive thoughts entangle themselves. This is nothing other than a spider tying itself up in its own silken thread, so we need to understand this.

Upon the fundamental nature in which there is neither coming nor going, settle in the true nature of pristine mind free of grasping and fixation, relaxed and set free in its own place. Just as the reflection of the moon in a container of water is not visible when the water is disturbed, but can be seen when it is left to settle, by doing what is contrary and leaving it without grasping, the key point to be grasped is seen clearly. Like the immovable steadiness of the king of mountains, we are taught there is no wavering from the self-nature of unshakeable unchanging rigpa. Thus unwavering unelaborate rigpa is such that it cannot be seen by looking, but is seen if we relax. This then is the key point of absence of an observer and something that is observed.

When Victorious Longchenpa speaks of rigpa transcending the name and designation of delusion and non-delusion, he enumerates the three essences of the foremost instructions, the three methods of resting in the view, and the three key points of unattached self-liberated conduct. The three essences of the foremost instructions are essence, nature, and compassion. The three methods of resting in the view comprise the following: outer appearance imperturbable presence, inner stirring imperturbable presence, and secret rigpa imperturbable presence. What are the three key points of unattached self-liberated conduct? They are taught to be appearances directly liberated, stirring self-liberated, and rigpa primordially liberated. Also, there are the four timelessly present singly incisive meditations, and so forth. These concern sixteen enumerations of practice, including distinctions, which are taught.

The ultimate key point, the real destination of self-settled non-conceptual rigpa, comes down to primordial purity residing as natural spontaneous presence which transcends the extremes of permanence and nihilation. Reaching final determination of the vast nameless exhaustion of phenomena, this is the supreme domain of experience of a yogi whose serene state of mind arises from within. Regarding this revelation of lofty experience and realisation, Longchenpa said:

> I felt this was the ultimate significance of the twelve vajra laughters being born in my mindstream.

Looking at how we ordinary beings have not progressed beyond a childish way of thinking, this is spoken of as merely the object of aspiration. The twelve vajra laughters are taught in the *Tantra of Self-arising Rigpa*, together with the eight great expressions which transcend cause and effect. However, regarding this, it is necessary to make correct distinction between provisional truth and definitive truth. If differentiation is not made, some who think in terms of definitive cause and effect may give rise to doubts regarding the naturally pure Dharma. So to make clear distinction of this point is extremely important.

I believe that for all practitioners of Dzogchen meditation, new and old, it is very important to forge the connection between the separation of view and conduct, so I would like to discuss this briefly. What is referred to by 'the twelve great vajra laughters' is the ultimate significance of true nature which transcends conceptual analysis. In tantra this is pointed out by the one who taught the tantra to the one who compiled it, in the manner of an instantaneous introduction. However, at the very moment of that indication, that which is taught and the act of teaching are naturally non-existent, as they do not waver from the expanse of the single true nature. It is said:

> I am the compiler, I am also the Dharma.

As the compiler, the teacher, and the tantra do not exist distinct from one another, then their experience of realisation resounds with wondrous laughter. As is taught in the *Magical Web of Manjushri*, this is supreme great laughter:

> Great laughter, far-reaching laughter,
> Widely resounding vajra laughter.

This is something that resounds to signify self-arising rigpa wisdom transcending origination, cessation, and elaboration of characteristics. It is the true fundamental mode of presence without transition or change, diminishment or development, primordially pure self-nature of the exhaustion of phenomena, the profound secret of the enlightened mind of the One Gone to Bliss himself. As this is the case, why is this laughter 'great'? It is the sound that destroys and annihilates the three realms. It is also the melody that obliterates existence.

In terms of the eight great expressions of amazement, it is taught that there is no difference between someone who murders the sentient beings of the three realms, and someone who continuously engages in the ten transcendent perfections. Upon hearing this, the ears of those with lesser aptitude will surely explode. At the stage of actually realising the true nature of the ultimate way things are, the fundamental non-existence of virtue and non-virtue is taught, illustrated by logical examples. To say that someone with an ordinary mindstream, someone who has not abandoned the eightfold group of consciousness of samsaric phenomena, who instantaneously kills the sentient beings of the three realms, and in contrast someone who accomplishes an equally vast amount of merit, are in no way different, would be to teach the negation of cause and effect. So, in this case, this is not to be taken literally. This is not teaching that cause and effect do not exist.

If something is constructed by virtuous and unvirtuous discursive thoughts, it is a conditioned phenomenon. However, its true nature is devoid of discursive thought. In this undeluded fundamental state, virtue and non-virtue, acceptance and rejection, do not exist. When such true nature is realised as it is, as the truth of the path is to be abandoned, it is taught that it does not depend on virtue and non-virtue, or cause and effect of the eightfold group of consciousness.

When we consider the example of the way non-virtue is purified, there are many different methods to do so. Non-virtue can be purified by what is known as 'purification through experience', 'purification through confession', and 'purification through remedy'. When the true nature of the ultimate way things are is realised nakedly, or when the true nature of the ultimate way things are is realised as it is, the undefiled root of virtue that has realised it naturally purifies the five aggregates and the eightfold group. At that time, habituations formed by earlier karma upon alaya have become exhausted, whereby the basis of virtue and non-virtue has gone. Therefore, if a person who has realised emptiness and merged appearances and mind into one taste, were to kill a living creature right now, it ensues that they would also be able to revive it instantly. It is taught for such a person there is no inherently existing virtue or non-virtue.

In this case, how should we understand these twelve vajra laughters and eight expressions of amazement? From one perspective, there is the way of understanding definitive truth which teaches that in fundamental true nature, virtue and non-virtue do not exist. An alternative way of looking at this is that both killing the sentient beings of the three realms, and equally practising the ten transcendent perfections, are no different and are of even taste. Someone who has not realised the meaning of true nature in this way, until they have reached such a level, is taught the provisional meaning: the necessity to uphold cause and effect with care, which is to cultivate virtue and reject non-virtue. Just as the Great Master taught:

> Your view should be higher than the sky, and your regard for karmic cause and effect finer than flour.

Therefore, these two perspectives of understanding should be comprehended according to the aptitude of your mindstream. If, when teaching Sutra, the expedient meaning, the real meaning, and the indirect meaning are not established, and at the stage of teaching Mantra, understanding is not reached through the six limits and four modes, then the four kinds of reliance will be understood in a contrary manner. If the four kinds of reliance become understood in a contrary manner, then reliance will not be on meaning but on words, reliance will not be on the ultimate but on the relative, and reliance will not be on the definitive but on the provisional.

At that time, if one relies not on wisdom but on consciousness, erring into hollow rhetoric and empty view, and gets left in mental formulations and the realm of theory, then one will arrive in a place that is not the path but a terrible ravine, from which it is difficult to find any means of rescue. Our Teacher, when he turned the first wheel of Dharma, taught us to know suffering, abandon its all-pervasive origin, realise cessation, and rely on the continuum of the path. At the stage of the middle wheel of Dharma, he taught that there is no suffering, no cessation, no path, no wisdom, no attainment, and also no non-attainment. So, if we do not know how to make the distinction between provisional truth and definitive truth, then we will not be able to avoid incompatibility and contradiction in the teachings. Until then, we will also not find the genuine path.

At first, a person of lesser aptitude should not rely on definitive truth, but provisional truth. In this case, for ordinary beings whose minds have not yet increased in aptitude, the truth that is the non-duality of liberation and non-liberation, the self-sound of vajra laughter, is merely the object of their present aspirations. However, even when sentient beings are deluded, the true uncompounded nature of the conditioned phenomena that is mind—the embodiment of the united three kayas which resides endowed with the three wisdoms—has never been separate even for a moment. If this is so, at this time, in addition to the pauper seeing that he has a golden treasure in his own home, in the true nature of rigpa free of origination and cessation, coming and going, if he passes through the stages of understanding, experience, and the birth of realisation, he holds in his hands the swift path to become manifestly enlightened without meditation. Due to this crucial point, All-knowing Jigme Lingpa said:

> You ripen the crucial point of heart-felt perseverance.
> I provide the nectar of the nine profound oral instructions.
> When the equivalent interdependent connection of life and
>   accomplishment conform,
> The future destination is revealed by Padma.

Likewise, if we can grasp the core of practice, the innermost essence of the nine profound foremost instructions and the tradition of the all-knowing father and son, from which the warm wind of blessings has not faded, then, just as it is said:

> In this life in which the time of death is uncertain,
> By grasping always with attachment, the ultimate goal is mistaken.
> If we allow thoughts of joy and sorrow, enemy and friend, to
>   disappear,
> The unproduced roots of joy are spontaneously present.

When we summarise a life of practice, it is like travelling on a journey to a distant place. Sometimes we have doubts, thinking 'Is this something that someone like me is capable of doing?' At other times we think 'Something is different now, a change has taken place in my mindstream'. Although various feelings of happiness and misery do occur, we should allow all discursive thoughts of hope and fear, joy and sorrow, to be discarded. Whatever arises, maintain the ever-changing array of the dharmakaya and transform whatever appears to enhance the path. By maintaining steadfast faith, respect, and devotion, there is no way of becoming mistaken.

In summary:

> **For this, although not even an atom upon which to meditate
>   is observable,**
> **It is of supreme importance to maintain it with undistracted
>   mindfulness.**

Teaching Day Four

Song Eighteen
Elucidation of Naked Rigpa

Once again, Shabkar sings a vajra song of the key points of the trekchö view to elucidate naked rigpa:

> **EMAHO!**
> **Once more, listen here fortunate children.**
>
> **This empty self-form of external objects, apparent yet non-existent,**
> **Is primordially empty, like the moon in water, so does not need to be purified.**
> **Internal thought processes vanish by themselves without trace,**
> **So there is no need to apply strenuous remedies to them.**
>
> **In relaxed wisdom of appearances and mind primordially liberated,**
> **There is no attribution of acceptance or rejection, hope or fear, whatsoever.**
> **For rigpa, nakedly free itself,**
> **Do not dress it in the clothes of analytical elaboration.**
> **Loose, free, unconstrained without trace,**
> **Settle relaxed in unbiased great evenness.**

For someone whose mind state is one of self-manifest rigpa, this teaches the method of settling of the introduction to the enlightened perspective of the primordial purity of the three realms. This external non-existent apparent object of empty self-form is primordially empty, like the reflection of the moon in water. Therefore, except for leaving it to be as it actually is, there is no need to purify something that is not empty in order for it to become empty.

That which seems like appearances and mind arising as various thought processes disappears of itself without trace, like a breeze in the air or a bird's path in the sky. Like the example of water that is left undisturbed so it naturally becomes clear, there is no need to make an effort to alter whatever thought processes arise. As both appearances and mind are primordially liberated, we are taught not to engage in attributing anything to relaxed self-arising wisdom that does not need to be changed, and thereby newly adding much acceptance or rejection, positivity or negativity, hope or fear, which leads to labelling the non-existent as existent.

Regarding unaltered and unchanged rigpa which is just as however it is, this bare and naked rigpa itself, 'analytical elaboration' refers to someone with a fixated mind that thinks 'It needs to be like this... It shouldn't be like that... This is how it should be...' with the self-fabricated positive presumption of making an improvement. That which is unelaborate does not wear the clothing of elaboration. What is called 'loose' is when the self-expression of primordial purity is laid bare, its innate glow arises spontaneously as stillness. What is called 'free' is to remain freely in a state of vividness while resting directly in uncontrived freshness. 'Unconstrained' refers to a groundless unobstructedness beyond words, an unfabricated radiance. In short, we are taught to remain self-settled and relaxed in natural evanescence without trace, unbiased great evenness, original immaculateness, infinite evenness. This teaches the view in connection with the method of settling.

The teaching that introduces meditation is as follows:

> **In this state, whatever thought processes arise,**
> **Knowing them to be the impartial self-arising natural radiance of rigpa,**
> **Without giving pursuit, when you let go into empty space itself,**
> **Appearances and mind unobstructed and unhindered,**
> **The evanescent shifting array of true nature,**
> **You will arrive immediately in the expanse**
> **Of Samantabhadra's enlightened intent.**

At the time of resting in the state of impartial samsara and nirvana, non-dual appearances and emptiness, there is no need to block out the appearances of the sixfold group of consciousness. Whatever occurs in the self-arising self-expression of rigpa, with non-duality of knowing and objects of knowledge, do not examine the past and do not welcome the future. This also includes not looking at our present consciousness and counting discursive thoughts, which are taught to be appearances and mind unobstructed, and so forth.

Up to now, what we call 'inherently luminous naked dharmakaya' seemed to be unfamiliar and unique, and to exist separately. But when we look at it, it is described as 'unobstructed, unhindered, and evanescent'. Perhaps this can be explained thus: as dharmakaya is without basis, it is unobstructed. As it is without support, it is unhindered, and as it is unidentifiable, it is evanescent. Moreover, the Great All-knowing One spoke of it as pristine openness, empty evanescence, impartiality, and so on, in the following contexts: not caught by the trap of antidotes, it is pristine openness. Original immaculateness is pure from the very beginning, so it is empty evanescence, and it is free of biases and grasping, and thus impartial.

For those who have proceeded onto high levels of yogic experience and realisation, that of which their individual self-knowing is aware, transcends conventional words, so when this is related to their followers in ordinary words, it can seem to be slightly misleading. But, except for gleaning a rough idea of that which is beyond the realm of expression and thought, how are we ordinary beings who rely on conventional thoughts and expressions able to decipher what they say? If we really need to decode these words, except for describing what they indicate in general, we are unable to define them precisely.

When we settle resting within the state of such unconfined infinite evenness of the vast enlightened intent of dharmakaya, there is no need to look for an ultimate result. We are taught we will have arrived already in the expanse of Samantabhadra's enlightened intent, so we need not hope for a result at a later time.

> **This is called the 'yoga of manifold self-liberation'**
> **Of Dzogpa Chenpo primordially liberated spontaneous presence.**
>
> **You have not gone anywhere, yet have arrived at the level of buddhahood.**
> **You have not practised, yet the result is accomplished spontaneously.**
> **Although not abandoned, afflictive emotions are pure in themselves.**
> **Your realisation is equal to the holy masters,**
> **You have followed them and finished all actions.**
>
> **This is the key point, so children, know it!**
> **Through the kindness of old father Chokyi Gyalpo,**
> **I, Tsokdruk Rangdrol, have now arrived**
> **At realisation of activity-free spontaneous presence.**

In the spontaneous presence of Dzogpa Chenpo primordially liberated and spontaneously present, there is no need to shoulder the burden of additional liberation. Knowing and the object of knowledge are non-dual. In the actuality of what is the even taste of appearances and mind, samsara and nirvana, it is appropriate to call this the 'yoga of manifold self-liberation', which is consistent in both name and meaning. How is it consistent? Without having gone anywhere, still one arrives at the level of buddhahood, self-abiding enlightened mind that knows its own nature. Without having practised, still the spontaneously accomplished result, the effortless imperturbable presence of primordial liberation, becomes spontaneously accomplished. While not being abandoned, the five afflictive emotions are pure in themselves as the complete five wisdoms. On this far shore, even the name 'afflictive emotion' does not exist.

That which is represented, this ultimate holy lama who is equal to the realisation of non-duality with the minds of the buddhas of the three times, or who is merged with the expanse of enlightened mind, is represented by the symbolic lama, the one who appears in human form in the perceptions of beings to be tamed. Through following and being guided by the lama, we can follow in their footsteps. This is the root of the key point that we pursue, the crucial point of Dzogchen primordially liberated and spontaneously present realisation. Therefore those wise and fortunate students who follow after Shabkar are taught to understand this accordingly.

'Old father Chokyi Gyalpo' refers to Chogyal Ngakyi Wangpo. Shabkar says it is through his master's kindness that he arrived at realisation of the kingdom of Dzogchen of activity-free spontaneous presence. When Chogyal Ngakyi Wangpo bestowed upon him the maturing empowerment, Shabkar was given the name 'Tsokdruk Rangdrol', 'six senses self-liberated'.

The All-knowing Lord of Dharma said:

> The state of the spacious expanse, spacious expanse, spacious great expanse,
> Is an immense expanse, a luminous expanse, a vast expanse,
> Thus it is a single expanse, non-dual. I have reached this converging blissful expanse
> Of manifold self-liberation at the level of the exhaustion of phenomena.

In addition to 'Longchen' or 'immense expanse', one of the other names the Great All-knowing One received was 'Natsok Rangdrol', which means 'manifold self-liberation'. We can see this quotation is similar in meaning to Shabkar's song, which is to be expected, as at the end of this text Shabkar mentions that he based it on the All-knowing Lama's works.

Following this, the key points of view, meditation, conduct, and result are taught, together with freedom from the defiles of straying and loss.

This is the key point, however some do not understand.

How some do not understand this key point is as follows:

> **Although everything is done primordially, they say 'I will do it'.**

How beginners who are mistaken stray onto the wrong path is as follows:

> **Although liberation is primordial, they say 'I will be liberated'.**
> **Although resting is primordial, they say 'I will rest'.**
> **Although meditation is primordial, they say 'I will meditate'.**
> **Although seeing is primordial, they say 'I will see'.**
> **Although arrival is primordial, they say 'I will arrive'.**

> **Those who place hope in a conceptually analysed view,**
> **Learn only meaningless words, understand only discursive thought,**
> **Realise only arrogance, meditate only conceptually,**
> **Analyse only dualistically, accomplish only samsara.**
> **Those who conceptually analyse true nature,**
> **Certainly have no karmic connection to Dzogchen Heart Essence.**

To follow after words mistaking the direction of truth with conceptual analysis is to change what is effortless into produced phenomena. An example of this is to dismount from a horse and ride a donkey. The elaborations of the mind of conceptual analysis are likened to measuring the sky in arm spans. As such people are not free from the trap of dualistic delusional discursive thoughts, the great darkness of ignorant habituation from beginningless time still remains in their hearts. So, from whichever point they begin their analysis, even if they hypothesise, contemplate, and expound, they do not transcend the confines of the mind of conceptual analysis. Regarding this, we are taught that for the time being, it is certain that such people do not have the karmic connection to be shown the utmost profound essence of the Dzogchen Heart Essence instructions.

Freedom from obstruction of such defiles of straying, loss, and error is as follows:

> **There is no need for action, actions do not achieve it;**
> **It is beyond the reckoning of action and non-action.**
> **In non-meditation beyond meditation, meditation only spoils it.**

> In non-viewing beyond viewing, what is viewed?
> In non-searching beyond searching, there is no finding.
> Thus rigpa is transparent unobstructedness.
>
> The person who does not listen to this as explained,
> Has no karmic connection to Dzogchen—how funny!
> Wherever you look arises as the realisation of
> Primordially pure great expanse, so samsara and nirvana are non-dual.
> To sing a song of such realisation,
> Will doubtlessly please the Victorious Ones of the three times.
>
> Should you ask 'If external apparent objects of confusion
> Are set free in their own place,
> Then won't one return to delusion again?'
> Ordinary people grasp at self, so are deluded.
> Yogis, knowing it to be groundless without root,
> Do not engage in contrivance or contamination, acceptance or rejection.
> By resting self-settled without grasping, they are unconfused.

Transcending action, effort, and achievement, having reached the expanse of the enlightened intent of Samantabhadra in which there is nothing to be done just as it is, there are no areas of straying, loss, or error. For example, before arriving at a destination, it is possible to take a wrong path, but having arrived at your goal, there is no need to worry about erring on the journey. Similarly, in primordially liberated spontaneously present Dzogchen, there is no effort or achievement of created or produced phenomena, grasping at characteristics of meditation as non-meditation, or striving to observe that which is unobservable, and so on. When in the truth of non-duality you engage in analysis of dualistic grasping, leaving yourself to search for something else, then such kind of person:

> Does not approach any closer to Dzogpa Chenpo.

We are taught that such foolish or perhaps senile people, who say they are going one way but set off in the other direction, can sometimes make us laugh.

In short, wherever we look, wherever we investigate and analyse, by singing such a song of the primordially pure great expanse that is already just what it is—fundamental nature free of effort and achievement, unfettered realisation of the exhaustion of phenomena of non-dual samsara and nirvana—we are taught that without a doubt, from basic space the Victorious Ones of the three times are uttering '*Ah la la ho!*' with wondrous laughter and delighted, smiling countenances.

While teaching the sublime unmistaken path which pleases the Victorious Ones, here Shabkar raises a doubt: 'If confused appearances, uncorrected in their own context and existing freely, continue to be allowed to run free and are left without modification, then won't we return to delusion?' If we understand 'ordinary' to mean actually being ordinary, then of course we will become deluded. However, here 'ordinary' has the meaning of 'uncontrived'. We are not taught to leave ourselves in ordinary proliferating delusion.

We are engaged in fabrication upon fabrication, change after change, like churning up water so it becomes cloudy. Thus not resting self-settled in innate fundamental nature, the mind of grasping onto grasped objects experiences confusion, and the environment, sense objects, and our bodies arise. At this stage, we need to rest in ordinary undistracted non-meditation, basic nature that is without distraction and free of grasping like the sky. Common sentient beings, including people and so forth, are deluded by grasping at a self. Yogis know fundamental nature which is groundless and without root, so when they remain at rest, self-settled without grasping, they are undeluded. Thus this teaches that if the key point of the truth of non-delusion is grasped, then there are no points of straying, loss, or error.

Once more, the introduction to dispelling defiles is taught:

> **If you ask 'Is there anywhere to go astray in this?'**
> **In this there is not one point of straying or erring;**
> **There are places to stray if you cling and are attached.**
> **Without any grasping to whatever arises,**
> **How could falling into points of straying occur?**
>
> **However, when rigpa arises upon an object,**
> **Whatever arises, looking at the essence of discursive thoughts**
> **Is itself not to be regarded as meditation.**
> **Uninterruptedly maintain the naked aspect**
> **Of distinct rigpa of that time.**
>
> **Furthermore, when rigpa is abiding without**
> **Proliferation or subsidence, the no-thought of the abiding aspect**
> **Is itself not the main practice of meditation.**

> Maintain the intense aspect of luminous clarity itself,
> The vivid limpidity of that time.
>
> Not understanding this key point, if you think
> Observing both arising and abiding itself is the essence of meditation,
> Then you will be confused, heart children.
> Mere abiding is the same as the samadhi gods.
> Mere arising is the same as ordinary thought.
> Even if you meditate on these, you will not attain enlightenment.

It is taught that at the level of all-good Samantabhadra there is nothing that is not good. Therefore, as mentioned earlier, when the everlasting kingdom of the enlightened intent of Samantabhadra is already embraced, there is nowhere to go astray, just as when the garuda flies in the sky there is no doubt about it falling into a ravine. However, if we become fixated and attached, all the points of straying, loss, and error are present. Without normal mind with alaya consciousness, without conceptual mind together with afflicted consciousness and conceptual consciousness, and without discursive thoughts fixating on the five doors as separate, not wavering from samadhi of luminous wisdom, and not eliminating that state which is free of distraction, confusion, and grasping, is taught to be the hidden meaning of compassion.

Free from mind, habitual latencies of meditative concentration are naturally exhausted, so there is no place of birth in the form realm. Being free from one-pointed mind without thought, there is no extreme of birth in the formless realm, and without conceptual grasped-grasping, there is no place of birth in the desire realm. When the four meditative concentrations and the non-conceptual wisdom of cessation, that to be abandoned and its remedy, its essence together with its aspects, have become self-purified, the points of rigpa going astray—mind and the habitual tendencies that grasp onto it—are purified. As mind has ceased, wisdom does not waver, and reaching a decisive experience of great non-grasping of appearances and rigpa is taught to be the ultimate realisation of secret Heart Essence.

In this case, to recognise discursive faults and to recognise rigpa are not the same thing. To look at the nature of thoughts is faulty meditation. When we settle free of an observer and the observed, although we do not identify the essence of rigpa of that time, its own luminous empty ineffable essence is seen by itself. The seer and the seen are non-dual, self-luminosity without grasping. Awakened from the abiding aspect, the stirring aspect not arisen, unobscured naked essence is distinct and bare.

Clearly distinct, this is naked lucidity unobscured by anything whatsoever. The aspect that is free of grasped-grasping is openness or arising equally extended, which is understood to be nakedness. Thus we should maintain this without interruption.

While residing, the darkness of no-thought is also not the true meditation of Dzogchen. It is taught that at that time, vividness, unobstructed transparency, and limpidity are unobscured, which together with an intensity of luminous radiance, arise from within. In this way, by practising the unity of shamatha and vipashyana, when rigpa wisdom appears nakedly, like staring into the cloudless primordially pure expanse of the sky, fundamentally what is known as 'samsara' has never existed. Seeing the essence of fundamental nature, the enlightened intent of the primordially pure three realms, immaculate vast complete purity, becomes manifest.

Not understanding this key point, although you may meditate by observing both arising and abiding, you will not become enlightened. This is samsaric mind. There is no point to this, other than attaining a result that resembles that cause. All-knowing Jigme Lingpa taught:

> Normal mind grasping at the luminous emptiness of shamatha;
> Conceptual mind deceived by conceptual analytical vipashyana;
> Basic space of indeterminate inaction;
> These three are excluded from Dzogchen.
>
> Meditation with fetters of remedial mindfulness;
> Rational mind with deliberate fixation on experiences of emptiness;
> Rational mind dwelling on muddled theory;
> You three are also excluded from Dzogchen.
>
> Normal mind's tense conceptual view and meditation;
> Rational mind trapped in the prison of fixation on meditative experiences;
> Conceptual mind's experiential awareness defiled with impurities;
> You three are also excluded from Dzogchen.

In short, these nine states are not included in the practice of Dzogchen. In summary, without modification, we need to maintain distinct emptiness, spacious openness without distraction or grasping.

Following this is a summary of the meaning:

> **In short, at all times until the rigpa aspect,**
> **Naked unobstructedness like a crystal sphere,**
> **Is mastered, maintain it distinctly.**

Having mastered it, do not separate from that state.

The key point of the trekchö view is said to be
'Strip rigpa bare and maintain it distinctly',
So this crucial point is of sole importance.
This is the confluence of a hundred lines,
So know it, fortunate heart children.

To summarise, at whatever time, whether arising or abiding, the rigpa aspect is unceasing with an intensity of luminous radiance, naked unobstructedness like a limpid crystal sphere, so do not separate from that state. It is said that to meditate is not most important, most important is to develop familiarisation. If one perfects familiarisation, then that is the supreme meditation. At one stage when mastery is attained, within the true nature of rigpa suchness, intellectually created philosophies which state 'conditioned phenomena are empty of their own essence' and 'true nature is empty of other essence', all such views from the sutra perspective, do not hold up to scrutiny.

Falling away self-liberated without trace, although apparent objects are unceasing in the nature of rigpa, rigpa does not mix with objects, it appears nakedly. When rigpa appears, we are taught all grasped-grasping fixation on samsaric appearances, that which is to be abandoned and its remedy, are self-liberated and disappear, like drawing a picture on water.

Generally speaking, what is referred to by the Tibetan term *'rig pa'* does not have one single meaning. At this juncture, if we want to distinguish the precise meaning, we know that in his *Stages of the Path*, Je Rinpoche uses the term *'rig pa'* when he states: whoever maintains that *rig pa* of mind remaining in no-thought without the intensity of the luminous aspect is shamatha, and with the intensity of the luminous aspect is vipashyana, is irrational, and he clarifies his point with a quotation. However, what Je Rinpoche refers to here is not in the context of discussing Dzogchen. He is referring to *rig pa* as 'awareness' which is the characteristic of mind which is clear and knowing. Thus, although the terms used in various teachings may be the same, their meaning differs depending on the context, and we need to apply this understanding to the Dharma language of the individual stages.

What does Je Rinpoche actually teach? Just preceding the above statement, he quotes from the *Stages of Meditation Part Two*, which accords with the foremost instructions of Prajnaparamita and the intent of the *Bhumi Sections*. It states that remaining in mind itself that possesses extreme pliancy is called 'shamatha', and while remaining in shamatha itself, thorough discernment of suchness, whatever it is, is vipashyana. What is this suchness? At the stage of Dzogchen it is the self-arising wisdom of rigpa. In the Dharma language of unexcelled Mantra it is distinguished by the terms 'vajra of the mind', 'genuine ultimate wisdom', and so forth. Also similarly, as Sakya Pandita stated, add anything to suchness and that view becomes elaborated. So if we know how to extract the hidden key point of all enlightened intent, then all the detailed explanations of experts and the experiences of accomplished masters actually come down to the same position.

In the teachings of the Three Manjushris of the Land of Snows, wherever contradictions come from, no contradictions remain. However, whichever scripture is taught, you need to elucidate it and reach a definitive conclusion according to your own tradition. Ultimately, by essentialising the instructions of practice for your own mindstream into a single key point, when this becomes medicine for the sickness of discursive thoughts of this rotten mindstream deluded by afflictive emotions, then that is appropriate. Whatever study and contemplation you do, consolidate it all into the main point of meditation practice. By concentrating the essence of this crucial point, if it comes to benefit your own experience, then I believe that such fortunate and great minded people as Shabkar's heart children should understand his instructions in this way.

The above primarily teaches the key points of threefold view, meditation, and conduct. Our final teaching tomorrow teaches primarily the result, the four great unerring vehicles, the four great unchanging nails, and so on, as we near the end of this foremost instruction scripture which teaches the meaning of trekchö primordial purity.

Closing Words

At the beginning of each of his songs, Shabkar Tsokdruk Rangdrol utters the exclamation of amazement 'EMAHO!' and calls out to us saying 'Fortunate heart children, listen!' By teaching the profound secret words of foremost instruction, heartfelt advice which is the very essence of his heart, abundantly and without concealment, he is saying 'Let me show this to you!' This is not like recounting some unseen distant legend, a fabulous tale of the abundance and pleasures of gods in heavenly realms. This is actually present in every mindstream of every person as a treasure trove of valuable jewels, yet we do not know we possess it. Looking outward, what is known as 'external happiness and comfort' or 'material abundance' appears to be attainable, so down a mistaken path we go from youth until old age. Now, having grown old and reached the point of death, there is nowhere else to go other than the place of death. We have reached the end of the path.

So we are told: 'Friends! Do not continue wandering blindly around like this, jumping about madly like fools! You are about to fall down into the final defile which lies directly ahead. Instead, turn around and go a better way. Crucially, let's address our life and the life of others, both now and in the future. Let me show you the sacred secret to lay the foundation of everlasting bliss, based upon the inner nature of our mind. I will give you the key to a new and joyful place of comfort.'

We all already know for certain that there is no joy or comfort to be found externally, because we have already put in so much effort trying to attain it. But when we have found inner undefiled joy of the mind, whatever we perceive becomes pure perception, and even the names of sorrow and suffering do not exist. We are taught that we need to discover this ourselves, based on training our own mind.

All perfect buddhas attained buddhahood through meditation. All accomplished masters and vidyadharas of the past also attained accomplishment through meditation. We have all read the biography of Jetsun Milarepa; he too attained accomplishment through meditation. First, when Jetsun Milarepa was a householder he killed a great many people and horses, but subsequently he developed renunciation and followed the profound guidance instructions of an authentic lama. He had such tremendous diligence that he would not retreat, even if a spear was pointed at his heart. Like this he persevered in practice, and through meditating, Milarepa finally attained accomplishment.

Each individual has their own reputation, a high or low status, and either prosperity or meagre wealth and possessions. Similarly, there is a huge diversity in ancestral heritage, genetic makeup, and so on. However, we are the same in that we all have the potential to become enlightened, we are all able to renounce samsara, and we all possess buddha nature in our fundamental mindstream. In that, there is no better or worse. Whoever meditates becomes enlightened. Whoever succumbs to grasping at solidification through fixated attachment wanders in samsara. Engaging in meditation does not cost us anything. It does not exhaust our provisions, nor require any effort. Except for the expression of amazement with which Shabkar begins his song, there is nothing else we can say about this amazing marvellous truth that we have heard, which we can enjoy without any gruelling physical effort.

What is known as 'meditation' is the enjoyment of pleasure and undefiled bliss, the experience of the essence of the nectar of mind. Therefore, we all need to engage in meditation. It is good to meditate in remote mountains, and it is particularly good if we can meditate in such places that have been blessed by holy beings, where samadhi develops naturally. Although this is the case, when we meditate together here, in such a large gathering of the spiritual community, qualities of experience and realisation yet to be born will surely develop, solely through the blessings of the gathered Sangha. What is more, those qualities that are already developed will increase further. Such is the inconceivable special power of the gathered Sangha.

A combination of such favourable circumstances is very difficult to assemble. It is difficult to come by and also rare to behold. Just like a hundred birds startled by a single slingshot, there are tales of an assembly of a hundred thousand practitioners attaining actual enlightenment simultaneously, flocking together on the level of perfect buddhahood. What is more, at the time of assembled group practice, the stories of those on the sidelines who serve the meals, birds that mark the time of day, even up to and including the local dairy yaks, becoming established at the level of vidyadharas, are of course also not without basis. Who can deny the swift path of actualising buddhahood without meditation, the realisation and conduct of former accomplished vidyadharas of the new and old schools of non-sectarian Secret Mantra?

It is said that every day, while Master Vasubandhu was reciting the sutras, a pigeon among the rafters would hear him. Due to this blessing, after a short while, the pigeon not only attained a physical basis of the higher realms, but also perceived the truth. With this in mind, who can grasp the extent of the benefit of just sitting among those meditating on the profound direct practical guidance of the explanatory tantras and hearing lineage of Secret Mantra? We should not think that these stories are tales from a time of good fortune long gone, or that those ancient times are very different from these modern times. Although nowadays, we are in the period of degeneration, in a time when the general blessings of the Dharma have partially faded, we should remember the analogy: *however black the darkness, that much brighter the lamp.* Likewise, it is taught that now is the time the blessings of the profound truth of Secret Mantra are especially swift.

Therefore, give rise to joyfulness, and if you can, right now this is an actual gathering of vidyadharas. This is a time of wonderful opportunity, where the value of each moment of every practice session of meditative equipoise cannot be measured in silver or gold. In this way, if we maintain our samaya commitments perfectly, then we will have the auspicious connection to attain enlightenment together in the future as a single group.

However, it is possible the feeling may arise that meditation is difficult or uncomfortable. This can occur for two reasons: firstly, because we do not know how to meditate, and secondly, because we are not familiar with meditating. To the extent that it is easy, effortless self-resting meditation seems too easy to some, as if it is not necessary to meditate at all, so they may go too far the other way. This happens because they do not accept meditation can be so easy, and so they do not know how to grasp the true secret significance of mind. By resting both body and mind self-settled, to maintain our true nature unmodified, subsumes many key points of Dzogchen meditation, and this does not require any hard work. To connect one thought after another we need to engage in much prior anticipation, present consideration, and subsequent analysis. So, to have to engage in countless activities of concern, which are like turbulent clouds, is actually very taxing. It is so unbearable for some they may even end up taking their own lives.

Unload all the mental burden of activities and remain in unwavering equipoise in a state of meditative concentration. This is a place of rest for the mind exhausted by the difficulties of a hundred hardships from beginningless time. However, lost down the tracks of familiar negative habituations from beginningless time, when you do meditate, if you think it is difficult to cut off thought, this is also an unnecessary burden of hardship which you are loading upon yourself. For a living breathing human being, is there anyone to whom thoughts do not arise? Thoughts occur, but it does not matter. Thoughts are the dynamic energy of true nature. If they arise, allow them to arise. If they do not occur, allow them not to occur. When abiding, this is the essence of true nature. When streaming forth, this is the manifest dynamic energy of wisdom. Do not pursue thoughts. If we chase after them we become confused, like water turning into ice. Leave thoughts naturally and they become self-liberated.

When we self-rest effortlessly within self-settled true nature, there is nothing bad called 'thought' that is left behind. When there is no need to engage in effort to prevent thoughts which we regard as bad, then it is easy. Effortless resting is not difficult. Aside from discussing the individual aspects of the terminology of known symbols which, from the perspective of their apparent mode, are called 'phenomena and true nature', 'delusion and non-delusion' in order to convey understanding to beginners, from the powerful perspective of the actual abiding mode, the characteristics of dualistic phenomena have never existed. There is nothing that is not subsumed within the vast equal taste of unity, the transcendent expanse of the single unelaborate bindu.

For fortunate beings who have pure vision and devotion, who recognise the wisdom of the fourth empowerment through the strength of the transference of blessings, there is nothing not to know about settling in the ongoing flow of the yoga of effortless non-distraction, free from exertion. Therefore, Shabkar teaches that if this is known, even a herdsman will be liberated. But if objects of knowledge are over-objectified and one becomes attached to elaborations, then even having the title 'pandita' is of no use. Therefore it is said:

> Not realising this, even panditas are deluded.

And also:

> One well-versed in words is not wise.
> One well-versed in unchanging truth is wise.

It was clarified earlier that if someone is not well-versed in meaning, then they are 'a pandita only in name'. Someone who is called 'a master' should not be called that just because they have learned a lot. It should mean that whatever they have learned, they have applied to their mindstream, where it has become medicine for afflictive emotions. So everyone here, abandon all timidity! Engage in fervent spiritual practice with enthusiasm and courage! Remember, the benefits of each session of meditation, each moment of meditation, cannot be rivalled by any ordinary gathering of accumulations or any ordinary purification of obscurations.

Teaching Day Five

Opening Words
Liberation

For practitioners of the Dharma, when we have entered its door, we should never part from the focus of the four mind changers in the beginning, in the middle, or in the end. That is why they are discussed whenever the Dharma conch is sounded. In particular, the teachings on karmic cause and effect concerning positivity and negativity, virtue and non-virtue, are in general very important, but during these present times, they are crucial. Why is that? Most of us here hail from the land of Tibet and believe in reincarnation and karmic cause and effect. However, has actual certainty in karma been born deep within us? If we have not connected this certainty to the key points to train our mindstreams, it will be as if the medicine is not being administered to the disease.

If we are unable to engage in careful acceptance and rejection of positivity and negativity, virtue and non-virtue, we will still be fooled by these appearances of samsaric activities, which like bubbles, are without essence. To exchange the meaningful everlasting purpose for the meaningless insignificant happiness of this life is the sign of not understanding its true significance. Because we are ordinary beings, it is difficult for us not to fall into an attitude of non-virtue and engaging in negative karmic actions. Of course, this is because we do not understand what the main source of our failing is, and so we come under the influence of confused ignorance.

What is called 'karma' is multifarious, like a mechanism of illusion which has numerous enumerations. There is karma experienced as observable phenomena, karma experienced after rebirth, karma experienced after several lifetimes, and so forth. These unimaginably numerous ramifications of karma do not decay by themselves, rot away, disappear, or anything like that. However, regardless of whatever type of karma we have, if it is confessed with the four remedial powers, through the power of confession it will thin out, just as the sun melts frost. Moreover, if precious bodhicitta is aroused in our mindstream, non-virtues will become self-purified, just as the sun illuminates darkness. Similarly, if we come to meet with the profound foremost instruction method of meditation practice which establishes emptiness in our mind, the root of existence will become extracted from its core within this lifetime. By embracing the permanent domain which accomplishes benefit for both self and others, we will come to arrive at the level where positive and negative karma is of neither benefit nor harm. This is because at the level of such accomplishment, in the ultimate analysis of rigpa nature, karma is inherently non-existent. In the Sutra section of the teachings, the Blessed One taught:

> Karma arises from conceptual thought, not from non-conceptuality.

Based upon this certainty in the mode of cause and effect, the two former mind changers: the difficulty of finding the freedoms and endowments and the impermanence of life, turn mind away from this life. The two latter mind changers: the defects of samsara, and karmic cause and effect, turn mind away from future rebirths. Together, these four mind changers turn mind away from samsara as a whole. As soon as powerful revulsion develops towards samsara, and we determine to escape from it and become free, the place to which we escape then becomes the crucial point. This is the search for liberation, and therefore we must identify what liberation is.

What are the different categories of liberation? There are three levels of enlightenment: shravaka arhat, pratyekabuddha arhat, and the enlightenment of a buddha, which does not abide in either extreme of existence or nirvanic peace. While we have the opportunity of choice, why would we select the lesser liberations over the greatest liberation? Of course we should select the level of omniscient perfect buddhahood. Even if we did attain the result of a shravaka or a pratyekabuddha, although we would attain the one-sided peace of our own freedom from the suffering of the three realms of samsara, in actual fact we would not have attained anything particularly good, either for ourselves or others. Also, however comfortable we ourselves would be, our loved ones and friends would still be experiencing suffering.

What are known as 'sentient beings' are incalculable and inexpressibly numerous. But even without considering such vast numbers, to abandon bringing benefit to others, even to just hundreds or thousands of sentient beings, and to search for our own happiness alone is not only not the way of the holy Dharma, it is the way of the lowest of worldly people. The parents of all our countless rebirths that we have previously taken are no different from our parents of this life. The result that is achieved upon entering the path of the lesser vehicle of shravakas and pratyekabuddhas does not only fail to accomplish any great benefit for others, but neither does it attain the perfection of abandonment and realisation—the enlightened qualities of perfect buddhahood—for our own benefit. The conditions which fail to attain these results are not embracing the special attitude of vast renunciation, only realising limited emptiness and nothing more, and not embracing bodhicitta.

Therefore, we know that the unmistaken goal to which we should aspire is the level of omniscient perfect enlightenment. However, just to know that the supreme object of attainment is the level of perfect buddhahood is not sufficient. Based on having this current potential for enlightenment, we can actualise it ourselves without spending many lifetimes. On this basis, we have arrived at the entrance to the path of our future goal, either for permanent good or permanent ill.

If each of us now turns within, we see we can enter onto any of the good paths of Sutra or Tantra which are complete and without error. This is no different from arriving at an innermost treasury which has gathered a wealth of enjoyment of everything desirable. Looking at this assembly of supportive circumstances, we have found the certainty of a precious physical basis which possesses the freedoms and endowments. With this, if we attain the supreme benefit of liberation, the level of perfect buddhahood, then benefit for all sentient beings, ourselves and others, will occur spontaneously without effort.

So if we consider with joy that on the path of luminous Dzogpa Chenpo, enlightenment can be attained in one lifetime on the basis of this very body, we should have high hopes. But, if from the outset we look downward and follow a lower path, then where else will we end up except in a hole? Alternatively, if we aspire to a lofty view but do not look to elevate our conduct from a lesser path, then our view will become too high and our conduct will be too low. This will leave view and conduct in discord, and it will be difficult to maintain good meditation and realise a positive result in this isolation.

In this case, as cause and effect indisputably produce a corresponding outcome, a result does not come about without regard to a cause. Therefore, whether we speak of the methods of the Sutra path—the ten levels and the five paths—or speak about the two stages of development and completion of the Mantra path—the path of the four kinds of vidyadhara—or if we speak about the wisdom path of luminous Dzogpa Chenpo of effortless basic liberation free of elimination or addition—primordially pure naked rigpa emptiness—in short, the result that is proclaimed to be perfect enlightenment which does not abide in duality, the manifestation of the epitome of the four kayas and five wisdoms, is accordingly the same.

If this is in accord, then in the manifestation of perfect enlightenment, compassion is like a bow, wisdom is like an arrow, and people skilled in means are skilful archers. As it is taught to be necessary to gather these three: compassion, wisdom, and skill in means as illustrated, this time we have attained a human body with the freedoms and endowments. We have also met with an authentic lama. Through faith and from the perspective of devotion, not only is the emanated body of the buddha always present, but the basis where the blessings of the lamas of the three lineages reside is the ordinary lama. So if your faith can support it, you can attain the blessings of a buddha appearing in actuality.

By receiving the nectar of oral instructions, we have the fortune to follow the dharmakaya doctrine of Samantabhadra. We have met with such fortune to be able to enjoy whatever we like of the secret treasury of instructions of maturation and liberation. This is even rarer than meeting a buddha in person. At this time when we have encountered the Dharma of greatly secret luminous Dzogpa Chenpo, we float along like a swan in a lake of lotus flowers, or a bee in a fragrant garden of blossoming flowers. For just a few moments in the morning and afternoon, through means of delighted striving, it is time for us to enter onto this path. On the protracted path of the causal vehicle, it is necessary to perfect oceanic completion, maturation, and cultivation for many countless aeons. Therefore, for those who are not able to manage to maintain consistently our meditation sessions each morning and afternoon, it is going to be difficult.

In terms of the close path of general Mantra, through meditating on the yogas with and without characteristics, it is taught one may become enlightened in sixteen, seven, or three lifetimes. Compared to the extremely swift path, this is not a short time. If one perfects maturation and liberation, generation and completion, of both Mahayoga and Anuyoga according to their respective paths, then it is taught one attains enlightenment in a single lifetime. But, for someone who is unable to manage neither the clear appearances of the generation stage, nor the meditative concentration of the completion stage, then there is no way to accomplish it.

If, on the effortless basic liberation path of luminous Dzogpa Chenpo, the natural face of primordially pure rigpa appears nakedly, and one can maintain this state of rigpa emptiness free of arising and cessation, the essence of the crucial points of all the lower vehicles is subsumed within it. How are all the practices of the lower vehicles subsumed in this? The Dzogchen practitioner abides in samadhi without normal mind, conceptual mind, or normal consciousness. When we speak of these, normal mind is alaya consciousness, conceptual mind is afflicted consciousness, and normal consciousness is consciousness of the five doors. When remaining in samadhi free of these, due to having no proliferation or subsiding of conceptualisation, the mind of the desire realm is reversed. As there is no normal mind of luminosity or an agent who is settled in luminosity, the mind of the form realm is reversed. Pristine luminosity free of all elaboration, self-arising wisdom, reverses the mind of the formless realm, and alaya together with the eightfold group attain the wisdom of complete liberation from the mind of the three realms, whereby what is known as the 'level of buddhahood' is not searched for elsewhere.

When abiding directly in the utter luminosity of rigpa wisdom, as there is neither grasping at an individual self nor grasping at a self-identity to phenomena, the intent of the view of shravakas, pratyekabuddhas, and bodhisattvas are subsumed within it. The pristine conduct of cleanliness of the three doors, and the three pristine wisdoms of the three sections from Kriya to Yoga, are also subsumed within this, together with the unity of non-dual appearances and rigpa. The incorporation of these three, actualisation of the extraordinary samadhi of realisation, also subsumes the enlightened intent of the three sections of inner Tantra. Therefore the lower practices of samadhi of faultless mind, and all the aspects of the qualities of realisation, are subsumed within this one practice. Thus the meaning of what is known as the 'thoroughly complete vehicle' is established by this reasoning.

Particularly, if one masters the dynamic energy of the four appearances on the path of trekchö primordial purity and tögal spontaneous presence, then through the unity of the utter luminosity of primordially pure emptiness and the utter luminosity of spontaneously present appearances, the coarse body dissipates into subtle particles or arises as a body of light in the kaya of great transference. The enlightened mind of a buddha, non-duality of the kayas and wisdoms, or alternatively the truth of the kayas and wisdoms without union or separation, is able to become complete instantaneously, and the level of supreme liberation can be attained.

To allow this to happen in this way, the basis: the essence of enlightenment, is complete within us. Based upon the condition of depending on a genuine spiritual master, the method to seize onto the key points of practising their direct oral instructions, is to train the mind with the four mind trainings. And by way of these, this is the way to seize the essence of the crucial points of practising the main practice. Thus, the spontaneously accomplished intent of the two kinds of benefit is fulfilled just as wished. This comprises a brief summary regarding the benefits of holy liberation.

Teaching Day Five

Main Teaching

Now we come to study the current text, which presents mind itself to be primordially the nature of enlightenment independent of generation and completion, the enlightened intent of Dzogpa Chenpo trekchö primordial purity. Shabkar Tsokdruk Rangdrol's teaching combines and explains in detail the foremost instructions of the essence of the enlightened intent of the vidyadhara lamas of the three mind, symbolic, and aural lineages, former masters who include Master Padmakara and Victorious Longchenpa.

From *Flight of the Garuda, Songs of the Trekchö View of Luminous Dzogpa Chenpo, Capable of Swiftly Traversing the Paths and Levels without Exception*, we have already completed the goodness of the beginning. From the goodness of the middle, we have completed most of the stages of guidance taught mainly for those who possess corresponding ordinary and extraordinary karmic fortune, presented primarily in terms of the view.

In the previous day's Dharma teaching, from the foremost instructions which mainly explain meditation, we learned that to which it is necessary to become accustomed, and abiding within that state, is the meaning of the view. Combining the four: view, meditation, conduct, and result, the crucial point of the view of trekchö is for rigpa to appear nakedly. This instruction was imparted to us by saying:

> This is the confluence of a hundred lines,
> So know it, fortunate heart children.

The meaning of this is the sphere of activity of those with sharp faculties whose mind state is one of self-manifest rigpa. The Chinese Master Shri Singha, direct disciple of the heroic holder of secrets Garab Dorje, bestowed the great empowerment of the dynamic energy of rigpa upon Master Padmakara through symbolic means, and the minds of master and student became equal. To speak of following after the enlightened intent of the one who indicated this method, the following three points gather together the enlightened intent of Dzogchen trekchö primordial purity: to reach decisive experience of the vast primordial purity of the exhaustion of phenomena, to encapsulate activity-free unimpeded nakedness, and to embrace the vast evenness of total liberation.

Thus, although rigpa arises, it is free of limitations. Inherently luminous naked rigpa is not spoiled by elaborations of concepts of characteristics. Even if negative thoughts arise, it is naturally pristine and naked. Even if positive thoughts arise, it is free of limitations and limpid.

Although it abides in its own state, it is uninterruptedly unimpeded. This suchness is not altered by remedies, nor spoiled by the flaws of myriad conditions. Without engaging in either renunciation or remedy, this rigpa aspect is demonstrated to be unimpeded naked dharmakaya. Here Shabkar teaches this using the terms of Longchenpa's *Treasury of Word Meanings* without any change in meaning, the only difference is his use of verse. In the *Treasury of Word Meanings* it states:

> At the time rigpa abides without proliferation and subsiding, the no-thought of the abiding aspect is not held to be meditation.

So what is meditation? Longchenpa continues by saying it is necessary to:

> Maintain openness without distraction of wakeful limpid pristine luminosity of naked rigpa of this time. But, at the time rigpa arises on an object, to observe whatever arises is not meditation. Maintain without distraction the naked aspect of luminous naked rigpa of that time. If this key point is not understood... mind merely residing is like the meditative concentration of the gods, and merely arising is the same as ordinary thought. One may meditate on these but buddhahood will not be attained.

Thus Longchenpa refutes these points with certainty, and similarly Shabkar teaches this in his songs.

Song Nineteen
Conduct that Liberates from Defiles

So, in connection with the stage of encapsulating activity-free unimpeded nakedness, today's first teaching primarily indicates conduct that liberates from the defiles of straying and loss with the four great guidelines, the four nails, the four that are brought to the state of exhaustion, and so forth, which are taught in stages. First, the four great guidelines are taught as follows:

> **EMAHO!**
> **Now again, heart children, listen with respect.**
>
> **To teach the four great guidelines that are without error,**
> **The great guideline for the view without error**
> **Is exactly this present distinct awareness.**
> **Since it is distinct and unerring it is called a 'guideline'.**

The great guideline for meditation without error
Is exactly this present distinct awareness.
Since it is distinct and unerring it is called a 'guideline'.

The great guideline for conduct without error
Is exactly this present distinct awareness.
Since it is distinct and unerring it is called a 'guideline'.

The great guideline for result without error
Is exactly this present distinct awareness.
Since it is distinct and unerring it is called a 'guideline'.

Just as a guideline marks a boundary, making the demarcation clearly distinguished and differentiated, the four: view, meditation, conduct, and result of Dzogchen Heart Essence are encompassed within this present rigpa—naked, inherently luminous, free of transition and change—and are complete in this alone. To master completely this distinct present unimpeded awareness, which is like a crystal sphere, and to maintain this state is clear and without error. As this does not become confused by any points of error, it is taught to be the guideline without error. This is described in exactly the same way in the Great Master's *Self-liberation through Naked Perception*. This teaches the four great guidelines without error.

Following that, the four unchanging great nails are taught as follows:

To teach the four unchanging great nails,
The great nail of the unchanging view
Is exactly this present distinct awareness.
Since it is steady throughout the three times it is called a
    'nail'.

The great nail of unchanging meditation
Is exactly this present distinct awareness.
Since it is steady throughout the three times it is called a
    'nail'.

The great nail of unchanging conduct
Is exactly this present distinct awareness.
Since it is steady throughout the three times it is called a
    'nail'.

The great nail of unchanging result

**Is exactly this present distinct awareness.
Since it is steady throughout the three times it is called a 'nail'.**

When something is pinned down with a nail it becomes fixed and firm, so the above are taught to have similar attributes. First Garab Dorje bestowed his final testament, the foremost instruction *Three Phrases Striking the Key Point*, to Master Shri Singha. Then later Shri Singha bestowed his final testament, called *'Seven Nails'*, to Master Manjushrimitra. Also, in the eleventh chapter of Longchenpa's *Treasury of the Basic Space of Phenomena* he teaches whatever is apparent to be purity equal to space using the eleven sky nails. These are the sky nail of direct encounter that liberates in its own place, the sky nail which demonstrates training rigpa dynamic energy in negative conditions, the sky nail of dispelling renunciation and remedy from the foundation, and so forth, up to the sky nail of total evenness of vast expansiveness.

Similarly here, the four: view, meditation, conduct, and result are all struck by the single nail of present awareness—distinct self-luminosity, primordial emptiness free of root, self-abiding essence of wisdom—to reach a decisive experience of the manifestations of supreme victor Samantabhadra. This is exactly the self-arising wisdom of dharmakaya in self-repose knowing its own essence. This does not change throughout the three times. How is it unchanging? Because grasping, fixation, and connections with the three times are severed, it does not change throughout the three times. Because this unchangingness is steady, this itself is singly the unchanging nail which strikes all view, meditation, conduct, and result.

From the teaching on the four that reach the state of exhaustion, first view reaching the state of exhaustion is as follows:

> There are a vast number of different views,
> But in present self-knowing, self-arising wisdom,
> There is no duality of viewer and that which is viewed.
> Do not look at the view, seek the one who looks.
> When the one who looks is sought but not found,
> At that time view reaches the state of exhaustion.
>
> This view, without anything to see,
> Does not become primordial nothingness, a completely blank void.
> Present awareness, uncontrived and distinct,
> Is exactly the view of Dzogpa Chenpo.

Teaching Day Five

Generally, when we speak of the 'view', whatever the object of comprehension may be, misconceptions regarding it become cleared through discriminating knowledge. Then, the concept that is held unequivocally to be certain is called the 'view'. However, because of misunderstanding, erroneous notions, partial understanding, and non-realisation of the true state, all variety of worldly and transcendent views exist. Similarly, we can posit as many various spiritual approaches as there are conceptual elaborations. In the Dharma terminology of the Nyingma tradition, in the single object of the basic space of phenomena, due to the differences of individual subjective perceptions, there is the tradition of teaching three: view which sees conditioned phenomena, view which sees true nature, and view which sees self-knowing.

At this stage, from the perspective of the extraordinary subjective perception of rigpa wisdom, phenomena which are subsumed by appearances and existence, samsara and nirvana—all external myriad appearances free of extremes and without basis—except for being merely apparent, have never existed and have never not existed, have never been true and have never been false. As they are without basis and are primordially pristine, they do not exist as phenomena of acceptance and rejection. As internal objects of our mind of arising and cessation do not exist, they transcend the extremes of identification of an essence. As the Dharma of view, meditation, and conduct which is transmitted and comes to be received, is unobserved and does not waver from the luminous space of the vast expanse of spacious truth, when the one who views is searched for but not found, this is taught to be view reaching the state of exhaustion.

At the stage of Dzogpa Chenpo, the terms 'exhaustion', 'nothingness', and 'emptiness' are not to be understood to refer to things that are actually exhausted into nothingness and become void. So then, can we say they exist? That is also not the case. These are called 'words which transcend conventional designation'. Therefore, as appearances of conditioned phenomena dissolve into their true nature, when the true nature of phenomena becomes totally inconceivable and ineffable, then this is the same perspective of understanding as saying 'exhaustion into true nature'.

When we say that in the view of true nature free of extremes there is no viewer or that which is viewed, do not understand this to be a primordially non-existent blank void. If the basic view is mistaken then meditation will be mistaken. If meditation is mistaken then conduct will also be erroneous, and ultimately the result will be like the story of Tarwa Nakpo who misunderstood, went astray, and was reborn as a rudra demon. Not ending up like that, present awareness—rigpa emptiness without arising and cessation, empty luminosity free of transition and change, the sole supreme monarch, uncontrived distinct limpidity—is itself the view of Dzogpa Chenpo. Therefore we are taught to reach a decision in the immediacy of exactly this.

As for meditation:

> There are a vast number of different meditations,
> But in unobstructed present ordinary awareness,
> There is no duality of meditator and that which is meditated on.
> Do not meditate on meditation, seek the meditator.
> When the meditator is sought but not found,
> At that time meditation reaches the state of exhaustion.
>
> This meditation, without anything to meditate on,
> Does not fall under the influence of drowsiness or agitation, gloom or fogginess.
> Uncontrived meditative equipoise in present awareness,
> Uncontrived and inherently luminous, is the meditation.

Now, just as there is a great abundance of views, similarly there are also many contradictory meditations. In effortless, spontaneously accomplished Dzogchen beyond the need to maintain the state of present awareness, or unobstructed rigpa luminosity-emptiness without grasping, there is nothing to divide dualistically into a meditator and something which is meditated on. Do not search for meditation externally, but seek a meditator inwardly. The innermost point of meditation will become resolved there. Whether it seemingly arises outwardly upon the objects of the sixfold group, or seemingly abides inwardly upon self-abiding awareness, this inherently luminous rigpa aspect that appears nakedly is unobstructed naked dharmakaya.

At any time, whether this mind is proliferating, abiding, or stirring, there is not a single moment that it is separate from inherently luminous unceasing rigpa. To search for a meditator apart from this, at the time one is not found, that is when meditation reaches the state of exhaustion. There, final resolution is reached. Generally, in Dzogpa Chenpo meditation of true nature primordially exhausted, there is no fixed reference endowed with characteristics whatsoever on which to meditate. Not to come under the influence of drowsiness or dullness, agitation or proliferation, and so forth, and particularly to avoid gloom and fogginess, we can bring forth the clarity of rigpa with an occasional forceful 'P'ET' sound.

What is taught to be 'present awareness' is not subtle mind, the nature of which is an indeterminate normal awareness of no-thought, like a foggy gloom, a complete blankness as if struck on the head by a stone and absent of any thought. Present awareness is an awareness without an object, free of grasping and fixation. From the aspect of its luminosity, it is like a kind of ordinary awareness. However, from the aspect of its non-grasping, it is not mind. These appearances of an agent who hears and an agent who feels are not stopped. So, how does it appear? Not following after objects, like the reflection of a person arising in a mirror, in the clarity aspect of rigpa, the arising aspect appears. This is called 'rigpa' or 'present awareness'.

What is referred to as 'present' means the sense of uncontrived ordinariness exists directly or as it always was.

> As it exists primordially, it is called 'timeless' (*ye*).
> As its nature is knowing, it is called 'awareness' (*she*).

This is the definition of wisdom (*yeshe*). Likewise, we are taught that to rest in uncontrived meditative equipoise in uncontrived inherently luminous present awareness, is meditation. Here Shabkar uses the word 'uncontrived' twice consecutively. The meaning of this is that upon the uncontrived ground, when one meditates on the uncontrived path, one pursues the uncontrived result: the level of spontaneous presence.

When we speak of 'uncontrived, unaffected, self-arising wisdom', 'self-arising' refers to wisdom which, from the aspect that it does not arise from something else or a cause, is called 'self-arising'. In that case, is it born from itself? We would have to say 'No'. Why? Because it is unborn. If it is unborn, then we would think logically it cannot exist. However, although that can be said of material things, for non-material things this does not disprove it. For example, we could say 'It is like space'. If we were to say that space is uncompounded, and so it is unacceptable to apply upon it a designation of existence, then we can ask 'Is space, and so forth, a phenomenon of the mind sense faculty?' If space is a phenomenon of the mind sense faculty, then it is established as a form of mentally known phenomena. As space, a vase, and so on, are all formed from the basic space of emptiness, then ultimately all of them are established as forms of emptiness.

Conduct reaching the state of exhaustion is as follows:

> **There are a vast number of different conducts,**
> **But in the single bindu of self-knowing wisdom,**
> **There is no duality of conduct and the one who engages in it.**
> **Do not engage in conduct, seek the one who engages.**
> **When the one who engages is sought but not found,**
> **At that time, conduct reaches the state of exhaustion.**

> This conduct, without anything to engage in,
> Does not fall under the influence of deluded habituation.
> In present awareness, uncontrived and inherently luminous,
> Not engaging in contrivance and contamination, acceptance and rejection, whatsoever,
> Is exactly completely pure conduct.

In general, for each vehicle there are many teachings on the categories of conduct. Similarly in Dzogchen, for ordinary beings to be tamed, twenty-one enumerations of conduct, or seven types of extraordinary majestic conduct, and so forth, are taught. However, because there is nothing that is not subsumed within non-attached basic freedom, the singly sufficient king of conduct is self-knowing all-encompassing wisdom, the single bindu of the basic space of phenomena, essence of non-dual basic space and rigpa. Within this, there is nothing to distinguish as a duality of separate conduct and a person who engages in it. Do not search to see if conduct exists or not, but search for the one who engages in conduct. If having sifted through the three thousandfold universe, you cannot find one who engages in conduct, then finding nothing is the supreme discovery.

At that time, conduct, having reached the state of exhaustion, has disappeared unimpededly into the state of the unborn. It is suitable to apply the term 'liberation' to this. Therefore, in conduct where there is nothing whatsoever in which to engage, not coming under the influence of negative tendencies of deluded habituations, in present awareness of uncontrived inherently luminous rigpa, do not engage in fabrication of contrivance or contamination, and so forth—any acceptance or rejection whatsoever—but rest in its own place. This itself it taught to be 'completely pure conduct'.

The teaching on result reaching the state of exhaustion is as follows:

> There are a vast number of different results,
> But in the self-knowing, effortless, and spontaneously present three kayas,
> There is no duality of accomplisher and accomplishment.
> Do not accomplish a result, seek the one who accomplishes.
> When the one who accomplishes a result is sought but not found,
> At that time, result reaches the state of exhaustion.
>
> This result, without anything to accomplish,

> Does not fall under the influence of acceptance or rejection, hope or fear.
> Present rigpa awareness, inherently luminous spontaneous presence,
> Manifest trikaya inherently luminous emptiness,
> Is itself the primordially enlightened result.

Whichever of the vast number of different results we discuss, there is nothing to find by searching for a result that comes from something else. The resultant self-knowing, effortless, and spontaneously present three kayas are complete in ourselves. How are they complete in us? Rigpa essence, limpid emptiness which is not established as anything whatsoever is ineffable and transcends the realm of thought and speech. This empty essence is dharmakaya. Unceasing nature arises inherently luminous in all samsara and nirvana. This luminous nature is sambhogakaya. The magical display of rigpa, all-pervading compassion which arises as anything, is nirmanakaya. Thus in this, there is no duality of accomplisher and accomplishment.

Therefore, do not try to accomplish a result, but seek the one who accomplishes. Having searched for one who accomplishes, this finding nothing is the unaccomplished result that is present in ourselves. At that time, rigpa reaches the state of exhaustion, and as there is no result whatsoever to accomplish, it is non-existent, and the state of inseparable rigpa emptiness is arrived at. In non-accomplishment of an alternative result that arises from elsewhere, we do not fall under the influence of acceptance or rejection, hope or fear. Other than present rigpa awareness, the inherently luminous spontaneously present three kayas which have become manifest, as there is no separate primordially enlightened result beyond this, we are instructed to arrive at a decisive experience of just this.

Teaching Day Five

Song Twenty
The Signs of Mastery

Here, a summary of the signs of the six masteries of view, meditation, conduct, fundamental nature, nirmanakaya, and the result, is taught as follows:

> **EMAHO!**
> **Now again, children of the family, listen well.**
>
> **Like that, if first you have maintained non-distraction,**
> **Later, even if you let go, in the ultimate sense,**
> **Even left ordinarily, there is no coming or going.**

Beginner practitioners first maintain non-distraction by the application of mindfulness. By practising in this way, gradually later, by settling in the state of effortlessness, even if they let go into the uninterrupted openness of whatever arises as naked rigpa emptiness—into whatever stirs as the dynamic energy of the dharmakaya monarch—in the ultimate sense, in ordinary mindfulness of true nature, mindfulness and the object of mindfulness are non-dual. Just as having arrived in a precious golden isle, even if we were to search for ordinary earth and stone, we would not find any. Rigpa emptiness-luminosity arises like the sun and moon in the sky, and we abide in a state of non-dual coming and going.

To indicate the signs and measure of this:

> **When both appearances and emptiness are inseparable,**
> **At that time the view has been mastered.**

By not falling into extremes regarding appearances, as appearances are not established with characteristics, they appear multifariously. By not determining emptiness to be isolated, as emptiness is not determined as separate, it extends all-pervasively throughout centre and edge. When inseparable appearances and emptiness, the enlightened intent of dharmakaya which transcends conceptual mind, becomes manifest, at that time the view has been mastered.

> **When both dreams and daytime are no different,**
> **At that time meditation has been mastered.**

If we strive at practice during the day and do not succumb to the influence of ignorant sleep at night, by merging night and day into one in the ongoing state of luminosity, if we can reside in the samadhi of true nature, luminous resting free of coming and going, then at that time meditation has been mastered. Generally speaking, a large portion of our lives is spent asleep, so at night do not slumber like an animal in an ignorant stupor. It is crucial to train in the yoga of the luminosity of sleep. Except for a difference in the level of grossness or subtleness, it is taught sleep and death are both alike, so for someone who is determined to accomplish enlightenment, it is very important to meditate on the yoga of the night. It is for this particular reason that in his guide to the six bardos, the Great Master saw fit to dedicate one part of the guidance to the bardo of dreams.

> **When both happiness and suffering are no different,**
> **At that time conduct has been mastered.**

In this life, while grasping at dualistic appearances has not been destroyed, there is differentiation between happiness and suffering. It would be very difficult to say that the feeling of massage on one side of your body and the feeling of being cut with a knife on the other side are the same. However, when we need to train our conduct up from a base level, then conduct that is without fear or concern and in control of appearances, in which suppression and promotion of dualistic grasping at acceptance and rejection is destroyed through gradual meditation, then that is the time conduct which sees happiness and suffering as identical has been mastered.

> **When both this life and the next are no different,**
> **At that time fundamental nature has been realised.**

For a yogi who is familiarised completely with true nature, they experience what is known as 'the way to die like a small child' in which there is no hope, fear, or consideration given to dying or staying alive. If there is no difference between this life and the next, and everything has merged into the basic expanse of the single true nature, at that time the ultimate mode of presence of fundamental nature is not mere words but has, in fact, become actualised or realised. If there were no key instructions of the Dharma of death to rely on, then what is known as 'death' would be feared by everyone, no matter who they are. However, when we do have the crucial instructions on the Dharma of death to rely on, there is no need to be afraid of dying. When we have accomplished the genuine Dharma of death, then death is the great entrance to liberation. The doorway to nirvana is also death.

What is known as the 'body' is something to be left behind: it incorporates unclean substances and is the basis of all undesirable sickness and negative influences. Leave it behind. Take up a body of pure light possessing the essence of wisdom. Not to delight in benefitting other sentient beings, and staying in this prison-like misery of samsara, we are suffering and our companions are suffering. What are we doing suffering together like this? Now renunciation that arises in our mindstream needs to be like a bird longing to fly away from suffocating smoke. Moreover, when we have the inner confidence of the realisation of fundamental nature, then we do not need to have so much fear of death.

> **When both mind and space are no different,**
> **At that time dharmakaya has been realised.**

The nature of mind, dharmakaya essence, empty luminosity without limit or centre, is like the example of the external sky, unwavering pristine lucidity, totally undelimited, and does not fall into any partiality whatsoever. When appearances and mind are non-dual, knowing and objects of knowledge are of one taste, and sky-like realisation and familiarisation equal to space is manifest. At that time, uncontrived unelaborate self-abiding dharmakaya is taught to be realised.

> **When your mind and buddha are no different,**
> **At that time the result has been realised.**

The rigpa essence of your mind is itself the very nature which possesses the three wisdoms. When Samantabhadra became enlightened, he did not become good. When sentient beings of the three realms are deluded in samsara, they do not become bad. This is unchanging wisdom pure from the first, innate limpidity free of elaboration which transcends abandonment and adoption, grasping and effort. Other than this, there is no separate buddha. Just as is taught in Indrabhuti's *Vishuddha*:

> Mind free of purification and achievement is buddha.

By actualising this, when both our mind and buddha become without difference, at that time the result has been realised. The above completes the teaching on freedom from the defiles of straying, loss, and error, and the signs and measure of familiarisation of the path of the yogi.

However we discuss things from the aspects of the view, meditation, conduct, or result, principally based upon deciding with the view, having maintained the state through meditation, at the time that familiarisation becomes mastered, conduct without suppression or promotion and the result free of hope and fear come about spontaneously. Thus, to decide in accordance with the view is the vast meditation of non-meditation. What does this mean? There is nothing whatsoever on which to meditate, and one does not become distracted for even a moment. At the time when the enhancement of meditation itself arises through conduct, faith without distinction and compassion without partiality which was not present before, arises spontaneously. At that time, whether from the perspective of view, meditation, or result, without the three: straying, blunder, or error, there is no other place at which to arrive, beyond reaching the result of the three kayas free of hope and fear: the dharmakaya kingdom.

In both a detailed and a medium-length manner of explanation, the above is a teaching in accordance with the minds of ordinary and extraordinary beings to be tamed, who are suitable vessels for Dzogpa Chenpo.

Teaching Day Five

Song Twenty-One
Yogic Practice

Now concisely, once again the complete key points of yogic practice for beings of ordinary mental capacity to be tamed are taught as follows:

EMAHO!
Now again, children of the family, listen to me!

With this encouraging request, Shabkar continues:

> Regard this material body as the moon in water.
> Utter verbal expression as echoes.
> Allow mental thought patterns to be cleared where they are.
> All appearances, sounds, and mental phenomena are illusions,
> Like mirages, dreams, reflections, moons in water,
> Cities of gandharvas, hallucinations, apparitions,
> Bubbles, and echoes—act without grasping!
> Undertake all conduct within this state.

The nature of the form aggregate of the corporal body, this gathering of the four elements like something we have borrowed, is an object that is subject to disintegration, unstable, unsteady, and essenceless. It is like the reflection of the moon in water, and so on, as taught here by the eight examples of illusoriness. This point is taught in detail in *Finding Rest in Illusion*. Like a reflection of the moon in water, our bodies are unstable, unsteady, and essenceless. Verbal expressions are like the sounds of echoes. Conceptual thought patterns in our minds also disappear naturally, becoming self-cleared without trace. Therefore, all apparent and existent phenomena are deceptive illusory apparitions, apparent while non-existent mirage oases, which through delusion arise as the further confusion of myriad dreams. Moreover, they are apparent as cities of gandharvas, hallucinations, apparitions, bubbles, and so forth. Thus the eight examples of illusoriness demonstrate that they are without essence.

Accordingly, unattached conduct without grasping is, moreover, not only mindful at a certain time, or seemingly careful with regard to a single area. With mindfulness, attentiveness, and carefulness yogis need to ensure they do not part from this mode of conduct. What is called 'mindfulness' is not forgetting, and not becoming distracted is 'attentiveness'. Avoiding negative actions is 'carefulness'. With these, we need to engage in all the modes of yogic conduct in accordance with the Dharma. This is the ongoing mode of conduct.

At the time of merging practice with meditation, how should this be done?

> **Link night and day continuously, without dividing practice sessions and breaks.**
> **In the self-settled state, do not engage in contrived alteration of thoughts.**
> **In luminosity-emptiness, self-expression self-liberated without grasping,**
> **Rest without truth, meditation, effort, or trace.**
>
> **Leave all past discursive thoughts that have gone**
> **Like the traceless path of a bird in the sky.**
> **Leave present awareness impeccable like space,**
> **Future thought like a mill with its water cut off,**
> **In free relaxation without engaging in fabrication or contrivance,**
> **Let loose in the state of self-settled unrestrictedness.**
>
> **Leave subtle and gross thoughts, the three and five poisons, and so on,**
> **Like thieves entering an empty house.**
> **Leave all the apparent objects of the sixfold group without trace,**
> **Like an illusory city that has collapsed.**

Generally speaking, meditation and post-meditation do not become inseparable until arriving at the level of no more learning. Before that, it is very difficult. However, by training in the successive stages of the five paths, not only do we need to arrive at the level of no more learning, but at the time of ordinary beings, the path is based on something similar in type to superior wisdom, which is then realised. This is the speciality of Mantra. Through the unelaborate yoga of Dzogpa Chenpo, when meditating on the continuous state of luminosity day and night uninterruptedly, at all times—during meditation sessions and breaks—do not separate from the practice of the session. In a state that is self-settled without contrivance or alteration, whatever ordinary thought processes that arise or stir, and as long as they remain, however displays of self-clarity arise, they all arise as self-liberated luminosity-emptiness without grasping.

In addition to this, here, four aspects which are not present are taught consecutively. They are no truth, no meditation, no effort, and no trace. All of truthless dependent origination with the self-form of the phenomena of appearances and mind, while not existent, is apparent from the aspect of delusion. However, the emptiness of this does not fall into straying from the view that is held as supreme. Although there is no reference point to say 'meditate on this' to meditate upon, there is not a single moment of becoming distracted. In non-meditation like the unceasing flow of a great river, in this continuous river of yoga, there is no particular effort of self-resting. By maintaining fundamental nature as it is, with respect to traceless great self-liberation, allow whatever arises to arise and whatever manifests to manifest.

For thought patterns of the three times, do not demarcate between past and future. Do not follow after previous discursive thoughts. Do not welcome forward the future that lies ahead. Present awareness in an unfabricated state, unceasing rigpa expression of mind itself, is free and vivid. As it is said:

> Freeness in unobstructed transparency,
> The experience of transparency is ineffable.

In a self-settled unrestricted state, what is referred to in the root text as 'loose' has the meaning of leaving uncontrived. At that time, whatever subtle or gross afflictive emotions and discursive thoughts arise, they are all just like a thief entering an empty house: there is nothing for the thief to gain and there is nothing to lose in the empty house. Like this example, for the entirety of whatever apparent objects of the sixfold group that arise, appearances are liberated upon appearing and mental stirring is liberated upon stirring. Like an illusory city that has collapsed without trace, we are taught to rest in a state without hope and fear.

Practising in this way, how to reach a decisive experience of vast primordial purity without grasping is taught as follows:

> **In short, threefold arising, cessation, and abiding; ground, path, and result;**
> **View, meditation, conduct, and result; time, place, expressions, and words;**
> **That which is settled and the one who settles; that which is liberated and the liberator, and so on,**
> **Are inherently luminous and unbiased without grasping, effort, acceptance, and rejection.**
>
> **Like streams merging into a great ocean,**

> **All phenomena are primordially pure in the basic space of mind.**
> **Develop confidence and reach a decisive experience of non-grasping.**

To combine the key points of practice and speak on the summarised essential meaning, whether we discuss it based upon the fundamental mode of presence of true nature free of threefold arising, cessation, and abiding, or we establish all phenomena of samsara and nirvana through the principles of ground, path, and result; at whatever time, in whatever place, however we explain it with whichever of the various key points of mental abiding of that which is settled and one who settles, and the method of liberation of that which is liberated and the liberator, and so forth, the point upon which to make a firm decision and reach decisive experience is naked rigpa.

Inherently luminous and without grasping, the empty factor is cut away, and there is nothing to be grasped onto in the luminous aspect. Whatever arises, there is no grasping or effort. There is no acceptance or rejection, regardless of what appears. To give an example, the streams of the land merge into the great ocean. They arise, yet they arise from the ocean. They merge away, yet they merge back into the ocean. Similarly, whatever the primordially pure basic space of the true nature of mind is, within that state all phenomena grasped by hope and fear are unobserved, becoming self-purified within their own context, free of something to be purified and any purification. Develop this as the core of confident practice and reach a decisive experience of, or determine this non-grasping.

Instructions for beginners on liberating thoughts in their own context are given as follows:

> **When meditating like this, many discursive thoughts may proliferate,**
> **However, do not be upset thinking 'Meditation does not come to me'.**
> **Mind proliferates but is empty, and abides but is empty.**
> **However it arises, it is the state of rigpa,**
> **So do not engage in suppression or promotion, acceptance or rejection.**
> **Rest released in the genuine uncontrived state.**
> **By doing so, discursive thoughts will certainly be liberated in their own context.**

From beginningless time up until now, from birth to the present day, except for looking outwards at others, we have not looked back at ourselves. In particular, we have never observed the fundamental nature of our inner mind. As if suddenly capturing a wild horse, when we initially turn inward, settle upon mind, and observe it, at first although we are engaged in meditation, we will get the impression that discursive thoughts have become more numerous. However, discursive thoughts have not become more numerous through meditating. The usual multifarious continuous confused permeation of discursive thoughts is like storm clouds. At this time, when we turn inwards and look, we see this.

At this stage we are taught we should not be miserable thinking that meditation is not coming to us. Why should we not be miserable? Just as if travelling on the road to a distant place, all kinds of the mind's movement of stirring and proliferating, happiness and sorrow, will be encountered. Therefore, it is not necessary to block discursive thoughts viewing them as bad. Mind proliferates, but it is empty luminosity without grasping. Similarly, it abides, but it is empty luminosity without grasping. However it arises, in whatever way it thinks, mind does not waver from the state of primordially pure rigpa. Therefore, do not engage in suppressing proliferation, promoting abiding, welcoming positive, shunning negative, and so on, together with any acceptance, rejection, suppression, promotion, discarding, or appropriation whatsoever. In the state of self-settled, unfabricated, genuine or fundamental nature, however it has always been, in that way, rest released and self-settled. By following this oral instruction, we are taught it is certain that whatever discursive thoughts arise, they will become self-liberated in their own context.

For beginners, once again, to enhance practice and dispel mental hindrances, intent focus on discursive thoughts is taught as follows:

> If people of lesser capacity cannot remain in this state,
> Alternate between analysis and resting, as at the stage of introduction.
> Alternatively, focus intently on thoughts like this:
> Provoke discursive thoughts, necessary or not,
> One after another in various forms.
> Elaborate until your mind is exhausted.
> Then, when you no longer wish to do so, rest loosely.

Generally, students who are vessels for the teachings of Dzogpa Chenpo have superior faculties in comparison to others. However, just as I have repeated many times before, this does not mean that there are no differences among us, between slightly sharper or slightly duller faculties. For those kinds of people from whom perception of rigpa is slightly hidden, referred to here as 'people of lesser capacity', at the stage of maintaining the state of rigpa, perhaps they do not know how to abide within it. Alternatively, they may be attached to the words of introduction and so not understand the real meaning, or perhaps they could be too tense.

In these cases, follow the words of the key points of introduction and recall their meaning. It might be useful to alternate between analytical meditation and resting meditation in equal combination. Another option which might help is to rely on the instructions to focus intently on discursive thoughts. Firstly, this is to provoke discursive thoughts, necessary or not, elaborating both good and bad thoughts in your mind until you become weary. At one stage, when you are unable able to think of anything else, feel fed up, and do not want to think any more, relax directly in that and settle. There is nowhere else to go beyond the fundamental nature of rigpa free of proliferation and subsiding.

In other cases, you may feel unhappy, that rigpa is unclear, and there is uncertainty as to what these unfavourable circumstances are exactly, as if some harm is coming from demons or spirits. In particular, now is a time when malevolent gyal spirits cause harm and gyalgong demons enter the hearts of those who engage in Dharma. Therefore among the methods to dispel such obstacles, this method is taught to be profound.

> **Alternatively, meditate on the genuine lama in the centre of your heart.**
> **Having held this in mind for a long time,**
> **Then rest in the state of non-grasping rigpa.**

This meditation on the lama is, in general, the essence of all practice. It is taught:

> Long ago, when there were no lamas,
> Even the name 'buddha' did not exist.
> The thousand buddhas of the aeon
> Appeared through relying on lamas.

Also:

> If you do not separate from perception of the lama,
> You also do not separate from the buddhas; they reside.

Through meditating on guru yoga, merge your mind inseparably with the enlightened mind of the lama. A more crucial key point of Dharma than this has not been uttered, even by the tongue of the Victorious One. Whether it is the time to dispel negative influences or to engage in practice, attain the empowerments, guidance, and foremost instructions with all the authentic attributes. In particular, meditate that in the jewelled pavilion of your heart, seated upon an eight-petalled lotus, is your root lama who introduces your mind to be the dharmakaya, their body brilliant with lustrous radiance. Through this meditation with characteristics, focus your mind on this and maintain it for a long time. After that, rest inseparably with the enlightened mind of the lama, ungrasping naked rigpa emptiness free of concepts and thoughts, proliferation and subsiding. If you familiarise yourself with this repeatedly, there is not a single hindrance to meditation that cannot be pacified.

Also, if you think you are falling under the influence of faulty meditation, drowsiness, agitation, or any such problem:

> Alternatively, visualise a bindu in the centre of your heart.
> Think that it descends downwards
> Until touching the mighty base.
> Doing so will certainly cut diffusion and agitation completely.
> When agitation is cut, rest in the state of rigpa.
>
> If drowsiness prevails, sharpen your gaze,
> Lay rigpa bare and maintain it distinctly.
> Or imagine the nature of your mind as a bindu
> And utter the sound 'P'ET'. Immediately it exits
> From the Brahma aperture like an arrow shot by a mighty archer,
> And think it merges completely with space.
> Then imagine the characteristics of space.
> It is impossible for this not to clear drowsiness.
> When drowsiness is cleared, rest in the state of non-grasping.
> This is the oral advice, so understand it.
>
> Without being bound by thoughts of wanting no-thought,
> Allow rigpa to be vast and elevated, let go into expansive openness.
> Be at ease, free and serene.

Meditation on the lama at the centre of your heart is supreme among all the ways to dispel hindrances. It is the root of all blessings. However, if you are unable to rouse so much devotion and longing, and as such do not succeed in dispelling hindrances, there are alternative foremost instructions in the oral advice. These are as follows: in the centre of your heart visualise a brilliant bindu as the essence of rigpa. Think that this descends down below the nine subterranean levels until reaching the mighty golden base. If you do so, this is certain to cut from the root all confusion of discursive thought and agitating hindrances. When agitation is cut, at that moment rest again in equipoise, in the state of inherently luminous rigpa.

If you feel that drowsiness is more prevalent, sharpen your gaze or invigorate rigpa, and maintain naked rigpa distinctly luminous in a state without obscuration. Alternately, visualise your mind itself again as a bindu, just as above, and meditate on this as having an appearance of light. Focus your attention again on this bindu. The P'ET syllable unites method and wisdom. The two sounds of PHA and TA sever dualistic grasping from the root to make the syllable P'ET. Upon uttering the syllable 'P'ET' forceful and brief, immediately the rigpa essence of mind itself in the form of a bindu exits from the Brahma aperture at your crown, like an arrow shot by a mighty archer which does not return. You should think that it merges completely or wholly, inseparable from the external basic space of the sky. Then, if we bring to mind the characteristics of empty luminous space without centre or limits, we are taught that it is impossible for any drowsiness not to be cleared. When drowsiness is cleared, at that time settle in a state of non-grasping self-clarity and maintain the continuous experience of practice without fault. These are called the foremost instructions that focus directly on drowsiness and agitation, referred to as oral advice, which is the oral transmission of the lama, and so we are instructed to understand them.

When we abide in the no-thought state of samadhi, do not be bound by thoughts of wanting no-thought. Do not fixate on a limited narrow attitude, but allow rigpa to be vast and elevated, transcending bias and without fixed dimensions. Let go into expansive openness, evenness, and limitlessness, and then ease, freedom, and serenity will arise spontaneously. As my lama Jigme Yonten Gonpo taught:

> Son, when fixation is exhausted, that is realisation.
> When deliberate grasping is exhausted, that is fundamental nature.
> When everything is without differentiation or exclusion
> In vast true nature, that itself is enough.

Here, measure of the signs of the path which focuses primarily on the gateway practice of calm abiding is as follows:

> At first, discursive thoughts are like a ravine torrent.
> In the middle, they are like the slow-flowing Ganges river.
> Finally, like the one-taste of all rivers in the ocean,
> Abide in the state of mother and child luminosity meeting.

Of the five experiences of movement, attainment, familiarity, steadiness, and perfection which occur gradually, here they are taught summarised into three. As mentioned before, when they are divided into five, the experience of movement is like a waterfall on a steep cliff. The experience of attainment is like a river in a narrow valley. The experience of familiarisation is like a great river. The experience of steadiness is like the ocean undisturbed by wind. The experience of perfection is explained to be like the king of mountains which does not move. Here, by means of the unity of shamatha and vipashyana, eventually discursive thoughts are liberated in true nature. If we settle in the meeting of mother and child luminosity, then according to the enlightened intent of trekchö primordial purity, this is taught to accord with the viewpoint that the four appearances arise in reverse order.

Following that, the ultimate mother perfection of wisdom which cuts through the four demons simultaneously, enhancement of the path of yoga of directly subduing in equal taste, is taught:

> In particular, whatever sickness, negative influence, or trickery occurs,
> Do not conduct any corrective rituals whatsoever.
> Engage in the conduct of directly subduing in equal taste like this:

This is the summary. Following that:

> Go to frightening and dreadful places such as
> Forests, charnel grounds, islands, groves,
> Caves, empty houses, or before the trunk of a solitary tree.
> Transform your body, the universal container and contents, appearance and existence, into nectar.
> Offer this to all the Victorious Ones and bodhisattvas of the ten directions.
>
> Visualise they are pleased, and with loving countenances
> They melt into light, and all of samsara and nirvana
> Completely fills with luminous nectar.
> The guests of qualities, the oath-bound Dharma protectors,

> The supreme field of compassion, the six classes of sentient beings,
> And all karmic creditors, harmful, obstructive, and elemental spirits,
> All beings equal to the extent of space,
> Are satisfied by this nectar which liberates upon taste.
>
> Determining that samsara and nirvana are of one taste,
> From the state of dharmakaya, uncontrived mind itself,
> Walk, sit, jump, and run,
> Speak, laugh, cry, and sing,
> Disturb and break things, and so on—engage in crazy conduct.

Go to places which ghosts, demons, goblins, and ogresses frequent, and where they reside: forests, charnel grounds, lonely trees, and so on, and directly subdue that which is unbearable. As Machik Labdron taught:

> This instruction to transform the physical body into food,
> Is the doctrine of Ama Jomo.

Transform your body into offering nectar and with this uncontaminated, desirable offering, offer it to the revered guests: the Precious Jewels, the Victorious Ones, and the bodhisattvas of the ten directions. Pleased, they melt into light, and from this blessing, all of samsara and nirvana becomes filled with the luminous nectar of wisdom. For the guests who embody positive qualities: glorious guardians, protectors, together with an oceanic gathering of oath-bound ones, the guests invited out of compassion, the six classes of sentient beings, the guests who are karmic creditors, those of the elemental class of spirits to whom you owe debts, and all other beings equal to the extent of space, this offering substance of nectar which liberates on taste arises as anything whatsoever, emanating as everything desirable. It has an essence of uncontaminated wisdom nectar which becomes the various forms of all that is desired. Thus visualise all guests are pleased, and in this way determine that all appearances of samsara and nirvana are the magical display of mind itself alone.

In the conduct of yogic discipline, whatever arises, whatever comes to mind, everything is unfeigned and uncontrived: walking, sitting, jumping, running, speaking, laughing, crying, singing, and so forth, which looks like someone who is mad. When the seven types of majestic conduct are taught, first is the conduct of a swallow entering its nest. Then there is conduct like a forest animal, and following that is conduct like a mute.

Then, in accordance with experience and realisation, comes conduct which is random and impetuous like a mad person, and conduct in which there is no difference between clean and dirty, good or bad, like dogs and pigs. Continuing through these, finally conduct comes about which is without anxiety or fear like a lion, king of the beasts.

Those yogis who maintain the conduct which masters appearances have the ability to revive the dead. They can convert others who lack faith, accomplish miracles, and have achieved rigpa arising as true nature. This enables them to exercise control over the external elements of earth, fire, wind, and so on—any object whatsoever. Other than something like this taking place, obviously not all practitioners are ones who can engage legitimately in crazy conduct. In this case, until we are actually able to act like that, maintain peaceful, mild, relaxed, and dignified conduct. It is important to avoid judging whether or not you are able to tame the mindstreams of others, but to monitor whether or not you have managed to tame your own mindstream. Crossing through spirit-filled places to wander alone through mountain hermitages, charnel grounds, snowy mountain ranges, and so on, is taught to be very useful for enhancing rigpa with yogic discipline.

> **Finally, rest in a peaceful and happy state.**
> **At night, sleep comfortably self-settled.**

In this way, maintain the conduct during the day. At night, the practice is to settle into genuine true nature and sleep comfortably.

> **Free of all recollection and thinking, proliferation and**
>   **subsiding, of discursive thought,**
> **Sleep in the genuine state of unborn complete recollection.**

We cannot just engage in crazy conduct. To undertake the conduct of distinguishing between samsara and nirvana, it is necessary to settle into genuine nature. So, likewise, finally rest in an unwavering peaceful and happy state. At night, sleep self-settled and in a comfortable way, free of all recollection and thinking, proliferation and subsiding, of gross discursive thought. Relax in the unborn ultimate fundamental nature, the primordially complete recollection and liberation of innate great bliss pervading fundamental nature, and sleep.

> **Do this, and sickness and malevolent influences will subside**
>   **by themselves.**
> **Then view and meditation will be enhanced, realisation will**
>   **be like space.**

> Meditation will be inherently luminous, conduct will be like a small child.
>
> Through the state free of all fixed reference, like a mad person,
> Without duality of self and other, like a noble being,
> Whatever is said is without grasping, like the sound of an echo.
> Unattached to anything whatsoever, like the garuda,
> Without anxiety or fear, like a lion,
> All is liberated from the very beginning, like a cloud-free sky.
>
> Such a yogi is an actual sugata vidyadhara,
> Worthy of homage from the touch of a hundred faithful crowns,
> Far more exalted than even a wish-fulfilling jewel.

Thus, the view is the evenness of samsara and nirvana. Meditation is primordial liberation inherently luminous. Conduct is unattached without fixation. Together with maintaining the conduct of yogic discipline of equal taste, when we engage in enhancement training of view and meditation, by embracing this suchness of confidence in the view, then realisation is sky-like without restrictions or extremes. Meditation without alternating between day and night does not go beyond inherently luminous rigpa of the three kayas. When conduct transcends that of ordinary people, it is free of grasping and without attachment, like an unconcerned small child. The suchness of the dynamic energy of realisation comes forth as compassion. From the aspect of not abandoning love for all limitless sentient beings, others become more cherished than oneself, just like a bodhisattva who abides on the level of a noble being.

As wisdom of the four empowerments is present in the mindstream, through the vase empowerment the body is purified, so wisdom with elaboration arises as its natural mode. Whatever is said with the speech, by having attained mastery of utterly unelaborate wisdom which transcends the object of what is spoken, speech becomes like the ungrasped sound of an echo. Through the secret empowerment, karma is purified. Through the unelaborate empowerment, wisdom which has no attachment to anything whatsoever arises as its natural mode, like the unintimidated garuda. Due to attaining the wisdom knowledge empowerment, extremely unelaborate wisdom masters self-manifestation self-liberating, so without fear or trepidation, lion-like fearless courageous confidence is found. Through the precious word empowerment, utterly unelaborate wisdom dawns self-arising, whereby whatever is apparent and whatever arises, everything is primordially liberated, like clouds vanishing in the sky. Such a person who has realised the pristine, luminous, unceasing wisdom of primordially pure enlightened mind has 'gone to bliss' having travelled the path to bliss and arrived at the blissful result of a sugata.

One who holds the yogic discipline of rigpa wisdom is known as a 'vidyadhara' or 'holder of rigpa'. We can also say that one who 'holds', through yogic unification with the genuine state, the actuality of rigpa wisdom just as it is, is called a 'vidyadhara'. There are many classifications of vidyadhara, but in terms of the four vidyadharas, they are: fully matured vidyadhara, power over life vidyadhara, great seal vidyadhara, and spontaneous presence vidyadhara. In our tradition, according to the position of the Great Omniscient One, although the body of a fully matured vidyadhara resides in a fully mature form, as soon as they are freed from this physical enclosure, they attain the body of the great seal. With this body upon the path of learning, one who possesses the undefiled wisdom of the enlightened perspective that unites with the level of buddhahood, is a vidyadhara with power over life. The body of one on the exceptional path of learning becomes the deity. Their activities are similar to those of a buddha, but the ultimate result is not actually achieved. They are taught to be a great seal vidyadharas. Having perfected abandonment and realisation, the path of no more learning is actualised, and they are asserted to be a spontaneous presence vidyadhara. There are minor differences between this way of explanation and the position accepted by the canonical lineage of Zur, however there are no great discrepancies in meaning.

If such a remarkably exalted person could be met with in such times as these, then with the three kinds of faith, and in addition by possessing irreversible faith enhanced by hundredfold admiration, such a being is worthy to be held above one's crown in devotional homage, and is far more exalted than even a wish-fulfilling jewel. They are great spiritual masters who accomplish spontaneously the two kinds of benefit: temporary and ultimate, in this life and the next, for everyone, themselves and others. The above teaches the instructions for the key points of the path including view, meditation, and conduct.

Teaching Day Five

Song Twenty-Two
The Result

The teaching on the result is as follows:

> **EMAHO!**
> **Now again, fortunate ones, listen to the song of this renunciant.**

From the ultimate result of the basic space of dharmakaya the sambhogakaya arises, whereby in order to appear as manifestations for whoever needs taming, they are endowed with the seven aspects of union. However, the five families of sambhogakaya Victorious Ones do not exist as anything other than this rigpa essence of the nature of mind, which abides within oneself. The way in which to actualise this is taught as follows:

> **Vairochana does not exist outside but exists within.**
> **The state of the basic space of phenomena, mind itself free of elaboration,**
> **The very essence of ignorance purified in its own place,**
> **Is the actual Bhagavan Vairochana.**

As the five kayas, five wisdoms, five lights, and so forth, are complete in rigpa wisdom, at the time of purity when the essence of wisdom becomes manifest, appearances in the impure state of the five afflictive emotions, five aggregates, five elements, and so on, are manifestly apparent as the five kayas, five wisdoms, and so forth. For this reason, searching for Vairochana outside, there is nothing to find. He is this inner rigpa. Rigpa essence of mind itself free of all extremes is the wisdom of the basic space of phenomena. As this is also nothing other than the very essence of afflictive emotions and ignorance purified in their own place, then the actual Bhagavan Vairochana is this rigpa.

> **Vajrasattva does not exist outside but exists within.**
> **The mirror-like state, rigpa dynamic energy's unceasing ground of arising,**
> **The very essence of aversion purified in its own place,**
> **Is the actual Bhagavan Vajrasattva.**

Similarly, Bhagavan Akshobhya or Vajrasattva do not exist outside but exist within. In the innate dynamic energy of rigpa, phenomena in general and its own clear reflection are mirror-like wisdom. Thus, aversion purified in its own place is mirror-like wisdom, and this abiding within its very essence is the actual Bhagavan Vajrasattva.

> **Ratnasambhava does not exist outside but exists within.**
> **The state of evenness without acceptance, rejection, suppression, or promotion,**
> **The very essence of pride purified in its own place,**
> **Is the actual Bhagavan Ratnasambhava.**
>
> **Amitabha does not exist outside but exists within.**
> **The state of discernment, bliss-emptiness subsiding into basic space,**
> **The very essence of attachment purified in its own place,**
> **Is the actual Bhagavan Amitabha.**
>
> **Amoghasiddhi does not exist outside but exists within.**
> **The all-accomplishing state, rigpa suddenly arising and self-liberating,**
> **The very essence of jealously purified in its own place,**
> **Is the actual Bhagavan Amoghasiddhi.**

By gaining experience in the primordially endowed enlightened qualities of rigpa, they become manifest. The suchness of Bhagavan Ratnasambhava abides in the state of evenness wisdom where pride is purified in its own place without any acceptance, rejection, suppression, or promotion. Bhagavan Amitabha, the suchness of rigpa wisdom of limitless light, similarly abides in the state of discerning wisdom where attachment is purified in its own place. Bhagavan Amoghasiddhi appears as the kaya which spontaneously accomplishes the two benefits, and abides in the state of all-accomplishing wisdom where jealousy is purified in its own place and there is no impediment or obstruction. In short, all are complete in the single essence of rigpa. Therefore, Bhagavans Ratnasambhava, Amitabha, and Amoghasiddhi all reside within and not externally. This teaches that this single essence of inner rigpa is the five families of Victorious Ones.

TEACHING DAY FIVE

SONG TWENTY-THREE
THE FUNDAMENTAL STATE OF LIBERATION

The final section of all the teachings is the instruction on the effortless primordially liberated fundamental state of liberation, which is as follows:

> **EMAHO!**
> **Now again, fortunate and only heart children,**
> **Listen to this vajra song with delight and joy!**

Having expressed this exhortation:

> **When you realise in this way, all appearances and existence entirely**
> **Are a mandala of the meaning of the oral instruction scriptures.**

Briefly outlined, the mandala which holds the foundation, empowerment, samaya commitments, practice, ritual offerings, and activities which are subsumed in method, mantra, and mudra: the ten attributes of Mantra, and so on, are all complete in the fundamental state. A detailed explanation of this is as follows:

> **On the paper of various appearances, white and red,**
> **The pen of self-arising wisdom rigpa**
> **Writes baseless primordially liberated non-grasping letters.**
> **Read the text in the state of non-dual appearance-emptiness.**

Thus, the manifestations of appearance and existence, the universal container and its contents, appear in all their variety, distinct and individually apparent. Upon this white and red paper, the pen of self-arising rigpa, pristine, luminous, and unceasing, writes letters which become a manifold dance of everything as baseless and primordially liberated, the non-grasping single taste of appearance and awareness. At this time, we are told to read the text that sees just as it is, the fundamental nature of non-dual appearances and emptiness, the fundamental mode of presence, however it is.

This is taught when a level of realised confidence of lofty experience and realisation is reached, having arrived at the stage of discussing the result. Alongside the main Dharma teachings, we have already mentioned the twelve great vajra laughters of tantra and the eight great expressions of amazement. The teacher of tantra uses great vajra laughter and expressions of amazement to teach whatever their own enlightened mind is like, just as it is, the sound of the definitive truth of the supremely secret true nature, exactly as it is.

This is not the same as a figurative teaching, an example of which would be an instruction to murder one's father and mother, or something similar, that would be taught with an implicit understanding of the true meaning. However, for someone of lesser faculties to whom true nature is not within their range of experience, first they gain a mere general understanding of the meaning of the fundamental mode of presence of true nature. Through engaging in inference, if they can determine the view, then when they gain familiarisation through meditation on a path that is somewhat similar in kind, so long as they have not just entered into conceptual analysis but have actually gained a little experience, then they have the hope of attaining the confidence to actualise realisation. Based on this intent, at one point when they do attain the result of actualised realisation, this is the time they become able to utter their own sound of great vajra laughter: resounding laughter just as it sounds, in the manner of Longchenpa, Shabkar, and so forth. Until then, realisation is merely the object of aspiration.

At the time when this true nature of the ultimate fundamental nature just as it is, is manifest and realised, in the fundamental state positivity and negativity do not exist. To murder the sentient beings of the three realms, or to engage continuously in the ten transcendent perfections, is the same. However, for a person who has not abandoned the eightfold group of samsaric phenomena—an ordinary being with an individual mindstream—the teaching that says murdering the sentient beings of the three realms and engaging continuously in the virtues of the ten transcendent perfections are both identical, does not teach that cause and effect is eliminated or non-existent. As realisation is mastered when samsaric phenomena of the five aggregates and the eightfold collection have become self-purified, positive and negative karmic habituations and their bases are exhausted. So, having come to the understanding of definitive meaning, in the ultimate essence of fundamental true nature, there are no phenomena with positive or negative characteristics. But until this has become manifest, it is necessary to be extremely careful with regard to cause and effect.

Then, once the result free of acceptance and rejection, hope and fear, is based on understanding the meaning of both the aspect of provisional meaning exactly as the terminology presents it, and the definitive meaning, then the view should be lofty. This establishes the ultimate result of the definitive meaning of the very pinnacle of the nine vehicles. Still conduct needs to be careful. From the very lowest level upwards, the initial entrance to the path of the nine vehicles, we begin with faith, renunciation, and the foundation of the path: taking refuge, together with purifying our mindstreams. We need to understand that, much more serious than being tricked by others, to deceive ourselves on this issue and not to go through this process correctly, will result in a major self-betrayal: we could mislead ourselves on a wrong path in all our successive lifetimes.

The point of engaging in the study and contemplation of the holy scriptures is not merely to become familiar with these topics and to research the Dharma. Nor do we come to listen to a lama teaching the Dharma in case we come to be tested on our understanding. When we receive the Dharma and listen to the oral instructions, we need to be able to identify what we have received. This is the meaning that is to be understood here.

> Upon the spontaneously present mandala of the entire three thousandfold universe,
> Droplets of the rain of naturalness sprinkle down,
> Pathways are the natural baselines laid out,
> And footprints are the coloured sand drawings.
>
> Your body is the apparent yet empty body of the yidam deity,
> Speech is resounding yet empty vajra recitation,
> And thoughts are the non-grasping self-liberated mind of the deity.
>
> All movements of limbs are mudras,
> Food and drink are offerings of true nature,
> All apparent forms are the deity's body,
> And all sounds and speech are music.
> Without guarding or breaking, this is self-settled samaya.
>
> Whatever such a yogi does,
> In the state of the luminous true nature, the oral instructions,
> Generation stage, and samaya are complete,
> So there is no need to rely on teachings of effort, cause, or effect.
>
> Effortless siddhis, wondrous, marvellous,
> And swift to attain are the special features
> Of Dzogpa Chenpo, fortunate heart children.

Generally speaking, the phenomena of samsara and nirvana are complete in the body and mind of the yogi: the aspects of method and wisdom are one's mother and father. The aspect of dharmakaya enlightenment is propelling karmic wind. The aspect of the primordial radiance of the five families is the seed of the five elements, and so on. From these, birth is nirmanakaya, abiding is sambhogakaya, death is dharmakaya, up to the arising of the empty aspect. As wandering beings primordially pass through ground, path, and result, in connection with the manner of liberation, and particularly the manner of reversing delusion, this body signifies the ground, its external apparent aspect signifies the spontaneously present manifestation of the ground, sickness signifies recognition of realisation, and ageing signifies the delusion of fixation on true existence vanishing. Death at the time of knowing one's own nature signifies reaching consummation at the level of primordial purity in inner basic space.

Because these are complete in the ground, when empowerment and oral instructions are recognised through introduction, it is tenable that liberation through meditating on the path can be accomplished. That which is present primordially complete in the ground is taught accordingly by the path, whereby that which becomes manifest as the result itself is inseparable ground and result. Therefore, all phenomena of samsara and nirvana, and threefold ground, path, and result are complete in the rigpa essence of mind itself. Because these are complete, as familiarisation with the path of practice becomes manifest, when in self-abiding wisdom the obscuring defilements are purified, the entire three thousandfold universal world realm arises as an uncreated spontaneously existing pure mandala whose droplets of the rain of naturalness sprinkle down upon the mandala base of accomplishment. All pathways, crossroads, and junctions are the mandala lines. All the footprints that have been left upon it are the coloured sand drawings.

The body of the one that moves is the non-dual appearance-emptiness form of the yidam deity. All resonant expressions of speech are resounding yet empty vajra recitations. Everything thought and remembered by mind is the non-grasping and self-liberated thought of the enlightened mind of the yidam deity. Everything expressed verbally is mantra. Whatever movements or gestures of the arms and legs that are made are all vajra dance and mudra. Whatever is eaten or drunk, everything is the feast gathering and undefiled offerings of true nature. All apparent forms are the deity's body. All sounds and speech are musical melodies. Without transgression, breaking, or limits to guard, this is self-settled samaya. This is also taught in the *Pearl Garland Tantra*:

> Rigpa itself is like this:

> The sun and moon are wisdom and method.
> Males are the ground, females are the path...

In the presence of self-manifest rigpa there are no phenomena of samsara or nirvana that are incomplete, and in the presence of a pure yogi everything is the pure mandala of the true nature of deity and mantra without rejection and absolutely complete, boundless and expansive. These special features are also taught in other tantras, not just once but in detail. For the yogi who realises in this way, whatever they do, however they do it, whatever appears, however things appear, as they abide in the state of the true nature of luminosity they do not need to rely on limited teachings of striving effort, cause and effect, or common elaborations. Everything exists as the effortless supreme accomplishment of this wondrous and marvellous Dharma. This is the special feature of Dzogpa Chenpo. Do we actually understand that this is the case? Shabkar appeals to us emphatically as his fortunate heart children with this vital point, so that we may manage to reach such a level of practice.

The teaching on the extent of liberation of excellent, middling, and lesser yogis is as follows:

> If practice develops such certainty,
> Like clouds vanishing into the sky,
> Conceptual thoughts of samsara and nirvana are purified in primordial ground.
>
> Like the unobscured luminosity of the orb of the sun,
> As self-aware luminous dharmakaya manifests,
> You will be able to revive the dead, understand secrets,
> And tame wandering beings by displaying myriad miracles.
>
> By utterly perfecting the qualities of the levels and paths without exception,
> People with excellent faculties are liberated in this life,
> Those with middling faculties at the moment of death, those of lesser faculties in the bardo.
>
> Having become liberated in the primordially pure ground,
> Perpetually residing in inner basic space inseparable from the wisdom of the three kayas,
> By emanating manifestations to tame beings in any way necessary,
> They bring benefit to sentient beings uninterruptedly.

Songs of Dzogchen Trekchö

**Keep the meaning of these words in your heart
And the sun of happiness is certain to arise from within!**

If you are practising according to the presentation of the view, meditation, and conduct, and the threefold ground, path, and result which is taught above, and the way in which they appear in the tantras, transmissions, and foremost instructions of Dzogchen, which is also indicated here, the two accumulations are completed automatically and the two obscurations are naturally purified. Although clouds appear, they appear from within the sky. Although they subside, they also subside within the sky. Just as clouds vanish, the appearances of samsara and nirvana and all conceptual thoughts arise from the ground of primordial purity and are purified in the ground. Just as the orb of the sun has never been covered by obscurations, self-aware luminous dharmakaya unobscured from the very beginning becomes manifest. At the same time, in the presence of everyone watching, not only is an accomplished practitioner able to revive the dead, they are also able to hear and understand concealed and secret language. With various miracles, and especially clairvoyance that knows the minds of others, by teaching the Dharma to whoever is to be tamed, they can tame sentient beings.

Similarly, all the ordinary and extraordinary qualities of the levels and paths are perfected. Particularly, on the common path of trekchö and tögal, at the time of focusing intently on the key points of the unity of basic space and rigpa, through the framework of the three kinds of extremely essential samadhi, the definite measure indicative of enlightened qualities arises. The three kinds of extremely essential samadhi are: samadhi of great imperturbable presence, samadhi of great immediacy, and samadhi of great sealing. When one has become accustomed to samadhi of great imperturbable presence, previously unseen phenomena become known automatically, many categories of samadhi spontaneously arise, mind does not engage with worldly activities, the faces of buddhas and bodhisattvas are seen, and previously absent vast compassion is born in one's mindstream.

When one has become accustomed to samadhi of great immediacy, appearances manifest as illusions and one is freed from fixation on the sense pleasures of existence. Rigpa appears nakedly and supreme realisation is manifest. Merging with the true nature of enlightened mind, samadhi of no-thought is born. As wisdom dawns self-arisen, the expanse of words and meaning emerges, naturally flowing forth. When familiarity with samadhi of great sealing has reached its fullest extent, appearances arise as luminosity, and one resides day and night in the true nature of phenomena.

Therefore, when we contemplate the full expression of familiarity with trekchö alone, whatever appearances arise, including one's own body, are seen to be partless particles. Because the particles of the four elements have become purified, one masters sublime insight and clairvoyance, and one is liberated in this very lifetime. Through the power of familiarity with trekchö, nothing is left behind except hair and nails. This is what we call in everyday language 'attainment of the rainbow body', and is referred to in the scriptures as 'the body vanishing into particles'. The perspective of the Heart Essence is that liberation up to and including the time when the death state arises as the luminous dharmakaya, is considered to be liberation in this very lifetime. The middling result is liberation in the bardo of the nature of phenomena, and the lesser result is liberation during the bardo of becoming and finding relief in the natural nirmanakaya realm.

We should understand the meaning of liberation in the primordially pure ground in more detail. At the time manifestations of the ground arise from the ground, everything is perceived as the spontaneously present realm, with appearance and existence arising as light and kayas. From the dynamic energy of its essence, the sambhogakaya manifestations arise. From the dynamic energy of enlightened qualities, the appearances of the spontaneously present nirmanakaya realm arise. From the dynamic energy of compassion, the door of samsara arises in personal experience like a dream. Although they do arise, in whatever way they arise, they do not exist as any delusion or non-delusion whatsoever. If we know our own nature, from the aspect that they form the conditions for liberation, they are the ground of liberation. If we do not know our own nature, from the aspect that they form the basis for delusion, they are labelled as the 'ground of delusion'.

Therefore, these manifestations of the ground are the ground of liberation, and primordial purity is the state of liberation. Primordial ground as basic space does not differentiate samsara and nirvana in any way, so it cannot be said that liberation occurs upon this. So, what is merging within the inseparable ground and result of primordial inner basic space likened to? For example, like the seed of a *se* tree which does not germinate, or extracting poison from mercury, they do not become harmful again. From primordially pure basic space, the radiance of external luminosity unfolds, and the two form kayas engage in the benefit of beings. This is the way in which it is taught.

Do not abandon these words and meanings with the assumption that you have understood them. By keeping them in mind and integrating them with your mindstream, engage in practice. Thereby the sun of happiness which accomplishes benefit for both self and others is 'Certain to arise from within'. With this instruction, we complete fully the goodness of the middle, the meaning of the text.

Teaching Day Five

Goodness of the End—The Conclusion

The goodness of the end, the conclusion, brings to completion how this teaching was undertaken, who sang these vajra songs, and how and when they were sung. Of these, first the name of the writer is defined:

The one who sang the songs of such enlightened intent
Appears to be the renunciant Tsokdruk Rangdrol.

The enlightened intent of Victorious Samantabhadra, these foremost instructions of Dzogchen trekchö, are songs of realisation of the view of inherent limpidity sang in the manner of dohas. The one who sang them, the yogi who has abandoned worldly activities of the three doors, appears to be Tsokdruk Rangdrol. In reliance upon this master, the meaning of the enlightened intent of the Victorious One, a new stupa of the dharmakaya, is made manifest to fortunate beings to be tamed.

Dedication of Merit

The dedication of merit to perfect enlightenment is as follows:

By this merit, may many fortunate beings to be tamed
Swiftly purify all defilements of ignorance, afflictive
   emotions, and thoughts
In the original basic space of primordial purity,
And attain the result in this very lifetime!

The merit of this composition is dedicated to the huge numbers of beings to be tamed who will come in the future and who possess the appropriate karma and fortune. The demon of ignorance at the root of existence is the cause of much karma and many afflictive emotions, and produces all the varieties of suffering that these sentient beings experience, so they wander in confusion obscured by the defilements of all-consuming thought. Through the merit of teaching in this way, may all the defilements of these all-consuming thoughts be purified totally and the fundamental nature of the undeluded ground, the true face of self-abiding rigpa itself, be seen. May all beings attain the result and arise as the youthful vase body in primordially pure original inner basic space in this very lifetime!

SONGS OF DZOGCHEN TREKCHÖ

Colophon and Prayer of Aspiration

These *Songs of the Trekchö View of Luminous Dzogpa Chenpo, Capable of Swiftly Traversing the Paths and Levels without Exception, 'Flight of the Garuda'*, were based on many Dzogchen treasures, including *Introduction to Naked Perception of Rigpa*, composed by Orgyen Rinpoche and revealed in the treasure of Siddha Karma Lingpa, **All-knowing** Longchenpa's *Seven Treasuries* **and** *Three Chariots*, which are the auto-commentaries on the *Trilogy of Rest: the Utterly Pure Chariot, the Noble Chariot,* and *the Great Chariot*, **the Sky Trilogy support teachings of Dzogchen**, which probably refers to the *Immaculate Sky* support text for trekchö and so on, and from the *Cloud Bank Trilogy:* **Cloud Banks of an Ocean of Profound Meaning**. As well as *Dzogchen Heart Essence of the Dakini*, the guidance instruction **Buddha in the Palm of the Hand**, and so on, as there is not a single Nyingma treasure teaching of Dzogchen that does not feature the complete trio of guru, great perfection, and enlightened mind.

> Additionally ornamented by my lama's foremost instructions and my own experience, this is spoken for the benefit of many faithful students by the renunciant Tsokdruk Rangdrol. May it become the cause to bring measureless benefit to the teachings and sentient beings.

This is the colophon and prayer of aspiration.

> These vajra songs were sung for all those with the fortune to pursue liberation, so the time to sing them is when the yogi is maintaining the view. The way to sing, how these songs should be sung, is as Vidyadhara Shri Singha said:
>
> > Buddha's enlightened mind is infinitely present,
> > Sentient beings' rigpa is partially present,
> > To make it as expansive as the sky is very beneficial.
>
> Accordingly, make rigpa as vast and lofty as the sky, and let go into expansive openness. Then, from the infinitely pervasive spacious state of the nature of mind, sing these vajra songs, and view and meditation will be enhanced.

This fully completes this teaching on the songs of Dzogchen trekchö, *Flight of the Garuda*.

Teaching Day Five

Final Words

Many of the teachings that I have given over the years have been transliterated from audio recordings, and these days everyone has access to these transliterated texts. Therefore, now it is useless for me to say that what I have taught is Secret Mantra, so you may not have permission to read it. Not only that, now all the collected works of the Secret Mantra tantras are available in market book stalls. Thinking about this, if having read these books, someone were to realise the complete profound meaning and see the essence of ultimate co-emergent wisdom, then this would be due to their own innately complete faith and pure vision, and the self-present blessings to see the true face of the realised ultimate lama. This must be due to a previous karmic connection becoming awakened.

If someone does not have this realisation and these letters and words become mere reflection, then perhaps we can say this has been decided by the method of self-secrecy. If someone has no concept of the presumptuousness of accessing the Dharma without permission, and other than having these words appear before their eyes, does not engage in any thought or analysis regarding their meaning, then maybe such people with impetuous conduct do not belong in Secret Mantra.

Whatever the case, those who have a dedicated interest in my published teachings, all fortunate friends of as yet unseen places and future times, can form the perception that reading these words is the same as hearing me speak them directly. To contemplate and analyse my teachings is the same as talking with me. And if there is anyone who gains benefit from these books, they can be counted among the closest of my Dharma friends, with the shared purpose of sailing together in this great ship of Dharma. However, in this present time when it is rare to possess impartial intelligence, there must be those who through aversion and attachment may judge these teachings, and at worst belittle and denigrate them. So, henceforth all such people should be the object of our practice of love and compassion.

The prayer of aspiration that I make continually is for all beings who see and come into contact with me, all who hear and think of me, all those who place their faith in me as their lama, as well as all those who consider me to be an enemy, condemn me, and make threats, may all those with both positive and negative karmic connections, all the way down to the creatures that fly in the sky and move on the land, and even the micro-organisms who consume my body with the concept that I am food, may they all be established in ever greater happiness.

These teachings of Dzogchen trekchö summarise the key points of the earlier and later Heart Essences, foremost instructions made easy to understand and explained in colloquial language. If there are a few pointers in what I have taught that are helpful, they have appeared through the power of the bodhicitta of our lineage lamas. But there is probably much that is erroneous, incomplete, and contradictory, because my mind speaks from a place that does not surpass the level of an ordinary being. So I pray, may you learn from this bad example and realise true dharmakaya wisdom.

www.ingramcontent.com/pod-product-compliance
Lightning Source LLC
Chambersburg PA
CBHW021805220426
43662CB00006B/192